Machine Learning and Cognitive Computing for Mobile Communications and Wireless Networks

Scrivener Publishing
100 Cummings Center, Suite 541J
Beverly, MA 01915-6106

Publishers at Scrivener
Martin Scrivener (martin@scrivenerpublishing.com)
Phillip Carmical (pcarmical@scrivenerpublishing.com)

Machine Learning and Cognitive Computing for Mobile Communications and Wireless Networks

Edited by
Krishna Kant Singh
KIET Group of Institutions, Delhi-NCR, Ghaziabad, India
Akansha Singh
Department of CSE, ASET, Amity University Uttar Pradesh, Noida, India
Korhan Cengiz
Electrical-Electronics Engineering Department, Trakya University, Edirne, Turkey
and
Dac-Nhuong Le
Faculty of Information Technology, Haiphong University, Vietnam

Scrivener
Publishing

Wiley Global Headquarters
111 River Street, Hoboken, NJ 07030, USA

For details of our global editorial offices, customer services, and more information about Wiley products visit us at www.wiley.com.

Limit of Liability/Disclaimer of Warranty
While the publisher and authors have used their best efforts in preparing this work, they make no representations or warranties with respect to the accuracy or completeness of the contents of this work and specifically disclaim all warranties, including without limitation any implied warranties of merchantability or fitness for a particular purpose. No warranty may be created or extended by sales representatives, written sales materials, or promotional statements for this work. The fact that an organization, website, or product is referred to in this work as a citation and/or potential source of further information does not mean that the publisher and authors endorse the information or services the organization, website, or product may provide or recommendations it may make. This work is sold with the understanding that the publisher is not engaged in rendering professional services. The advice and strategies contained herein may not be suitable for your situation. You should consult with a specialist where appropriate. Neither the publisher nor authors shall be liable for any loss of profit or any other commercial damages, including but not limited to special, incidental, consequential, or other damages. Further, readers should be aware that websites listed in this work may have changed or disappeared between when this work was written and when it is read.

Library of Congress Cataloging-in-Publication Data

ISBN 978-1-119-64036-3

Cover image: Pixabay.Com
Cover design by Russell Richardson

Set in size of 11pt and Minion Pro by Manila Typesetting Company, Makati, Philippines

Contents

Preface

The rapid advancements that have recently taken place in communication and network technology have resulted in numerous information services and applications being developed globally. These technological advances continue to have a high impact on society by affecting the way we lead our lives, and although they have undoubtedly improved quality of service and user experience, there is still much to be done. With that in mind, our main objective in writing this book is to address the many challenges associated with this technology and to provide a platform for machine learning-enabled mobile communications and wireless networks.

Since it is highly desirable to develop smart technologies for communication to improve the overall services and management of wireless communication, in addition to providing mathematical and conceptual background on the latest technology, various areas still needing improvement are discussed in this book, including seamless wide-area coverage, high-capacity hotspots, low-power massive connections, and low-latency and high-reliability wireless networks. In addition to mobile communications and wireless networks, machine-learning techniques are also discussed, including machine-learning architecture and framework, deep reinforcement learning for wireless networks, machine learning–based security and privacy protection for communications/networks, spectrum-aware mobile computing, wireless technology in the Internet of Things (IoT), infrastructure in mobile opportunistic networks, and spectrum allocation in cognitive radio.

Machine learning and cognitive computing have converged to provide some groundbreaking solutions for smart machines. With these two technologies coming together, machines can acquire the ability to reason similar to the human brain. Since the research area of machine learning and cognitive computing covers many fields that can be used effectively for topology management, such as psychology, biology, signal processing, physics, information theory, mathematics, and statistics, the utilization of machine-learning techniques like data analytics and cognitive power will lead to a better performance of communication and wireless systems.

Based on the dominance of the emergent field of machine learning and cognitive computing as applied to mobile communications and wireless networks and the aforementioned facts, this book is an essential guide for all academicians, researchers, and those working in industry in the related field. Because it is an amalgamation of theory, mathematics, and examples of the discussed technologies, this book will also be relevant to all levels of students—from undergraduate and postgraduate to research students—studying computer science or electronics.

Krishna Kant Singh
Akansha Singh
Korhan Cengiz
Dac-Nhuong Le
May 2020

Machine Learning Architecture and Framework

Nilanjana Pradhan* and Ajay Shankar Singh

School of Computer Science and Engineering, Galgotias University, Greater Noida, Uttar Pradesh, India

Abstract

Machine Learning is one of the fastest developing fields in computer science with wide range of applications. The machine learning architecture involves lot of complexity. The machine learning architecture will implement learning algorithm in the application engine which will perform the predictions, perform various complex queries in database and finally use analytics tools to produce predictions based on application areas. An effective machine learning architecture helps in designing better data centers, promote human welfare, solving critical system failures. A good architecture will cover all important risks involved with data privacy and security areas. In order to set up an effective machine learning architecture the problem area must be well defined. Training data (text, images, audio, video, structured data, user generated content etc.) must be collected for machine learning development process. In most cases data are incorrect and useless. The quality of the data matters in building and effective ML system. Good data visualization, data filtering, encryption tools and analytics tools are required. The machine learning system must be tested with test data. The model must get validated. In business domain ML algorithms are implemented on business processes, business services, people, skills, culture, risk management, partners, business functions, business organization.

Keywords: Machine learning, analytics, encryption, prediction, algorithm

*Corresponding author: nilanjana.pradhan@galgotiasuniversity.edu.in

Krishna Kant Singh, Akansha Singh, Korhan Cengiz and Dac-Nhuong Le (eds.) *Machine Learning and Cognitive Computing for Mobile Communications and Wireless Networks*, (1–24) © 2020 Scrivener Publishing LLC

1.1 Introduction

Machine learning is a branch of AI in which we require large volume of data and analyze those data with efficient algorithm. It aims at extracting knowledge or patterns from a large volume of observations. In supervised learning the observations contains data which trains the machine learning system to recognize certain rules.

ML systems recognize patterns from input data and predict or classify an object. In reinforcement learning, given evaluations help in distinguishing the situation. Examples are various types of ML applications which make a computer capable of playing games or drive vehicles. Machine learning emerged from artificial intelligence; however it focuses more on cognitive learning. AI attempts to model human function and intelligence which helps to resolve various problems. An important aspect of ML that makes it particularly appealing in terms of business is that it does not require as much explicit programming in advance to acquire intelligent insight. This ability uses various learning algorithms that simulate some human intelligence. Once data is collected and prepared for machine learning, algorithms are selected, modeled and interpreted [1]. Every learning system progresses through various learning iterations on its own to reveal hidden business value from data. Machine learning does not require too much of advance programming. Large amount of raw data is required coupled with high computing power on the execution platform to perform all the computations required for learning. However programming is still required for the application of machine learning, especially if it is applicable to automation.

The fundamental of ML involves large volumes of information data for the learning procedure. This information could emerge out of an assortment of sources, for example, venture frameworks, centralized server databases, and IoT edge gadgets. IT may be organized or unstructured in nature. Extremely high volumes of information are frequently nourished into machine since more information regularly yields better bits of knowledge. In this computerized business time, different sources and volumes of data are detonating. Learning in ML is commonly utilized for business reason for existing is either directed or unaided. In these classifications, be that as it may, there is a wide range of sorts of calculations and ML schedules, which are utilized to achieve different goals.

There are various eager learning methods which start computing before receiving new test data. They generally depend more on upfront evaluation of training data in order to predict without the need for new data. As a result, eager learning methods tend to spend more time on processing the training data. Another kind of learning method known as lazy learning method delays processing and data evaluation until it is fed with new test data. Machine learning is used to provide results that are either predictive, i.e. provide forecasts, or prescriptive, i.e. suggests recommended actions. Various data sets and feature regions are required for investigation using machine learning algorithm [1]. This yield information is by and large put away for examination and conveyed as reports and encouraged as contribution to other venture applications or frameworks.

The large volume of data that are collected from IoT sensors and other new information sources is increasing the capabilities of businesses to evaluate them and retrieve value and insights from them. Machine learning can relatively quickly and efficiently evaluate these mountains of data; many businesses are capturing the opportunity to discover the hidden insights that could deliver a competitive edge.

1.2   Machine Learning Algorithms

As of late individuals crosswise over various controls are exploring artificial intelligence to enhance their professional work. Artificial intelligence is used by economists to foresee future market costs in order to make a benefit. In restorative science [1], computer based intelligence is utilized to arrange whether a tumor is harmful or not. In meteorology AI is used for weather prediction. AI is used by human resource recruiters to analyze the résumé of applicants which helps in finding out if the applicant meets the minimum criteria for job. To achieve all these application of AI we need to implement machine learning algorithms. Every machine learning enthusiast begins with learning various ML algorithms and then moves toward building the ML architecture for various applications.

1.2.1   Regression

Regression is actually a method of building predictive model. This algorithm is mainly used for forecasting a predictive analysis. Here a set of predictor variables predicts an outcome, i.e. dependent variable. Regression estimates the relationship between one dependent and one independent variable and determines the strength of predictors and effect of forecasting. Various kinds of regressions are linear regression, multiple regression, logistic regression, ordinal regression, multinomial regression, and discriminant regression [2].

In the above figure the x hub speaks to autonomous variable and y—pivot speaks to subordinate variable. The dots represent the various observations. We need to minimize the error, i.e. the difference between estimated value and the actual value.

1.2.2   Linear Regression

One of the most well known algorithms in machine learning is linear regression. Machine learning helps in reducing the error of a predictive model resulting in making most accurate predictions. One of the examples of both statistical algorithm and machine learning algorithm is linear regression. Linear regression which is a linear model establishes a linear relationship between input variables and a single output variable [2]. If there are multiple input variables it is known as multiple linear regression. In simple regression problem the model is represented by

$$y = mx + c$$

where x represents the input data and y represents the output or predict and m and c are the variables which the model will try to learn.

In multivariable regression the model will use the following equation to learn

$$f(x, y, z) = a_1 x + a_2 y + a_3 z$$

where the variables x, y, z will represent distinct pieces of information for every observation. The prediction function helps in estimating the sales of a given company in comparison to the expenditure on television advertisement. Linear regression assumes that, independent variable (X) and dependent variable (Y) have a linear relationship between them. At each value of X, Y is distributed normally. For each value of X variance of Y is similar and all observations are independent.

1.2.3   Support Vector Machine

Support vector machine (SVM) is one of the popular machine learning algorithms. A hyperplane in an N-dimensional space (N—the quantity of highlights) that particularly classifies data points is discovered with the help of this algorithm [3].

1.2.4 Linear Classifiers

Linear classifiers are very simple with easy computational methods using linear functions. It divides the feature space into two different regions as shown in Figure 1.1 and Figure 1.2 with the help of classifier margin. The classifier margin can be in two dimensional or three dimensional space. The characteristic of the object is mainly presented as feature vector.

The classifier margin of a linear classifier and the width of the boundary can be incremented before hitting a data point. It helps in separating two data sets of different class. It is generally drawn in between data sets of two different classes. The specific distance from the decision boundary to the closest data point confirms the margin of the classifier. The SVM where data points are classified by linear classifier is the simplest kind of SVM and is called LSVM [3].

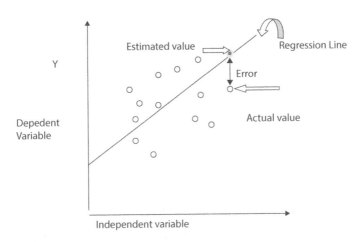

Figure 1.1 Linear classifier.

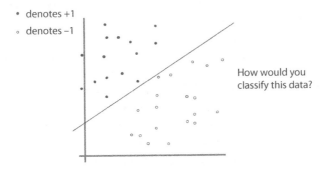

Figure 1.2 Linear classifier for SVM. Source: https://towardsdatascience.com/a-friendly-introduction-to-support-vector-machines-svm-925b68c5a079.

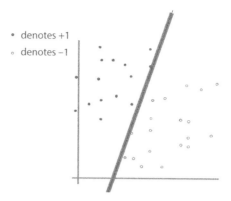

Figure 1.3 Linear classifier with hyperplane in SVM. Source: https://towardsdatascience.com/a-friendly-introduction-to-support-vector-machines-svm-925b68c5a079.

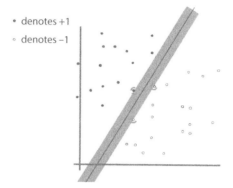

Figure 1.4 Linear classifier for SVM with wider hyperplane. Source: https://towardsdatascience.com/a-friendly-introduction-to-support-vector-machines-svm-925b68c5a079.

The position and orientation of the hyperplane are influenced by the support vectors which are the data points located close to the hyperplane is represented in Figure 1.3 and Figure 1.4. The margin of the classifier is maximized by these support vectors. The position of the hyperplane will change if we delete the support vectors.

One of the well known classification problems with machine learning is overfitting or overtraining. This happens when we are unable to classify unseen examples correctly and we have learned the training data very well. In this condition the classifier fits the training data rigidly. It does not work well on the test data. It is one of the causes of poor performance of any machine learning model [3].

In nonlinear SVM as shown in Figure 1.5, the input features can be mapped to higher dimensional feature space as represented in Figure 1.6 where they become separable [3]. Figure 1.7 represents hyperplane and support vectors in higher dimension.

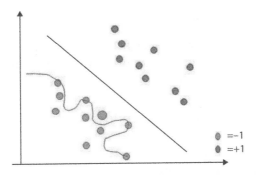

Figure 1.5 Non-linear SVMs: Feature spaces. Source: https://towardsdatascience.com/a-friendly-introduction-to-support-vector-machines-svm-925b68c5a079.

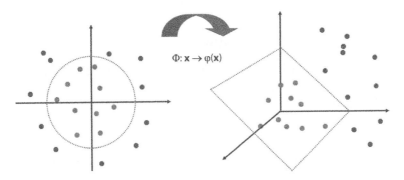

Figure 1.6 Non linear SVM where features are converted into higher dimension. Source: https://towardsdatascience.com/a-friendly-introduction-to-support-vector-machines-svm-925b68c5a079.

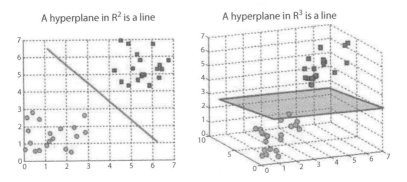

Figure 1.7 Hyperplanes and support vectors. Source: https://towardsdatascience.com/a-friendly-introduction-to-support-vector-machines-svm-925b68c5a079.

1.2.5   SVM Applications

In many real world problems we apply SVM algorithm and it is based on supervised learning algorithms and hence it classifies unrecognized data. Following are some of the application areas of SVM [3].

- Text and hypertext categorization
- Face recognition
- Image classification
- It is used in bioinformatics for protein classification and cancerous cell classification.
- Character recognition of handwritten words
- Disease prediction

1.2.6   Naïve Bayes Classification

Naïve Bayes classifier is a probabilistic machine learning model which is based on Bayes theorem. If there are several thousand data points and few variables naïve Bayes classifier can be used. The various real time applications of naïve Bayes classifier are:

- Spam classification—predicts whether an email is spam or not
- In medical science it helps to predict whether a patient suffers from a specific disease.
- Forecasting of climatic conditions
- Digit recognition
- Sentiment analysis
- Recommendation systems

According to *naïve Bayes assumption* all features are independent given the class label Y. Following equation denotes naïve Bayes model:

$$P(X_1,\ldots\ldots,X_n|Y = \prod_{i=1}^{n} P(X_i|Y)$$

After selecting Naïve Bayes classifier we need to train it with some data.

1.2.7 Random Forest

The kind of classifier that is composed of many decision trees is random forest. Tin Kam Ho of Bell Labs first proposed random forest and the term came from random decision forests. Decision trees which are considered as individual learners are combined to form random forest and are commonly used for data exploration. CART or classification and regression tree is one type of decision tree. It divides feature space into sets of disjoint rectangular regions and it is greedy, top-down binary, recursive partitioning [4].

The random forest is one of the algorithms which give correct classification results and efficiently runs on large databases. There are thousands of input variables which it can handle without data deletion. The variables which are important for classification are estimated by it. An internal unbiased estimate of the generalization error is generated as the forest building progresses. It helps in maintaining accuracy as it has an effective method for estimating missing data in case a large volume of data is missing [4].

1.2.8 K-Nearest Neighbor (KNN)

The entire data set is used as training set instead of splitting the data set into a training set and test set in case of KNN algorithm. The KNN algorithm traverses the entire data set to find the k-nearest instances to the new instance in order to find a new instance. For K number of instances the total mean and mode of the outcomes are calculated for a classification problem where the value of K is user specified. Euclidean distance and Hamming distance methods are used for calculating the similarity between instances.

1.2.9 Principal Component Analysis (PCA)

Principal component analysis (PCA) is utilized to investigate information effectively and make representation by diminishing the quantity of factors. By catching the greatest difference in the information and arranging it into another framework are called "chief parts" is achieved.

In PCA every segment is a direct mix of the first factors and is symmetrical to each other. Connection between these segments is zero and they are symmetrical to one another [5].

The course of the greatest inconsistency in the information is caught by the main principal component. All the progressive principal components (PC3, PC4, etc) catch the rest of the fluctuation while it is uncorrelated with the past segment [5].

1.2.10   K-Means Clustering

K-means algorithm is an unsupervised learning which involves unaided realizing which is utilized when we have unclear classes of information. This calculation targets discovering bunches in the information. Variable N means the quantity of clusters. The calculation iteratively doles out data point to one of N clusters [6].

Clustering is a technique used to perform statistical data analysis in various fields. The centroids of the K clusters in K-means clustering are utilized to mark new information. Each information point is relegated to a solitary group. Clustering enables you to look and break down the clustering that has developed naturally [6].

Every single centroid of a cluster is an accumulation of highlights which characterize the subsequent gatherings. Looking at the centroid highlight loads can be utilized to subjectively translate what sort of gathering each bunch speaks to.

1.3   Business Use Cases

The K-means clustering algorithm is used to discover clusters which have not been unequivocally assigned the information. This can be utilized to affirm business presumptions about what kinds of clusters exist or to recognize obscure clusters in complex informational indexes. When the algorithm has been run and the clusters are portrayed, any new data can be adequately consigned to the right clusters [6].

This is a flexible algorithm that can be used for a clustering. A few examples of use cases are:

- Behavioral division
- Segmentation of historical sales data
- Segmentation of exercises on application, site, or stage
- Define interests dependent personas
- Create profiles dependent on action observing
- Inventory order
- Group stock with deals action
- Group stock with assembling measurements
- Sorting sensor estimations
- Detection of various types of movements with the help of sensors
- Grouping of pictures

- Segregation of various types of sound
- Identify cluster identification in wellbeing checking
- Detecting bots or abnormalities
- Separate legitimate action clusters from bots
- Group substantial movement to tidy up anomaly discovery

Note that these segments of the design guide to a large number of the ML stages (see Figure 1.8) examined in the past area—for instance, getting, handling and demonstrating information, and afterward executing ML schedules and sending the outcomes. An all out big business ML design, containing every one of the highlights above, presumably won't be fundamental when simply beginning with ML. From the get-go, experts may buy a little scale ML platform to suit a special use case, and buy off-the-rack apparatuses to help a littler scale, "ML Lite" (lightweight) design appropriate for early use cases. After some time, they can iteratively fabricate, scale and bind together this into an "ML Enterprise" design that can efficiently bolster numerous use cases. The accompanying segments investigate the distinctive real segments of this design in more detail [7].

For data acquisition in the information obtaining segment of the ML design, information is gathered from an assortment of sources and

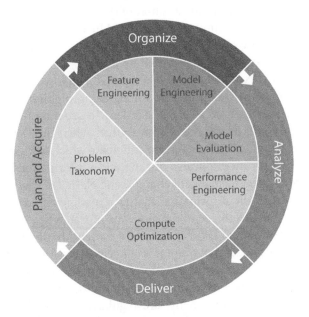

Figure 1.8 Continuous ML model and control framework (Source: Sapp, C. E. Preparing and architecting for machine learning. *Gartner Technical Professional Advice*, p 18).

arranged for ingestion for ML information handling stage as shown in the above figure. This segment of the engineering is significant on the grounds that ML frequently starts with the accumulation of high volumes of information from an assortment of potential sources, for example, ERP databases, centralized servers or instrumented gadgets that are a piece of an IOT framework [7].

Information Processing/Integration: In the information handling part of the design, the place information is sent for the development reconciliation and handling required to set up the information for ML execution. This may incorporate modules to play out any information change, standardization, and cleaning encoding steps that are important. Likewise, whenever regulated learning is utilized, information should have test determination steps performed to get ready arrangements of information for preparing [7].

Processing throughput is required here and you may execute a Lambda design. Moreover, you may use memory preparing for rapid handling. Different decisions for incorporating information in this layer may incorporate whether to utilize an independent information joining application or a mix stage as an administration (iPaaS). Highlight analysis of the information ingested for preparing may incorporate highlights that are excess or superfluous. Along these lines, specialized experts must empower the capacity to choose and examine a subset of the information so as to lessen preparing time, or to improve the model. Much of the time, highlight examination is a piece of test choice. In any case, it is critical to feature this subcomponent so as to change information that may damage security conditions or advance exploitative expectations. To battle security and moral concerns, clients should concentrate on expelling highlights from being utilized in the model. It is a decent standard to separate however much information as could be expected from sources when they are accessible. This is on the grounds that it is hard to anticipate which information fields are valuable. Acquiring duplicates of generation information sources can be intense and subject to stringent change control. In this way, it is smarter to get a superset of the information that is accessible and after that limit the information really utilized in the model using database [7]. In the event that during improvement it turns out to be evident that further information ends are required, at that point it is conceivable to just unwind the see criteria, and the additional information is promptly accessible. Capacity is cheap, and this makes the procedure substantially more light-footed. Information planning instruments are regularly used to perform highlight examination and choice. We should search for apparatuses that help self-administration information arrangement so as to furnish information science groups and designers with the capacity to control information to help ML calculations or models. Administration will assume a noteworthy job in the segment of your design. Moreover, consider verifying the learning and classification parts of your engineering to guarantee security or moral contemplations aren't ruptured through antagonistic ML [7]. Information Modeling: The demonstrating bit of the engineering is that the place calculations are chosen and adjusted to address the issue that will be inspected in the execution stage (see Figure 1.9). For instance, if the learning application will include bunch investigation, information grouping calculations will be a piece of the ML information model utilized here. On the off chance that the figuring out how to be performed is administered, information preparing calculations will be included also.

Execution ML algorithms can be very nondeterministic, and they may yield sudden practices, contingent upon preparing and information arrangement. Specialized experts must structure for nondeterminism by empowering flexible figure situations. Think about the open cloud as one of those versatile situations.

Information Acquisition: In the information securing segment of the ML engineering, information is gathered from an assortment of sources and arranged for ingestion for ML information handling stage (see Figure 1.10). This segment of the design is significant on the grounds that ML frequently

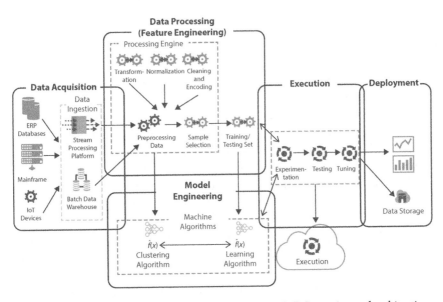

Figure 1.9 Machine learning architecture (Source: Sapp, C. E. Preparing and architecting for machine learning. *Gartner Technical Professional Advice*, p 20).

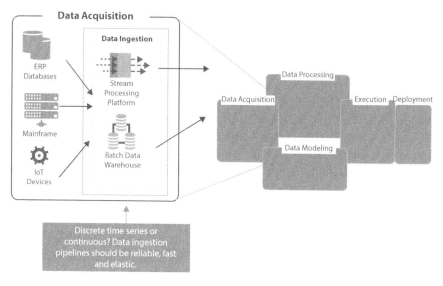

Figure 1.10 ML architecture: data acquisition (Source: Sapp, C. E. Preparing and architecting for machine learning. *Gartner Technical Professional Advice*, p. 21).

starts with the accumulation of high volumes of information from an assortment of potential sources, for example, ERP databases, centralized computers or instrumented gadgets that are a piece of an IOT framework.

1.4   ML Architecture Data Acquisition

Data Processing/Integration: The data processing portion of the architecture is where data is forwarded for the advance integration and processing required to prepare the data for ML execution. This may include modules to perform any data transformation, normalization, and cleaning encoding steps that are necessary. In addition, if supervised learning is used, data will need to have sample selection steps performed to prepare sets of data for training.

Computing throughput is required here and you might choose to implement a Lambda architecture. Additionally, you might choose to use in memory processing for high-speed processing. Different decisions for coordinating information in this layer may incorporate whether to utilize an independent information mix application or a joining stage as an administration (iPaaS).

Feature analysis of the informative data ingested for handling may incorporate highlights that are repetitive or irrelevant. Hence, specialized experts must empower the capacity to choose and dissect a subset of the information so as to lessen preparing time, or to disentangle the model. When in doubt, incorporate examination is a bit of test decision. Regardless, it is extremely important to include this subcomponent so as to change information that may disregard security conditions or advance untrustworthy forecasts. To battle security and moral concerns, clients should concentrate on expelling highlights from being utilized in the model. It is a decent guideline to separate however much information as could reasonably be expected from sources when they are accessible. This is in light of the fact that it is difficult to predict which data fields are useful. Acquiring duplicates of creation information sources can be extreme and dependent upon stringent change control. In this manner, it is smarter to acquire a superset of the information that is accessible and after that limit the information really utilized in the model using databases [7]. On the off chance that during improvement it turns out to be certain that further information ends are required, at that point it is conceivable to just unwind the see criteria, and the additional information is quickly accessible. Capacity is cheap, and this makes the procedure substantially more light-footed.

Data preparation tools are often used to perform feature analysis and selection. We must look for tools that support self-service data preparation in order to provide data science teams and developers with the ability to manipulate data to support ML algorithms or models. Governance will play a major role in the component of your architecture. Additionally, consider securing the learning and classification parts of your architecture to ensure that privacy or ethical considerations aren't breached through adversarial ML.

The demonstrating bit of the design is that the place calculations are chosen and adjusted to address the issue that will be inspected in the execution stage. For instance, if the learning application will include group investigation, information bunching calculations will be a piece of the ML information model utilized here. In the event that the figuring out how to be performed is directed, information preparing calculations will also be included.

1.5 Latest Application of Machine Learning

The magical touch of machine learning has made our life more comfortable than before. The contribution of science is just undeniable in our everyday life. Effect of science in our life cannot be overlooked. In our regular life we are gaining lot of advantages from Internet. For example we use Google map to travel in unknown roads. We use social networks and blogs to express our thoughts or feelings. Online news portals help us to remain updated about recent news and so on. Our perception of life is becoming more digital and because of various machine learning applications.

1.5.1 Image Identification

Picture acknowledgement is one of the most critical machine learning applications. In advanced picture it helps in distinguishing and recognizing an element or an article. This technology is used in example acknowledgment, face location, face acknowledgment, optical character acknowledgment and numerous more. Machine learning approach for picture acknowledgment is exceptionally powerful. In AI approach for picture acknowledgment, key highlights are separated from the picture and these highlights are sustained as contribution to an AI model.

1.5.2 Sentiment Analysis

Feeling investigation is another AI application which causes us to separate feelings from the content and decides the frame of mind or assessment of the speaker or the author.

The primary worry of assessment investigation is to discover the contemplations of other individuals. On the off chance that somebody gives a negative criticism about the film we have to discover the real idea (positive or negative) from the content and it is the real assignment of assessment investigation. Examination application can be applied to the further application, for example, in audit based site, basic leadership application [8].

The AI approach helps in extracting information from the information. This methodology can utilize enormous information to build up a framework. In AI approach two kinds of learning calculation, regulated and unaided, can be utilized in supposition examination.

1.5.3 News Classification

Another benchmark utilization of an AI is news order. Because of this in present days the volume of data has duplicated colossally on the web. Since each individual have his individual intrigue or decision along these lines, to pick or assemble a bit of suitable data turns into a major test to the clients.

1.5.4   Spam Filtering and Email Classification

Machine learning algorithms are executed in order to characterize email and channel the spam naturally. One of the popular technologies called multi-layer recognition is utilized to channel the spam. The standard based spam separating has a few disadvantages to channel the spam while spam sifting utilizing the ML approach is increasingly effective.

1.5.5   Speech Recognition

Expressed words are changed into content with the help of speech recognition. It is called programmed discourse acknowledgment, PC discourse acknowledgment or discourse to content. This field is profited by the headway of ML approach and huge information.

At present, all business reason speech recognition frameworks utilize an ML way to deal with perceiving the discourse. Why? The speech recognition framework utilizing ML approach is superior to the discourse acknowledgment framework utilizing a customary technique.

This is because, in an ML approach, the framework is prepared before it goes for the approval.

Fundamentally, the ML programming of discourse acknowledgment works in two learning stages:

1. Before the product buy
2. After the client buys the product

1.5.6   Detection of Cyber Crime

Machine Learning algorithm is widely used in cyber security to prevent online misinterpretation. This extensive ML application decreases the misfortune and amplifies the benefit. Utilizing Machine learning in this application is much more beneficial than any other traditional rule based system.

1.5.7   Classification

A powerful classifier framework can be built by using machine learning approach and eventually fabricate a compact model which improve its productivity.

Each occurrence in an informational collection utilized by the ML algorithm is spoken to utilizing a similar arrangement of highlights. These occasions may have a known mark; this is known as the ML algorithm. Supervised and unsupervised are two varieties of the ML methodologies that are utilized for problems related to classification.

1.5.8   Author Identification and Prediction

The unlawful utilization of online resources for inappropriate or illicit purposes has increased with the quick development of the Internet and has turned into a noteworthy worry for society. For this respect, creator distinguishing proof is required. Author recognizable proof additionally is known as initiation ID. The creator distinguishing proof framework may utilize an assortment of fields, for example, criminal equity, the scholarly community, and humanities. The way toward saying something dependent on the past history is known as prediction. It very well may be climate forecast, traffic prediction and many more. A wide range of estimates should be possible utilizing an ML approach.

1.5.9   Services of Social Media

Do you ever consider how they utilize the Artificial Intelligence and Machine learning to deal with your social record? For instance, Facebook consistently sees your exercises like with whom you talk, your preferences, working environment, and study place. Furthermore, AI/ML consistently acts dependent on experience. Along these lines, Facebook gives you a proposal dependent on your exercises.

1.5.10   Medical Services

AI techniques and devices are utilized broadly in the territory of medicinal related issue, as an occurrence to recognize an infection, treatment arranging, restorative related research, and expectation of the ailment circumstance. Utilizing AI based programming in the social insurance issue gets a leap forward in restorative science.

1.5.11   Recommendation for Products and Services

Assume that we obtained a few things from an online shop a few days prior. Two or three days after, you will see that the related shopping sites or administrations are suggested for you.

Internet based life is utilizing the AI way to make alluring and awesome highlights, for example individuals you may know, recommendation, and response alternatives for their clients. These highlights are only a result of the AI procedure.

1.5.11.1   Machine Learning in Education

Instructors can utilize machine learning to check the amount of exercises that understudies can devour, how they are adapting to the exercises educated and whether they are viewing it as a lot to expend. Obviously, this enables the instructors to enable their understudies to get a handle on the exercises.

1.5.11.2   Machine Learning in Search Engine

Web indexes depending on machine learning to improve their administrations is no mystery today. Actualizing these, Google has presented some astounding administrations, for example, voice acknowledgment, picture search and some more. How they concoct additionally fascinating highlights is the thing that the truth will surface eventually.

1.5.11.3   Machine Learning in Digital Marketing

This is the place machine learning can help fundamentally. AI permits an increasingly applicable personalization. Consequently, organizations can cooperate and draw in with the client. Refined division centers around the fitting client at the ideal time, additionally with the privilege message. Organizations have data which can be utilized to get familiar with their conduct. Nova uses machine learning to compose deal messages that are customized. It realizes which messages performed better in the past and likewise recommends changes to the business messages.

1.5.11.4   Machine Learning in Healthcare

This application appears to stay an interesting issue throughout the previous three years. There are a few promising new businesses of this industry as they are outfitting their exertion with an emphasis on social insurance. These incorporate Nervanasys (obtained by Intel), Ayasdi, Sentient, and Digital Reasoning System among others.

PC vision is the most noteworthy supporters in the field of machine learning, which uses profound learning. It's a functioning human service application for ML Microsoft's InnerEye activity that begun in 2010 and is presently chipping away at a picture analytic device.

1.6   Future of Machine Learning

People have endeavored to develop machines post-industrialization which work like a human. Self driven machines have changed various business standards and one of the most prominent gifts to humankind is a thinking machine. Self-driving vehicles, propelled accomplices, mechanical handling plant staff, and canny urban zones have shown that sagacious machines are possible in the progressing years. Man-made insight has changed most industry sections like retail, creating, support, restorative administrations, and media and continues assaulting new locales.

In view of current innovation patterns and methodical movement machine learning is moving toward maturity. It will consistently stay a necessary piece of AI, enormous or little. ML expects expanded significance in business applications. The significance of ML is expanding and there is a likelihood that the innovation presents a cloud technology which is referred to as "machine learning-as-a-service." ML algorithms will be empowered by machine learning algorithms to adapt ceaselessly depending on the data which developed over the web. Equipment merchants upgrade CPU capacity to encourage ML information handling and it's a major surge in this procedure. Equipment sellers will be used to overhaul their machines in order to improve the forces of ML. Machine learning will help machines to comprehend setting and significance of data [9].

Quantum AI calculations have the capacity of changing the field of AI. For example, these calculations can utilize the upsides of quantum calculation to improve the capacities of old style techniques in AI. If quantum PCs are facilitated into AI, it could incite speedier planning of data, which could stimulate the ability to join information and draw bits of learning—and that is what's coming up for us. Quantum-filled structures will give a much snappier and even more solid computation to both directed and solo figuring. The extended introduction will open shocking AI capacities, which probably won't have been recognized using old style PCs.

Psychological administrations include a great deal of AI SDKs, APIs, and organizations, which empower designers to consolidate clever limits into their applications. With such administrations, designers can empower their applications to finish various commitments, for instance, vision affirmation, talk distinguishing proof, and talk understanding. As this development is continuing to propel, we are most likely going to watch the improvement of significantly keen applications that can logically talk, hear, see, and even reason with their condition. Subsequently, designers will more likely than not develop all the more enthralling and discoverable applications that can feasibly unravel customers' needs established on trademark correspondence techniques.

AI calculations are used to offer proposals to customers and entice them to complete certain exercises. With such calculations, you can consolidate the information in a data and make reasonable conclusions, for instance, a person's favorable circumstances.

Machine learning algorithms enable computers to understand the importance of information.

A prepared client of ML systems shares his bits of knowledge into the universe of ML, recommending that all these patterns are fast approaching in the domain of ML.

Utilization of Various Technologies in ML: The development of the Internet of things has profited machine learning from multiple points of view. The utilization of various mechanical techniques to accomplish better learning is as of now is in sync with machine learning algorithms; later on increasingly "shared learning" by using various innovations is obvious.

Customized Computing Environment: Developers will approach API packs to structure and convey "increasingly savvy application." In a way, this exertion is much the same as "helped programming." Through these API units, designers will effortlessly insert facial, discourse, or vision-acknowledgment highlights into their frameworks.

The processing speed of ML algorithms in higher-dimension vector handling will significantly be upgraded by quantum computing which will result in the victory in the domain of ML. Higher profit in business will occur with the progress of ML in future. ML-empowered administrations of things to come will turn out to be progressively precise and significant. For instance, the recommendation engines of things to come will be undeniably increasingly applicable and more like an individual client's close to home inclinations and tastes. A fast gathering of the most striking innovation patterns for 2018 is the result of innovative machine learning trends. Gartner's Top 10 Technology Trends of 2017 entireties up the all-plaguing computerized fever as the presence of individuals, machines, and business forms in a brought together framework.

The research and development in AI and ML lead to digital security which have taken ML algorithm to the following degree of realizing, which recommends that the security-driven ML use cases to come will be set apart for their speed and exactness. The entire research pattern is accessible in machine learning, artificial intelligence and the future of cyber security. Data scientists and digital security specialists may come closer because of this developing pattern to accomplish regular programming improvement.

Machine Learning algorithm may change the application-improvement markets of tomorrow because of which it is difficult to overlook the world-wide effect "man-made intelligence washing" in the present business market.

Toward the start of industrial revolution, simulated intelligence and ML have mutually been given a similar significance as the disclosure of power. These outskirts advances, much the same as power, have introduced another period in the historical backdrop of information technology.

Business and industry areas are controlled by ML framework. These advancements are step by step achieving transformative changes crosswise in different parts of industry.

Step by step, human specialists and machines will work together to convey improved results. Propelled machines will be relied upon to convey exact and auspicious discovery of patient conditions and the experts will be able to concentrate on more patients.

The most recent advancements like blockchain are affecting India's capital markets and are examined by computer based intelligence and machine learning. Blockchain is utilized to anticipate developments in the market and to identify misrepresentation by capital showcase administrators. Man-made intelligence innovations not just give chances to more up to date plans of action in the money related market but also harden the AI technologist's situation in the business-venture biological system. The tedious assignments in a normal DBA framework give chance to AI advancements to mechanize procedures and undertakings. The present DBA is engaged with cutting edge instruments.

1.7   Conclusion

The following are some imminent trends in machine learning field: Machine learning uses multiple technologies. Machine learning is benefitted by IOT in various ways. Multiple technologies help to achieve better learning. In this way we can achieve better "collaborative learning." In personalized computing environment API kits are accessible by the developers to design and deliver exceptional "intelligent application." Facial, speech, or vision-recognition features are embedded systems with intelligent API kits by developers. In high-dimensional vector processing the speed of execution of machine learning algorithms will be greatly enhanced by quantum computing and will be the next scope in the domain of ML research [10]. Higher business outcomes will be obtained using unsupervised machine learning algorithms. In the future, ML enabled services will become more accurate and relevant. Inside a significant number of programming bundles, machine learning and artificial intelligence (AI) and related advancements will be available crosswise over numerous enterprises, and will become part of our day by day lives by 2020.

Shockingly, however the guarantee of new income has pushed programming entrepreneurs to put resources into AI advancements, actually most associations don't have talented staff to grasp AI. A certain note of caution in numerous industry reviews on machine learning and its effect on ventures is that product sellers should initially concentrate potential business profits by machine learning and understanding the business-client needs. In various capacities of tech-empowered arrangements many trust deficiencies that exist today will disappear in the next 10 years. Another strong purpose behind standard clients is that various AI fueled applications customers are confronting to defeat the trust obstruction after some time. The Citizen Data Science people group will prepare for another innovation request world with more presentation and more access to mechanical answers for their day by day business.

Competitive business agents can be created using AI and ML techniques while advances like the Cloud carry nimbleness to business procedures, and hence influence business results.

References

1. Alpaydin, E., *Introduction to machine learning*, pp. 200–300, MIT press, Cambridge, Massachusetts, 2009.
2. Harrell, F.E., Ordinal logistic regression, in: *Regression modeling strategies*, pp. 311–325, Springer Series in Statistics, Springer International Publishing, Switzerland, 2015.
3. Meyer, D. and Wien, F.T., Support vector machines. *Interface Libsvm Package e1071*, 28, pp. 1–8, 2015.
4. Liaw, A. and Wiener, M., Classification and regression by random Forest. *R News*, 2, 3, 18–22, 2002.
5. Jolliffe, I., *Principal component analysis*, pp. 1094–1096, Springer, Berlin, Heidelberg, 2011.
6. Guojon, G. and Michael., K.P., K-means clustering with outlier removal. *Pattern Recognit. Lett.*, 90, 8–14, 2017.
7. Sapp, C.E., Preparing and architecting for machine learning. *Gartner Tech. Prof. Adv.*, 1–37, 2017.
8. Kharde, V. and Sonawane, P., Sentiment analysis of twitter data: a survey of techniques. *arXiv preprint arXiv:1601.06971*, 139, 5–15, 2016.

9. S. Tanaka and M. Kori, Data acquisition device, data acquisition method and computer readable medium, U.S. Patent Application No.10289719., Washington, DC: U.S. Patent and Trademark Office, 2019.
10. Wang, W. and Siau, K., Artificial Intelligence, Machine Learning, Automation, Robotics, Future of Work and Future of Humanity: A Review and Research Agenda. *J. Database Manage. (JDM)*, 30, 1, 61–79, 2019.

Cognitive Computing: Architecture, Technologies and Intelligent Applications

Nilanjana Pradhan[1]*, Ajay Shankar Singh[1] and Akansha Singh[2]

*[1]School of Computer Science and Engineering, Galgotias University,
Greater Noida, Uttar Pradesh, India*
*[2]Department of Computer Science and Engineering, ASET,
Amity University Uttar Pradesh, Noida, India*

Abstract

Huge popularity of cognitive computing in both academic and industry is as a result of rapid development of computer software, hardware technologies and artificial intelligence. Logical methods are used by cognitive computing in psychology, biology, signal processing, information theory, mathematics and statistics to build machines which have reasonable ability similar to human brain. An effective cognitive computing architecture can be constructed using 5G network, robotics, deep learning, cloud and IOT infrastructures. Voice recognition, computer vision, cognitive healthcare, smart city, and smart transportation are some of the application areas. Cognitive computing framework connects with big data analytics as it requires huge amount of data to assimilate critical thinking capability of human being. Reinforcement learning is one of the machine learning techniques that can be used in cognitive computing architecture. Deep learning algorithms, open source frameworks and computer vision are also used to build an effective cognitive computing architecture. The architecture will define resource, workload and computation process rules which regulate application performance, It also helps in information hiding, autonomic scaling, optimize reliability and mobility of data which promotes DL/ML systems.

Keywords: Cognitive computing, deep learning, reinforcement learning

*Corresponding author: nilanjana.pradhan@galgotiasuniversity.edu.in

Krishna Kant Singh, Akansha Singh, Korhan Cengiz and Dac-Nhuong Le (eds.) Machine Learning and Cognitive Computing for Mobile Communications and Wireless Networks, (25–50) © 2020 Scrivener Publishing LLC

2.1   Introduction

The pattern of behaviorism slowly declined in middle and later times of the twentieth century. Just as the promotion of PC innovations, the quick advancement of phonetics, data hypothesis and information science has brought a noteworthy and interesting psychological transformation.

Processing of information in human mind has given rise to an interdisciplinary subject called psychological science. Intellectual researchers investigate mental ability of individuals through perception on perspectives, for example, language, recognition, memory, consideration, thinking and emotion. The intellectual procedure of individuals is basically considered the accompanying two phases. Right off the bat, individuals become mindful of surrounding physical conditions by means of their sensory organs which helps to gather outer information [1]. The information passes through nerves for preparing, stockpiling, investigation and learning within brain. The output results are encouraged different sections of body through sensory system and after that the respective body part delivers proper conduct reaction. In this way, a total shut circle that spreads basic leadership and activity is framed. The cognitive framework is incredibly intricate; it is fundamental to utilize the devices and the techniques from different subjects.

With the advancement of computerized reasoning increasing over the globe, IT organizations are searching for approaches to patch up their engineering to make progressively vigorous. Progressively, specialists are going to mind motivated engineering with co-found memory and handling, bringing about PCs which are multiple times quicker than customary PCs. Such is the energy around AI equipment, that this stage has been named as a "renaissance of equipment" as sellers are racing to manufacture space explicit or outstanding task at hand explicit designs that can fundamentally scale and improve computational productivity [1].

Also, as we move forward in the portable time, the remaining tasks at hand are going to look amazingly divergent since the necessities of registering are evolving. Organizations need to depend on an alternate design, each implied for a specific outstanding task at hand. The place sellers are making a move from Von Neumann registering design and are endeavoring to improve the exhibition of figuring with multi-center CPU structures.

As talked about above, subjective registering frameworks are regularly founded on numerous advancements like characteristic language handling and questions, AI calculations, continuous processing, etc. Undertakings must be furnished with essential advanced methodology and mechanical foundation to incorporate these frameworks into key business procedures to lift the offer of administrations on any scale [2].

The privilege SaaS items can have a lot of effect on rising new companies, SMEs and enormous associations alike. For instance, to boost the effect of psychological activities, computerized design must have cloud coordinated into the framework. It is so in light of the fact that for subjective registering frameworks to process a monstrous measure of information for investigation, design distinguishing proof and expectation, a broad figuring force is required.

Furthermore, cloud application administrations demonstrate to be the most cost-productive and sharpest choice as they don't require any physical foundation for their establishment and offer more noteworthy capacities, for example, between operability and simpler customization. With the virtual establishment of cloud set up, undertakings can use computerized frameworks of intellectual figuring to deal with their center business activities, for example, deals arranging, overseeing accounts and production network, showcasing, and so forth just as to design each phase of the client lifecycle, starting from revelation to building dependability [2].

2.2 The Components of a Cognitive Computing System

An all out intellectual figuring framework incorporates the accompanying segments:

Artificial Intelligence (AI): AI identifies with a machine detecting or generally seeing its condition and after that finding a way to accomplish the objectives it was intended to reach. Early AI was increasingly simple, for example, information search, and intellectual registering is commonly viewed as a propelled type of AI.

Algorithms: Algorithms are sets of guidelines that characterize the methods that should be pursued to take care of a specific sort of issue.

Machine Learning and Deep Learning: Machine learning is the utilization of calculations to burrow through and parse information, gain from it, and after that apply figuring out how to perform assignments later on. AI demonstrates on the neural system of the human mind that uses a layered structure of calculations. There are a lot bigger measures of information and it takes care of issues from start to finish, rather than breaking them into parts, as in conventional AI draws near.

Data Mining: Data mining is the way toward inducing information and information connections from massive historical datasets.

Decision Automation and Reasoning: This is the procedure of an intellectual processing framework that applies its figuring out how to accomplish. Destinations are called reasoning. It's not much the same as human thinking, yet is intended to copy it. The result of a thinking procedure might be choice mechanization, in which programming self-governingly produces and actualizes an answer for an issue [3].

Speech Recognition and Natural Language Processing (NLP): Natural language handling is the utilization of registering methods to comprehend and produce reactions to human dialects in their normal—that is, customarily spoken and composed—structures. NLP traverses two subfields: Natural language understanding (NLU) and Natural language generation (NLG). A firmly related strategy is discourse acknowledgment, which changes over discourse contribution to composed language that is appropriate for NLP [3]. Visual acknowledgment utilizes profound learning calculations to examine pictures and recognize objects, for example, faces.

Emotional Intelligence: For quite a while, psychological figuring avoided attempting to mirror passionate insight; however intriguing activities, for example, the MIT startup Affectiva, are attempting to assemble processing frameworks that can comprehend human feeling through such markers as outward appearance and after that create reactions. The objective is to make intellectual figuring frameworks that are strikingly human-like due to their capacity to peruse passionate signs [3].

2.3 Subjective Computing Versus Computerized Reasoning

Considering subjective figuring a structure computerized reasoning is right, it misses an essential qualification that makes it so amazing.

When we talk about computerized reasoning, frequently we are looking at something that is fundamentally an extraordinary complex practical calculation. That is, an AI is an incredibly, complex choice tree—one we may not have the option to pursue ourselves—that when given particular information, will deliver an anticipated yield [4].

This is the way independent vehicles work, by taking in a beginning stage and a goal as info and exploring between the two as per an incredibly long arrangement of if–else proclamations. Cognitive frameworks utilize the majority of a similar AI, normal language handling, and information mining strategies that the above AI utilizes; however it makes things a stride further and looks to imitate the manner in which the human mind reasons and decides, frequently with clashing or out and out conflicting data [4].

It crunches the majority of this information and thinks about every one of the parameters and factors at play and deals with each the manner in which people may pick which café to eat at or which vehicle to purchase. When it completes its investigation, a psychological computational framework like IBM's Watson will give what it supposes is the best decision for a given issue from a variety of potential arrangements. This isn't really the correct decision, in any case. It leaves it to the human who is utilizing the framework to choose what the correct game-plan is in a given circumstance.

The fundamental qualification between psychological stages and man-made reasoning frameworks is that you need an AI to accomplish something for you. A subjective stage is something you go to for joint effort or for guidance. The applications for these stages go from prescription to client administration. Specialists can utilize these frameworks to help them in diagnosing patients, using their capacity to examine a patient's restorative history against each medicinal course reading at any point composed, distinguishing potential maladies a doctor may never have considered, or even think about. Organizations can utilize it to consolidate a wide range of hazard factors into a choice before furnishing an organization with a suggestion about a speculation or an area to construct another satellite office. The conceivable outcomes for this innovation later on are tremendous, and no industry will be left immaculate by it in the following decade [4].

2.4   Cognitive Architectures

The objective of this exertion is to build up an adequately proficient, practically exquisite, conventionally intellectual, amazing bound together, subjective engineering on the side of virtual people (and ideally canny operators/robots—and even another type of brought together hypothesis of human cognizance—too). An intellectual engineering is a theory about the fixed structures that give a psyche, regardless of whether in common or counterfeit frameworks, and how they cooperate—related to learning and abilities typified inside the design—to yield canny conduct in a decent variety of complex situations [5].

A terrific bound together design incorporates crosswise over (ostensibly representative) higher-level points of view in addition to some other (ostensibly subsymbolic) angles basic for fruitful conduct in human-like situations, for example, recognition, engine control, and feelings. A conventionally subjective engineering traverses both the formation of man-made reasoning and the displaying of common knowledge, at an appropriate degree of reflection. A practically rich engineering yields a wide scope of capacities from the associations among a little broad arrangement of instruments—basically what can be thought of as a lot of psychological Newton's laws. An adequately productive design executes rapidly enough for its foreseen applications, for instance, taking close to 50 msec for each intellectual cycle for ongoing virtual people [5].

Figure 2.1 represents flowchart of building a cognitive structure and represent our accentuation is on the improvement of the Sigma (Σ) plan, which explores the graphical designing hypothesis that progression currently depends after blending what has been picked up from over three decades worth of self-governing headway of mental structures and graphical models, an exhaustively fitting top tier formalism for structure canny segments. The result is a combined (discrete+continuous) and mixed (symbolic+probabilistic) approach that has yielded starting results transversely over memory and learning, basic reasoning and fundamental administration, mental imagery and acknowledgment, talk and standard language, and believing and thought. Figure 2.2 also presents cognitive architecture which provides us an idea of basic HCI model.

General human-level man-made cognizance, or AGI, has certain specific essentials. These can't be met by current AI/significant learning

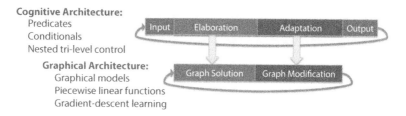

Figure 2.1 Flowchart of cognitive architecture (Source: http://cogarch.ict.usc.edu).

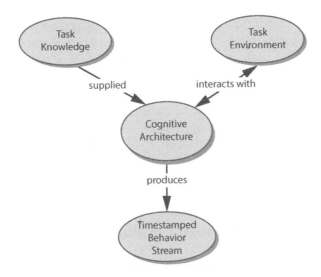

Figure 2.2 Structure of a model based on a cognitive architecture (Byrne, M. Cognitive architecture in HCI: Present work and future directions, 11th International Conference on HCI, Las Vegas).

approaches alone, nor by any dainty techniques. In this case we need an emotional designing (or self-decision administrator) approach [5].

2.5   Subjective Architectures and HCI

The research on human–computer interaction might not be instantly clear. Externally, this category of research appears to be speculative mental science, especially when the experts engage in talks based on any outcome of information processing. In any case, all things considered, scholarly structures may in sureness be presumably the significant work on emotional science i.e. human–computer interaction. Various occupations are available in which HCI research and development are expanding. Much research is going on in the field of HCI space models for research on mental planes.

It was deduced that various HCI structure and appraisal issues could, in all honesty, be reinforced by quantitative system. In at least the last twenty years, this science base has created and current amalgamations of the science base are directly best addressed in scholarly structures. As such, models reliant on abstract structures can serve to help the usability engineer in plan and evaluation. As referenced, designing based models all around produce as yield a period ventured stream of exercises, both plain (e.g., keystrokes) and mystery (e.g., recuperations from whole deal memory).

It may not be promptly evident what type of research on cognitive models emphasize HCI. Superficially, this sort of research regularly looks like profoundly hypothetical psychological science, especially when the analysts get involved in banters about the implications of low-level highlights of the design). In any case, for reasons unknown, cognitive models may in truth be the absolute most HCI-important psychological science work accessible. There are various jobs which cognitive architectures can fill in HCI research and practice, and in the other course, there are significant inquiries the HCI space models for look into on cognitive design [6].

2.6   Cognitive Design and Evaluation

At the point when an electrical or aeronautics designer plans, or assesses a structure, she has available to her a wide assortment of apparatuses, both subjective and quantitative, to help with the assignment. These building controls have a solid quantitative science base at their center which empowers such devices. The equivalent has commonly not been valid for the ease of use engineer. The ease of use engineer by and large needs to depend on a blend of rules, experience-based heuristics, direct experimental assessment (e.g., an ease of use test), and different less proper techniques. These are surely helpful procedures that have added a lot to the ease of use of a gigantic exhibit of PC frameworks, and progressively customary designing professionals additionally utilize such methods. Be that as it may, the quantitative conventional techniques accessible to different specialists have a lot of significant worth and are for the most part thought to be fundamental to the training, to such an extent that undergrad educational programs in such territories regularly requires numerous courses in the science and numerical base before understudies are even allowed to take medium-and upper-level courses in their building discipline. From numerous points of view, this is on the grounds that the science base for these controls is viewed as further developed than it is for the ease of use engineer. Notwithstanding, this is evolving. Numerous HCI structure and assessment issues could, indeed, be bolstered by quantitative procedure. In the last twenty or more years, this science base has developed and current unions of the science base are presently best spoken to in psychological models. In this way, models dependent on intellectual structures can serve to help the ease of use engineer in plan and assessment. As referenced, engineering based models by and large produce as yield a period stepped stream of activities, both unmistakable (e.g., keystrokes and mouse snaps) and secretive (e.g., recoveries from long haul memory) [6].

Thus, dependent upon nuances and assumptions made, emotional models can anticipate customer execution on an arrangement of measures including task times, learning rates and moreover inconveniences, eye check ways, move, and screw up rates. Unmistakably, countless these are really the sorts of things accommodation designers plan to get from usability tests. Also, these models can as often as possible give bits of information that convenience tests can't give. Cognitive models can much of the time make such reasons indisputable. In addition, the gauges made by such models are generally quantitative. While on some non-model-based from the previous reason it may be possible to envision that interface A will beat interface B, it is remarkable that various systems give a check of how much better A will be [6]. This isn't to recommend that mental models will out and out supplant usability tests; certifiable accurate tests both in the examination focus and in the field are still driven in other planning controls too. Regardless, mental models can empower the usability to fabricate focus convenience tests around features or tasks at risk to be noteworthy and can enable standard to out early arrangement choices, thusly reducing the amount of cycles of convenience testing and maybe even the amount of customers required. This is particularly engaging when the customer masses is pretty much nothing or incredibly difficult to get to as a result of specialization or cost, or when the endeavors or conditions required in the tests are unsafe or expensive. For example, testing business air ship pilots in flight is very trying since pilots are difficult to enroll and their time is exorbitant, outfitting business jetliners with new equipment requires noteworthy time and structuring effort, and poor results can have deadly outcomes. A part of these issues can be overpowered by the usage of test frameworks instead of certifiable cockpits; anyway, high-consistency test frameworks are themselves indulgent. Similar issues come up when arranging or surveying structures for use by remedial specialists (particularly impelled geniuses); one can imagine any number of exceptional masses that would raise a couple or all (or much continuously) such issues.

Relative issues come up when arranging or surveying structures for use by remedial specialists (particularly impelled professionals); one can imagine any number of extraordinary masses that would raise a couple or all (or much dynamically) such issues. By and by, it is emphatically the target. Along these lines, subordinate upon doubts made, energetic models can predict customer execution on a mix of measures including task times, learning rates and furthermore irritates, eye check ways, move, and mess up rates. Obviously, interminable these are amazingly the sorts of things

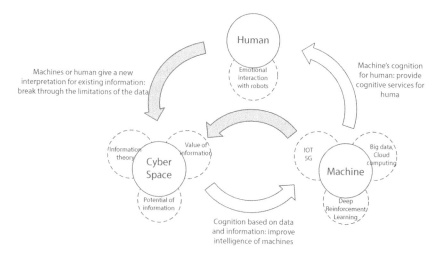

Figure 2.3 Human-centered cognitive cycle. (Source: Min Chen, Francisco Herrera, Kai Hwang, Cognitive Computing: Architecture, Technologies and Intelligent Applications, Published in IEEE Access 2018,Computer Science.)

comfort modelers expect to get from settlement tests. Figure 2.3 represents a cognitive cycle in which information from cyberspace is collected and sent to the machine. The machine processes the information and send to human expert or robot who in return forms a new interpretation and again send it to the cyber space. Furthermore, these models can a noteworthy piece of the time give bits of information that solace tests can't give. For example, while it may be possible to show up with no inconvenience of utilization test that interface A produces best endeavor execution times relative over interface B, it is routinely obscure the reasons key the well-spring of the division. Cognitive models can consistently make such reasons self-evident [6]. Additionally, the examinations made by such models are ordinarily quantitative. While on some non-model-based from the past reason it may be possible to anticipate that interface A will beat interface B, it is exceptional that various structures give an extent of how much better A will be. This isn't to recommend that mental models will thoroughly supplant convenience tests; veritable accurate tests both in the examination focus and in the field are up until now decided in other sorting out controls also. Regardless, mental models can connect with the convenience to create focus usability tests around features or assignments resolved to be huge and can enable standard to out early arrangement alternatives, in like manner lessening the proportion of cycles of usability testing and potentially the proportion of customers required.

This is particularly enrapturing when the customer people is close nothing or unfathomably difficult to get to as a result of specialization or cost, or when the endeavors or conditions required in the tests are hazardous or expensive. For example, testing business flying machine pilots in flight is astoundingly endeavoring since pilots are difficult to choose and their time is expensive, furnishing business jetliners with new equipment requires tremendous time and sorting out effort, and poor results can have savage outcomes. A bit of these issues can be overpowered by the utilization of test frameworks as opposed to genuine cockpits, regardless that high-consistency test structures are themselves liberal.

Subjective Models in Lieu of Human Users: Figure 2.4 represents the cognitive functioning of right brain and left brain. The way that these models are executable progressively (or quicker) implies they have various other HCI relevant applications which follows Figure 2.4 and that may not be promptly clear. One such use is in wise coaching frameworks (ITSs). Consider the Lisp mentor; this mentoring framework contained a design based running computational model of the information important to execute the applicable Lisp capacities, and a module for evaluating which

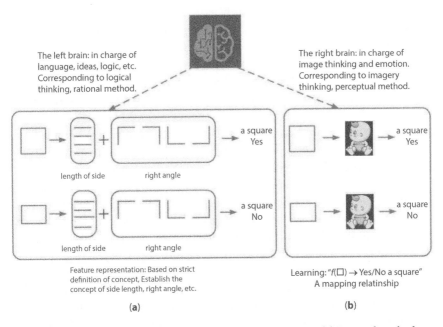

Figure 2.4 Perceptual and rational method to recognize a square. (a) Rational method. (b) Perceptual method (Source: Chen, M., Herrera, F., & Hwang, K. (2018). Cognitive Computing: Architecture, Technologies and Intelligent Applications. *IEEE Access, 6,* 19774-19783).

bits of this learning was aced by the understudy. Since the model was executable, it could anticipate what move the understudy would make if the understudy had right learning of how to take care of the issue. At the point when the understudy made an alternate move, this told the ITS that the understudy was missing at least one pertinent bit of learning. The understudy could then be given input about what learning was absent or inadequate, and issues which practiced this information could be chosen by the ITS for further practice by the understudy. By recognizing understudies' learning, and the holes in that information, it was conceivable to create progressively powerful instructive encounters. Issues that contained learning the understudy had effectively aced could be dodged, to not exhaust the understudy with things they definitely knew. This opened up the understudy to focus on the material they had not yet aced, bringing about improved learning. While the Lisp coach is an old research framework, ITSs dependent on the equivalent basic subjective design with a similar basic philosophy have been created for all the more squeezing instructive needs, for example, secondary school variable based math and geometry and are presently sold industrially. There is another significant and HCI-important application for high-constancy psychological models: populating reenactments or reproduced universes. For instance, preparing a tank administrator is costly, even in a test system, since that learner needs to confront sensible restriction. Sensible restriction comprises of other prepared tank administrators, so preparing one individual requires removing a few prepared administrators from their ordinary obligations (i.e., working tanks on genuine missions). This is troublesome and costly. Assuming, in any case, different administrators could be reproduced reasonably, at that point the student could confront resistance that would have helpful preparing esteem, without expelling officially prepared administrators from their obligations. There are many preparing circumstances like this, where the best way to prepare somebody is to include numerous human specialists who should all be detracted from their customary employments. In any case, the requirement for costly specialists can conceivably be killed (or possibly diminished) by utilizing compositionally based intellectual models instead of the human specialists. The U.S. military has just begun to try different things with simply such a situation. There are different areas other than preparing where having sensible adversaries is attractive, for example, computer games. Other than things like surface mapped 3D illustrations, one of the highlights frequently used to sell games is system play. Figure 2.5 represents a system architecture of cognitive computing which utilize cloud technologies, tensor flow, various database tools to build any cognitive applications.

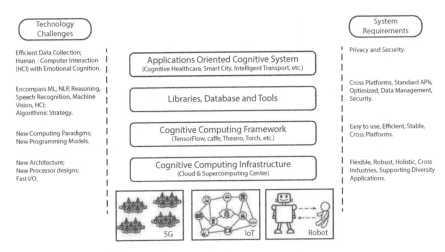

Figure 2.5 The system architecture of cognitive computing (Source: www.
semanticscholar.org/paper/Cognitive-Computing).

This engages players to attract enemies whose limits are more essentially indistinguishable from their own than average PC created rivals. In any case, even with framework play, it isn't always plausible for a gamer to find an appropriate opponent. In case the PC made enemy were an even more high-steadfastness proliferation of a human in regard to abstract and perceptual motor capacities, by then PC game players would experience no difficulty finding appropriate enemies without relying upon framework play. While this presumably won't be the most deductively entrancing usage of mental structures, it has all the earmarks of being certain that emotional models will be used. This is by no means whatsoever, a complete summary; there are various other potential uses for abstract models in HCI. Regardless, this should give enough with the objective that the value (or if nothing else the potential worth) of such endeavors to the HCI social order is apparent. This is certifiably not a totally promissory note, either, as there have been various productive usages of mental models in HCI past those referenced here. Most issues of journals, for instance, human–computer interaction and all of the methodology of the ACM SIGCHI meeting contain papers which use building based mental models. There was an uncommon fragment of the journal human–computer interaction focused on such models in 1997, a tantamount remarkable issue of the International Journal of Human-Computer Studies in 2001, and an unprecedented region of the journal Human Factors in 2003 that contained a couple of papers reliant on such models. The association between cognitive models and HCI is very challenging.

HCI challenges for cognitive science out of the blue, the relationship between academic models and HCI is comparable. Subsequently as theoretical structures can contribute genuinely to and practice in HCI, managing HCI issues is valuable and instructive for research in insightful models. As referenced, mental science has grasped a gap and-vanquish strategy to the assessment of human knowledge; models and hypotheses in a singular domain of study (e.g., memory) reliably touch base at models and theories in different spaces (e.g., vision). Thus, the undertakings utilized in different labs are ordinarily exceptionally phony, stripping on and on an assortment of impacts so the agent can concentrate on their specific region. Individuals in HCI don't have this guilty pleasure. Hence, HCI is an amazing space to push on the coordination limits of mental plans. Furthermore, HCI is an astoundingly commonplace locale for individuals who make Cognitive models. Such individuals participate in insightful cerebrum research or programming structuring, in any case by and large have a superior than normal package of broadly instructing in the other control. Since these are two of the focal controls reflected in HCI, there will all things considered be a basic spread in interests between individuals in conceptual models and individuals in HCI. Furthermore, since most structure producers in like way put over the top extents of imperativeness pulled in with their PCs, they are immediate affected by advances in HCI.

Open Issues and Future Work: While the reputation of insightful structures in HCI is dazzling, they are from various points of view still works in progress. There are different inconveniences that legitimately can't be tended to by enthusiastic structures. Fortunately lot of research has been done to solve these issues and everything considered early reports of movement are promising.

Theoretical Coverage: While academic models endeavor to be done, joining the full degree of discernment, information, and engine control is indisputably a significant test. Obviously, there are a critical number of holes in what has been checked by academic plans. If all else fails, discernment and engine control are essentially appeared at a sensible level; these structures for the most part don't cover point by point bits of how light is changed into impression of things and surfaces, nor are the subtleties of complex engine upgrades represented.

Along basically undefined lines, models made in mental courses of action don't express smooth or focus penchants, something real customers obviously do. Another game plan of parts which has not yet gotten exquisite thought are factors like insufficiency, stress, nonappearance of rest, and such. While these unequivocally may pass on with them stacked with inclination or energetic parts, such factors in like way effectively sway human insight and execution.

Astoundingly, hypothetical structures have usually not been used to exhibit the effects of such specialists. Over once more, regardless, evaluation into how such effects can be showed up with mental structures is in movement.

This enables players to attract foes whose limits are more for all intents and purposes indistinguishable from their very own than average PC delivered rivals. Nevertheless, even with framework play, it isn't always doable for a gamer to find a reasonable opponent. In case the PC made foe were an even more high-faithfulness propagation of a human in regard to emotional and perceptual motor capacities, by then PC game players would experience no difficulty finding legitimate foes without relying upon framework play. While this presumably won't be the most deductively intriguing usage of mental structures, it gives off an impression of being inevitable that emotional models will be used thusly. This is by no means, an all out once-over; there are various other potential uses for emotional models in HCI. Regardless, this should give enough with the objective that the value (or if nothing else the potential worth) of such endeavors to the HCI social order is clear. This is anything but a totally promissory note, either, as there have been various productive uses of mental models in HCI past those referenced here. Most issues of journals, for instance, human–computer interaction and all of the techniques of the ACM SIGCHI meeting contain papers which use designing based mental models.

The contribution of HCI in cognitive science is indefinite, hence the relationship between academic models and HCI is comparable. In this way as dynamic structures can contribute sincerely to research and practice in HCI, managing HCI issues is helpful and instructive for research in insightful models. As referenced, mental science has grasped a gap and-vanquish strategy to the assessment of human knowledge; models and hypotheses in a singular domain of study (e.g., memory) reliably touch base at models and theories in different spaces (e.g., vision). Thusly, the undertakings utilized in different labs are regularly remarkably phony, stripping on and on an assortment of impacts so the specialist can concentrate on their specific region. Individuals in HCI don't have this extravagance. In this manner, HCI is an astounding space to push on the coordination limits of mental plans. Also, HCI is an astoundingly ordinary locale for individuals who make mental models. Such intelligent people have done insightful research in human brain programming ,therefore in any case for the most part have a superior than normal bundle of broadly educating in the other control. Since these are two of the focal controls reflected in HCI, there will all things considered be a basic spread in interests between individuals in theoretical models and individuals in HCI. Also, since most structure creators in like way put unbelievable extents of essentialness pulled in with their PCs, they are immediately affected by advances in HCI.

Another piece of emotional structures that does not actually meet the full extent of limits imperative to demonstrate HCI endeavors is that such plans are in general scholarly; they model essentially parts of thinking, and basically enough perception and motor control to support that thinking. They all around don't consider components like impact and social effect. Regardless, as impact and feeling have been subjects which have gotten critical thought generally in the HCI social order, wear down planning impact with scholarly structures is rising rapidly. Along practically identical lines, models made in mental plans don't express sleek or extract tendencies, something real customers obviously do. Another plan of parts which has not yet gotten tasteful thought is factors like shortcoming, stress, absence of rest, such factors in like manner influence human brain discernment and execution. Incredibly, abstract structures have ordinarily not been used to show the effects of such authorities. Afresh, be that as it may, assessment into how such effects can be shown with mental structures is in advancement. Taking everything into account, most emotional showing has been made arrangements for showing the lead of a single customer at some random minute. Clearly, various assignments of unprecedented eagerness to HCI investigators and experts incorporate social occasions or gatherings of customers. While there is nothing on a fundamental level which thwarts the usage of abstract structures to construct different models and have those models partner with one another, such use has not been the standard and it isn't clear how much these would really get the sumptuousness of human social association. Regardless, there has been some reassuring work on this front, any way that work did not dive significantly into social components.

Wipro offers Wipro HOLMES Artificial Intelligence Platform™ which helps enterprises hyper-automate processes, redefine operations and reimagine their customer journeys. It helps customers offload specific cognitive tasks to the AI software to gain cost efficiencies and agility, thereby adopting hybrid modes of working. It has capabilities such as language understanding, vision, learning, prediction, reasoning, and inferences, which enable businesses, build and deploy cognitive solutions for the digital age.

The solution areas include HOLMES for Business (e.g. Enterprise Know Your Customer (e-KYC), Engineering Drawings, Contract Management, Tax Forms, etc.), HOLMES for IT (IT Infrastructure Automation, Application Services Automation) and Business Process Service Delivery Automation [7]. Cognitive cloud computing and IT as a help hold the way to big business resurrection. Numerous organizations feel undermined by the advanced age. They glance around and never again observe a similar challenge. Since 2000, the greater part of the organizations that had earned a spot in the esteemed Fortune 500 have failed, were procured or just stopped to exist. New organizations have quickly risen in their place, and a significant number of them are disturbing how things are done on their way to the top.

2.6.1   Architectures Conceived in the 1940s Can't Handle the Data of 2020

Distributed computing gives new companies the mental fortitude to point their slingshots at longstanding business monsters both inside and outside their enterprises. New businesses take piece of the pie and keep administrators alert around evening time due to the opportunity they have by being brought into the world computerized. Free of conventional imperatives, for example, overhead and coordinations, they flourish with application based plans of action that incite adaptability and help them benefit as much as possible from their information.

Undeniably, information drives business. Experts as of late placed that every one of the information on the planet added up to 4.4 zettabytes. To place that in context, a zettabyte is around 10 to the intensity of 21 bytes. That will appear to be an insignificant detail by 2020, when worldwide information could conceivably build multiple times over to 44 zettabytes. What should concern associations isn't only the sheer measure of information however the way that 80 percent of it is unstructured. Dull information contains video, writings, online networking posts, sound clasps—things that are additionally significant to organizations in light of the fact that the data conveys incredible knowledge on shopper conduct [8].

Organizations can't tap dull information utilizing customary registering, the vast majority of which depends on engineering that was structured in 1945 by Princeton mathematician John von Neumann. While Von Neumann's creation propelled advancement for a considerable length of time, it can never again appropriately serve the numerous mechanical needs confronting associations today.

2.7   Cognitive Technology Mines Wealth in Masses of Information

Associations should not be questionable or scared of where the advanced future is going. The change from battle to quality requires just a cloud-local stage that is prepared cognitively.

The motivation behind why customized innovation can't start to deal with the present information requests is that it needs sorted out data and modified rationale to work. Cognitive frameworks adapt deliberately and consistently, all while dealing with dissimilar and shifted information.

Cognitive technology comprehends unstructured data, for example, the symbolism, normal language and sounds in books, messages, tweets, diaries, web journals, notions, pictures and recordings. It discovers meaning since it can reason through information and offer new settings to gauge and consider. Our customers see this with IBM Watson and its capacity to gain from high volumes of information at amazing velocity. Watson programming peruses 800 million pages for every second. For one of our customers, Watson innovation at first ingested 80 million records and is steadily including 30,000 extra reports each day.

At the point when utilized in an ideal half breed cloud condition, subjective innovation can reliably build the bits of knowledge you produce against your information, while at the same time growing your universe of information. All your dull information sees the light of investigation and activity, and with recently discovered dexterity and adaptability, your association continually shows signs of improvement at everything.

2.7.1   Technology Is Only as Strong as Its Flexible, Secure Foundation

It's essential to push that best in class design underlies these momentous gains in information knowledge. IBM customers, for instance, rely upon us to incorporate the correct blend of versatility administrations and after that faultlessly organize and work them. By joining intellectual innovation and IT robotization, Watson can anticipate issues and keep the IT condition solid just as offer bits of knowledge so administrators can improve business and IT performance. Many IBM customer ventures have encountered emotional improvement in effectiveness: inside 6 years and a half after reception of IT mechanization, the manual remaining tasks at hand have dropped between 20 to 70 percent.

The overall sustenance movement organization association Sysco, for one, participated with IBM Global Technology Services to improve its vehicle of 1.8 billion occasions of generally transient sustenance. Our Dynamic Cloud Automation of 4,000 servers subsequently settles scene and issues tickets, diminishing Sysco's fundamental issues by 89 percent and the typical objectives time from 19 hours to 28 minutes.

So additionally, IBM Watson redesigned the customer duty tries of retailer The North Face. We made a propelled gadget that redoes The North Face customers' shopping experiences. A URL on their devices incites when they're in a store to empower them to find the right item, while The North Face site taps Watson to get some information about their zones and when they'll wear dress to check atmosphere and lead them to fitting incidental decisions [9]. CTOs and CIOs regularly ask me where they should begin. I guide them to initially take the surest way to progress: Identify a utilization case with a customer or client and get a speedy success. At that point, they can demonstrate to investors that venture IT as a Service and intellectual figuring can improve things.

At that point, they can have dexterous advancement, react to the challenge's plans of action and present their own plans of action—they can be disruptors. To perceive how your association can be renewed as a coordinated disruptor, get familiar with IBM Global Technology Services [9].

Psychological processing vows to be the following huge development in registering frameworks—yet what's going on here? In spite of the buzz, there is no firm accord on what accurately establishes intellectual registering, a propelled field of man-made brainpower. We have additionally gathered together bits of knowledge from pioneers in psychological innovation and gave accommodating infographics that separate the ideas.

2.8   Cognitive Computing: Overview

Here's a working meaning of the term: Cognitive figuring depicts registering frameworks that are intended to copy human or close human insight, so they can perform undertakings generally appointed to people in a way that is comparative or even better than the human's presentation of the errand.

IBM, whose Watson PC framework demonstrated in Figure 2.6 with its regular language handling (NLP) and AI capacities is maybe the best known "face" of psychological registering, authored the term subjective processing to depict frameworks that could learn, reason, and communicate in human-like style. Psychological processing traverses both equipment and programming.

All things considered, intellectual figuring unites two very various fields: psychological science and software engineering. Subjective science ponders the functions of the cerebrum, while software engineering includes the hypothesis and plan of PC frameworks [10]. Together, they endeavor to make PC frameworks that copy the psychological elements of the human

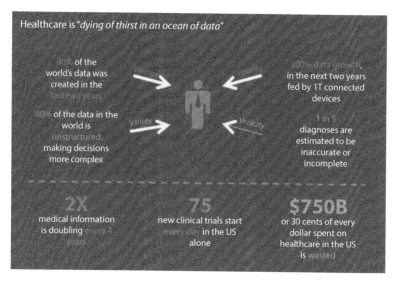

Figure 2.6 IBM Watson utilized in healthcare (Source: https://www.slideshare.net/mobile/AndersQuitzauIbm/ibm-watson-in-healthcare).

mind. For what reason would we need PC frameworks that can work like human minds? We experience a daily reality such that produces bountiful measures of data. Most gauges find that the computerized universe is multiplying in size as least at regular intervals, with information growing in excess of multiple times from 2010 to 2020. Sorting out, controlling, and understanding that tremendous measure of information surpasses human limit. Subjective PCs have a mission to help us.

You've presumably encountered intellectual figuring applications as of now, maybe without knowing it. Presently, psychological registering is helping specialists to analyze sickness, meteorologists to anticipate tempests, and retailers to pick up knowledge into how clients carry on.

Probably the best interest for subjective figuring arrangements originates from enormous information investigation, where the amounts of information outperform human capacity to parse however offer benefit creating experiences that can't be disregarded. Lower-cost, cloud-based intellectual figuring innovations are winding up progressively available, and beside the set up tech goliaths—for example, IBM, Google, and Microsoft—various littler players have been making moves to get a bit of the still-youthful subjective registering market [9].

Little wonder, at that point, that the worldwide market for psychological registering is required to develop at a galactic 49.9 percent compound yearly development rate from 2017 to 2025, prospering from just shy of $30 billion to over $1 trillion, as indicated by CMFE News.

Psychological procedures utilize existing learning and create new information. The idea of comprehension is firmly identified with abstract ideas, for example, psyche and insight. They can perform assignments that solitary people utilized to have the option to do. So as to accomplish this new degree of registering, intellectual frameworks must be:

1. Versatile
2. Intuitive
3. Iterative and stateful
4. Relevant

Cognitive computing mimicking the capacity of a human cerebrum is represented in Figure 2.7 and handling mankind of issues. Mix of advancements to comprehend human association and give answers. Subjective figuring frameworks use machine learning calculations. Such frameworks constantly procure learning from the information.

Three periods of figuring are:

1. Classifying system—including objects
2. Programmable system—preparing numbers
3. Subjective registering understand information, forecast

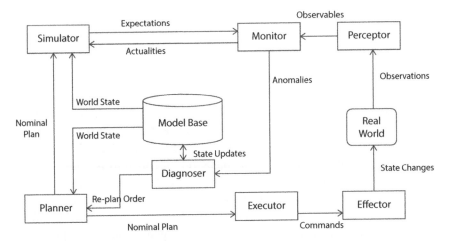

Figure 2.7 High autonomy cognitive architecture (Source: Cognitive computing 2016, https://www.slideshare.net/jimsiah1/cognitive-computing-2016).

When computer becomes brains the human mind incorporates memory and handling together. It responds to things in its environment. But a PC has separate memory and processing. It does its work by a clock. For the first run through in figuring history, it's feasible for machines to gain for a fact and enter the unpredictability of information to distinguish affiliations. The field is called subjective analytics enlivened by how the human mind forms data, makes inferences as opposed to relying upon predefined guidelines and organized questions. Psychological examination can push past the constraints of human comprehension, enabling us to process and see enormous information continuously. Setting based theories can be shaped by investigating massive quantities of changes of potential connections of impact and causality—prompting ends. Any branch of engineering mainly have three components: (a) executive layer organizer and recreation; (b) coordination layer diagnoser, model base, screen, and agent; and (c) execution layer effector and perceptor. Engineering WATSON Super PC was created by IBM Research and named after IBM's originator—Thomas J Watson. Research group was driven by Principal Investigator Dr. David Ferrucci and modified by 25 IBM scientists. Watson is capable of addressing addresses presented in regular dialects, and is able to manufacture information and learn, comprehend common language and collaborate more normally with people [9]. IBM Watson question noting technology utilize more than a hundred procedures to categorize various languages [9]. Deep comprehension of human language Software-DeepQA. It runs on group of intensity 750 computers, 10 racks holding 90 servers, 2880 3.55GHz power processor cores. 16 TB memory holds around one million books.

How does Watson answer a question? This procedure takes a sum of 3 seconds. The goal of Watson according to IBM is "to have PCs begin to cooperate in normal human terms over a scope of uses and procedures, understanding the inquiries that people pose and giving answers that people can comprehend and legitimize." The objective of psychological figuring is to make robotized IT frameworks that are equipped for taking care of issues without needing human support. It is used in healthcare industry. The data explosion—medical information is required to twofold every 73 days by 2020. The great unknown—80% of wellbeing information is undetectable to current frameworks since they are unstructured. Watson Health can see them. A quick study shows that Watson can peruse 40 million reports in 15 seconds. Cognitive computing is making farming progressively gainful. Cognitive computing is making autos more intelligent. Figure 2.8 represents various applications of cognitive computing. Cognitive computing is making our homes and workplaces increasingly secure, just as our outskirts. Future aspects include augmented virtual reality, sentient systems, specialized deep

Cognitive Computing Applications

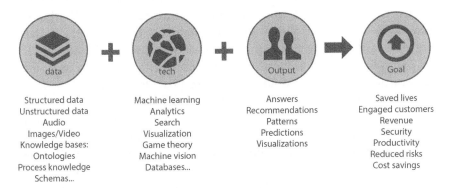

data	tech	Output	Goal
Structured data	Machine learning	Answers	Saved lives
Unstructured data	Analytics	Recommendations	Engaged customers
Audio	Search	Patterns	Revenue
Images/Video	Visualization	Predictions	Security
Knowledge bases:	Game theory	Visualizations	Productivity
Ontologies	Machine vision		Reduced risks
Process knowledge	Databases...		Cost savings
Schemas...			

Figure 2.8 Cognitive computing applications (Source: Understanding cognitive applications: A framework—Sue Feldman, https://www.slideshare.net/diannepatricia/understanding-cognitive applications-a-framework-sue-feldman).

learning on big data sets, and generalized artificial intelligence systems [9]. Cognitive registering has been portrayed as a set of self-governing and keen information preparing speculations and advances emulating the components of the cerebrum past customary basic information handling. To comprehend what psychological processing is intended to do, we can profit by first understanding the quality it tries to imitate: intellectual insight. Psychological knowledge is the human capacity to think in dynamic terms to reason, plan, make answers for issues, and learn. It isn't equivalent to enthusiastic insight, which is, as indicated by clinicians Peter Salovey and John D. Mayer, "the capacity to screen one's own and others' sentiments and feelings, to separate among them, and to utilize this data to control one's reasoning and activities." Put basically, subjective insight is the utilization of mental capacities to take care of issues and answer questions, while enthusiastic knowledge is the capacity to viably explore the social world. Subjective knowledge is predictable with analyst Phillip L. Ackerman's idea of insight as information, which sets that learning and procedure are both piece of the acumen. Intellectual figuring tries to structure PC frameworks that can perform subjective procedures similarly that the human mind performs them.

2.9   The Future of Cognitive Computing

In spite of the fact that neurosynaptic chips brought revolutionary changes in technology, they don't start to approach the multifaceted nature of the

human mind, which has 80 billion neurons and 100 trillion neurotransmitters and is strangely control effective. IBM's most recent SyNAPSE chip
has just 1 million neurons and 256 million neurotransmitters. Work proceeds on neuromorphic designs that will rough the structure of the human
cerebrum: IBM says it needs to assemble a chip framework with 10 billion neurons and 100 trillion neurotransmitters that devours only one
kilowatt-hour of power and fits inside a shoebox. One significant achievement of things to come is the exascale PC, a framework that can play out
a billion estimations for each second, a thousand times more than petas-
cale PCs presented in 2008. Exascale registering is thought to coordinate
the handling intensity of the human cerebrum at the neural level. The U.S.
Division of Energy has said that at any rate one of the approaching exascale
machines would have liked to be worked by 2021 will utilize a "novel engineering." Another historic suggestion for subjective registering originates
from researchers and specialists who need to saddle the huge and multiplying measures of logical information [10]. They propose the improvement of a psychological "brilliant associate" that could examine learning
and contextualize it so it could distinguish and quicken research addresses
expected to meet all-encompassing logical goals, and even encourage the
procedures of experimentation and information survey.

While IBM is as yet a worldwide pioneer in psychological registering,
expecting to "intellectually empower and disturb businesses," it faces rivalry
from subjective processing new companies in explicit segments. A zone of
the intellectual registering scene that will probably observe significant development is custom subjective figuring. Custom psychological registering
depends on the rule that designers who need to bring intellectual capacities
(for example, PC vision and discourse acknowledgment) to their applications
ought not need to stress over the intricate procedure of preparing these astute
capacities, since preparing requires making monstrous curated datasets.

The connection between scholastic models and HCI is practically identical. Hence as hypothetical structures can contribute really to research
and practice in HCI, overseeing HCI issues is important and educational
for research in clever models. As referenced, mental science has gotten a
handle on a hole and-vanquish technique to the appraisal of human information; models and speculations in a solitary area of study (e.g., memory)
dependably get in contact at models and hypotheses in various spaces (e.g.,
vision). In this manner, the endeavors used in various labs are commonly
uncommonly fake, stripping endlessly an arrangement of effects so the
operator can focus on their particular area. People in HCI don't have this
indulgence. Without a doubt, it can be imagined that customers should
interface with a wide level of scholarly, perceptual, and motor breaking

points. Subsequently, HCI is an astonishing space to push on the coordination furthest reaches of mental plans.

Moreover, HCI is an astoundingly a typical distinct technology for people who make cognitive models. Such people have actually started consistent and tough research on human brain programming. Since these are two of the central controls reflected in HCI, there will everything considered be an essential spread in interests between people in applied models and people in HCI. Moreover, since most structure makers in like manner put over the top degrees of importance pulled in with their PCs, they are quickly affected by advances in HCI.

Open Issues and Future Work: While the notoriety of wise structures in HCI is astonishing, they are from different perspectives still works in advancement [10]. There are various burdens that honestly can't be tended to by energetic structures. Luckily research has been begun unending these issues and everything considered early reports of development are promising.

Theoretical Coverage: While scholastic models try to be done, joining the full level of wisdom, data, and motor control is undeniably a critical test. Clearly, there are a basic number of openings in what has been checked by scholarly designs. As a last resort, insight and motor control are basically showed up at a reasonable level; these structures generally don't cover point by point bits of how light is changed into impression of things and surfaces.

References

1. Chen, M., Hao, Y., Gharavi, H., Leung, V.C., Cognitive information measurements: A new perspective. *Inf. Sci.*, 505, 487–497, 2019.
2. Sheth, A., Internet of things to smart iot through semantic, cognitive, and perceptual computing. *IEEE Intell. Syst.*, 31, 2, pp108–112, 2016.
3. Tarafdar, M. and Beath, C.M., Wipro Limited: Developing a Cognitive DNA, *Thirty ninth International Conference on Information Systems*, San Francisco, vol. 3, pp. 6–7, 2018 .
4. Wang, Y., Zhang, D., Kinsner, W. (Eds.), *Advances in cognitive informatics and cognitive computing*, vol. 323, Springer, Berlin, Heidelberg, 2010.
5. Vallverdú, J., Talanov, M., Distefano, S., Mazzara, M., Tchitchigin, A., Nurgaliev, I., A cognitive architecture for the implementation of emotions in computing systems. *Biol. Inspired Cognit. Archit.*, 15, 34–40, 2016.
6. Konar, A., *Artificial intelligence and soft computing: behavioral and cognitive modeling of the human brain*, CRC Press, Boca Raton, Florida, 2018.
7. Amato, F., Marrone, S., Moscato, V., Piantadosi, G., Picariello, A., Sansone, C., HOLMeS: eHealth in the Big Data and Deep Learning Era. *Information*, 10, 2, 34, pp. 1–20, 2019.

8. Yao, Y., Three-way decisions and cognitive computing. *Cognit. Comput.*, 8, 4, 543–554, 2016.

9. Chen, Y., Argentinis, J.E., Weber, G., IBM Watson: how cognitive computing can be applied to big data challenges in life sciences research. *Clin. Ther.*, 38, 4, 688–701, 2016.

10. Kelly, J.E., III and Hamm, S., *Smart machines: IBM's Watson and the era of cognitive computing*, Columbia University, Press, New York, 2013.

Deep Reinforcement Learning
for Wireless Network

Bharti Sharma[1]*, R.K Saini[1], Akansha Singh[2] and Krishna Kant Singh[3]

*[1]Department of Computer Application, DIT University,
Dehradun, Uttarakhand, India
[2]Department of Computer Science Engineering, ASET,
Amity University Uttar Pradesh, Noida, India
[3]Department of ECE, KIET Group of Institutions, Ghaziabad, India*

Abstract

The rapid introduction of mobile devices and the growing popularity of mobile applications and services create unprecedented infrastructure requirements for mobile and wireless networks. Future 5G systems are evolving to support growing mobile traffic, real-time accurate analytics, and flexible network resource management to maximize user experience. These tasks are challenging as mobile environments become increasingly complex, heterogeneous and evolving. One possible solution is to use advanced machine learning techniques to help cope with the growth of data and algorithm-based applications. The recent success of deep learning supports new and powerful tools that solve problems in this domain. In this chapter, we focus on how deep reinforcement learning should be integrated into the architecture of future wireless communication networks is presented.

Keywords: Big data, cellular network, deep learning, machine learning, neural network, reinforcement learning, wireless network, IoT

3.1 Introduction

Wireless networking landscape is undergoing a major revolution. The smart phone-oriented networks of the past years are slowly turning into a huge

---

*Corresponding author: Bharti.sharma@dituniversity.edu.in

Krishna Kant Singh, Akansha Singh, Korhan Cengiz and Dac-Nhuong Le (eds.) Machine Learning and Cognitive Computing for Mobile Communications and Wireless Networks, (51–72) © 2020 Scrivener Publishing LLC

ecosystem of the Internet of things (IoT), which integrates a heterogeneous combination of wireless devices, from smart phones to unmanned aerial vehicles, connected vehicles, wearable devices, sensors and a virtual reality device. This exceptional transformation will not only lead to an exponential increase in wireless traffic in the foreseeable future, but also lead to the emergence of new and unverified cases of using wireless services that are significantly different from conventional multimedia or voice services. For instance, beyond the need for high data rates which has been the main driver of the wireless network evolution in the past decade—next-generation wireless networks must be able to deliver ultra-reliable, low-latency communication [1–4] that is adaptive, in real-time to a rich and dynamic IoT environment.

Future wireless networks, large volumes of data must be collected, periodically and in real-time, across a massive number of sensing and wearable devices. Such massive short-packet transmissions will add to a substantial traffics over the wireless uplink, which has traditionally been much less congested than the downlink. This same wireless network must also support cloud-based gaming [5], immersive virtual reality services, real-time HD streaming, and conventional multimedia services. This ultimately creates a radically different networking environment whose novel applications and their diverse quality-of-service (QoS) and reliability requirements mandate a fundamental change in the way in which wireless networks are modeled, analyzed, designed, and optimized.

As an important enabling technology for artificial intelligence, machine learning has been successfully applied in many areas, including computer vision, medical diagnosis, search engines and speech recognition [4]. Machine learning is a field of study that gives computers the ability to learn without being explicitly programmed. Machine learning techniques can be generally classified as supervised learning, unsupervised learning and reinforcement learning. In supervised learning, the aim of the learning agent is to learn a general rule mapping inputs to outputs with example inputs and their desired outputs provided, which constitute the labeled data set. In unsupervised learning, no labeled data is needed, and the agent tries to find some structures from its input. While in reinforcement learning, the agent continuously interacts with an environment and tries to generate a good policy according to the immediate reward/cost fed back by the environment. In recent years, the development of fast and massively parallel graphical processing units and the significant growth of data have contributed to the progress in deep learning, which can achieve more powerful representation capabilities. For machine learning, it has the following advantages to overcome the drawbacks of traditional resource management, networking, mobility management and localization algorithms.

The first advantage is that machine learning has the ability to learn useful information from input data, which can help improve network performance. For example, convolution neural networks and recurrent neural networks can extract spatial features and sequential features from time-varying received signal strength indicator (RSSI), which can mitigate the ping-pong effect in mobility management [6], and more accurate indoor localization for a three-dimensional space can be achieved by using an auto-encoder to extract robust finger print patterns from noisy RSSI measurements [7]. Second, machine learning based resource management, networking and mobility management algorithms can well adapt to the dynamic environment. For instance, by using the deep neural network proven to be an universal function approximator, traditional high complexity algorithms can be closely approximated, and similar performance can be achieved but with much lower complexity [8], which makes it possible to quickly response to environmental changes. In addition, reinforcement learning can achieve fast network control based on learned policies. Third, machine learning helps to realize the goal of network self-organization. For example, using multi-agent reinforcement learning, each node in the network can self optimize its transmission power, sub-channel allocation and so on? At last, by involving transfer learning, machine learning has the ability to quickly solve a new problem. It is known that there exist some temporal and spatial relevancies in wireless systems such as traffic loads between neighboring regions [9]. Hence, it is possible to transfer the knowledge acquired in one task to another relevant task, which can speed up the learning process for the new task. However, in traditional algorithm design, such prior knowledge is often not utilized.

This book chapter includes the increasing use of machine leaning methods in different subfields of wireless network like resource management, networking, mobility management, localization and computation resource management and covering the use of deep reinforcement learning in wireless networking as cutting edges technologies in mobile network analysis and management are jointly reviewed from other machine leaning algorithms angle.

The remainder of this chapter is organized as follows: Section 3.3 discusses related work and Section 3.4 describes the growth of machine learning to deep learning. Section 3.4.1 describes a brief introduction of advance machine learning techniques. Applications of machine leaning including deep reinforcement learning in wireless network are discussed in Section 3.5. The advantages of deep reinforcement are tackled in Section 3.5.4, followed by the conclusion.

3.2   Related Work

Wireless and deep learning problems have been researched mostly independently. Only recently crossovers between the two areas have emerged. Several notable works paint a comprehensives picture of the deep learning and/or wireless networking research landscape. LeCun *et al.* discussed the goal of deep learning and introduced many frequently used models, and focused on the potential of deep neural networks [10]. Schmidhuber gave the detailed survey of deep learning including the evolution, methods, applications, and open research problems [11]. Liu *et al.* reviewed the fundamental principles of deep learning models, and discussed the deep learning developments in selected applications, [12]. Arulkumaran *et al.* presented fundamental algorithms and many architectures for deep reinforcement learning, covering trust region policy optimization, deep Q networks and asynchronous advantage actor–critic [13] and in this study authors highlighted the performance of deep neural networks in different control problem and the applications of deep reinforcement learning have also been surveyed in [14]. Zhang *et al.* discussed the application of deep learning in recommender systems [15]. In this study author also focused on the potential of deep learning in mobile advertising. As deep learning becomes increasingly popular, Goodfellow *et al.* provided a broad lecture series on deep learning in a book that included prerequisite knowledge, underlying principles, and frequently used applications [16]. Intelligent wireless networking is a popular topic of research in the area of research nowadays and related research works by different researchers in the literature have been reviewed in the same direction [17–21, 24].

Jiang *et al.* discussed the capabilities of machine learning in 5G network applications covering massive MIMO and smart grids [25]. In this study author also identified research gaps between ML and 5G. Li *et al.* discussed the potential and challenges of artificial intelligence (AI) into future wireless network architectures and discussed the importance of AI in the 5G era [26]. Klaine *et al.* presented the several successful ML algorithms in self-organizing networks (SONs) and discussed the pros and cons of different algorithms, and discovered the future research directions [27]. Potential of artificial intelligence and big data for energy efficiency purposes [28] was discussed. Chen *et al.* presented traffic offloading approaches in wireless networks, and proposed a novel reinforcement learning based solution [29] which opened a new research field in embedding machine learning to greening cellular networks.

More recently, Fadlullah *et al.* presented a broad survey on the development of deep learning in different areas including the application of deep learning in the network traffic control systems [30]. In the study author also focused on the several unsolved research issues for future study. Ahad *et al.* introduced various algorithms, applications, and rules for using neural networks in the wireless networking problems [31]. This study discussed traditional neural networks models in depth and their applications in current mobile networks. Lane *et al.* investigated the strength and advantages of deep learning in mobile sensing and focused on the potential for accurate inference on wireless devices [32]. Ota *et al.* presented deep learning applications in mobile multimedia. Their survey included the state-of-the-art of deep learning algorithms in mobile health and mobile security and speech recognition. Mohammadi *et al.* surveyed recent deep learning methods for Internet of things (IoT) based data analytics [33]. They reviewed the detailed existing works that incorporated deep learning into the IoT domain. Mao *et al.* reviewed the deep learning in wireless networking [34]. Their work surveyed the state of-the-art of the deep learning in wireless networks and discussed research challenges to be solved in the future.

3.3   Machine Learning to Deep Learning

Machine learning is a combination of computer programs that can be trained from data as a replacement for pre-programmed instructions (as traditional programming language). Machine learning concepts are usually categorized into supervised learning, unsupervised learning, and reinforcement learning. Nowadays, many researchers have had increasing interest in combining supervised and unsupervised approaches to form semi-supervised learning. In supervised learning, the model is made by the mapping of input to output using a given dataset. Classification is a frequently solved problem using supervised learning. In classification, every sample in the dataset belongs to one of the M classes. The class of each sample is given by a label that has a discrete value $\{0,...,M-1\}$. When the labels in the above example are real values (continuous), this task is known as regression problem. In unsupervised learning, the dataset is a collection of samples without labels. Typically, the aim of unsupervised learning is to find patterns that have some form of regularity. Usually, some model is fit to the data with the goal of modeling the input distribution. This is known as density estimation in statistics. Unsupervised learning can also be used for extracting features for supervised learning. In semi-supervised learning, the number of labeled samples is too small, while there are usually a large number of unlabeled samples. This is also a typical case in real-world situations. The goal of semi-supervised learning is to find a mapping from input to output but also to somehow make the unlabeled information useful for the mapping task. At least, the performance of the semi-supervised model needs to improve compared to the supervised model.

In recent times, deep learning has gotten a lot of consideration over machine learning algorithms due to its performance in many applications. Deep learning does better than the traditional machine learning approaches due to its different characteristics like greater computation power, automatic feature extraction, and the development of GPUs. Deep learning paid attention to a famous problem in machine learning i.e. the problem of representation. The inspiration for deep learning is to model how the human brain works. Figure 3.1 shows the fundamental difference between machine and deep learning. Deep learning has been able to attain major discovery in speech recognition, object recognition, image segmentation, and machine translation. The scientific contributions and developments of the deep learning method provided the ground work for the advances in such a large variety of applications [35]. So, in the same way cellular networks can obtain the benefits of deep learning research, especially in the era of 5G [36, 37].

3.3.1   Advance Machine Learning Techniques

3.3.1.1   Deep Learning

The fundamental concepts of deep learning is based on the same concepts of machine learning. The recent success of deep learning is mainly dependent on

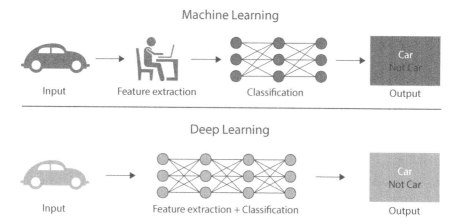

Figure 3.1 The machine and deep learning pictorial representation [38].

the artificial neural networks (ANN). Research on artificial neural networks was started back with the attempt to find something new in the 1940s [35]. Initially, ANNs were not very popular, and that is the reason the current recognition appears new. Broadly, there have been three eras of research in deep learning: the early 1940s–1960s, when the field was known as cybernetics; the 1980s–1990s, when it was called connection-ism; and the current surge that started in 2006, which is called deep learning. Initial growth on deep learning algorithms was motivated by computational models of how the brain learns. This is the reason that research in deep learning went by the name of artificial neural networks (ANN).The first neuron model was presented in [39]. Later, the first perceptron learning algorithm was presented in [40]. Since then, many varied models and learning algorithms have been introduced such as the Hopfield networks [41], self-organizing maps [42], Boltzmann machines [43], multi-layer perceptions [44], radial-basis function networks [45], autoencoders [46], and sigmoid belief networks [47]. Deep learning solves the problem of representation learning by enabling computers to build complex concepts out of simpler concepts.

3.3.2   Deep Reinforcement Learning (DRL)

Behavioral psychology has inspired a new machine learning technique, and that is reinforcement learning that has emerged as an advanced technology

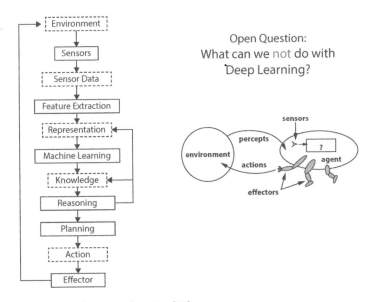

Figure 3.2 Deep reinforcement learning [48].

and as a new subcategory in machine learning. Figure 3.2 shows the learning method of reinforcement learning. DRL is concerned with an agents's reward or utility connected to surroundings via perception and action which produces an adaptation. In reinforcement learning (RL), the agent aims to optimize a long term objective by interacting with the environment based on a trial and error process.

Specifically, the following reinforcement learning algorithms have been applied by different researchers.

3.3.2.1   Q-Learning

One of the most commonly adopted reinforcement learning algorithms is Q-learning. Specifically, the RL agent interacts with the environment to learn the Q values, based on which the agent takes an action. The Q value is defined as the discounted accumulative reward, starting at a tuple of a state and an action and then following a certain policy. Once the Q values are learned after a sufficient amount of time, the agent can make a quick decision under the current state by taking the action with the largest Q value. More details about Q learning can be referred to [49]. In addition, to handle continuous state spaces, fuzzy Q learning can be used [50].

3.3.2.2   Multi-Armed Bandit Learning (MABL)

In an MABL model with a single agent, the agent sequentially takes an action and then receives a random reward generated by a corresponding distribution, aiming at maximizing an aggregate reward. In this model, there exists a tradeoff between taking the current, best action (exploitation) and gathering information to achieve a larger reward in the future (exploration). While in the MAB model with multiple agents, the reward an agent receives after playing an action is not only dependent on this action but also on the agents taking the same action. In this case, the model is expected to achieve some steady states or equilibrium [51]. More details about MAB can be referred to [52].

3.3.2.3   Actor–Critic Learning (ACL)

The actor–critic learning algorithm is composed of an actor, a critic and an environment with which the actor interacts. In this algorithm, the actor first selects an action according to the current strategy and receives an immediate cost. Then, the critic updates the state value function based on a time difference error, and next, the actor will update the policy. As for the strategy, it can be updated based on learned policy using Boltzmann distribution. When each action is revisited infinitely for each state, the algorithm will converge to the optimal state values [53].

3.3.2.4   Joint Utility and Strategy Estimation-Based Learning

In this algorithm each agent holds an estimation of the expected utility, whose update is based on the immediate reward, and the probability to select each action, named as strategy, is updated in the same iteration based on the utility estimation [54]. The main benefit of this algorithm lies in that it is fully distributed when the reward can be directly calculated locally, as, for example, the data rate between a transmitter and its paired receiver. Based on this algorithm, one can further estimate the regret of each action based on utility estimations and the received immediate reward, and then update strategy using regret estimations. This algorithm is often connected with some equilibrium concepts in game theory like logit equilibrium and coarse correlated equilibrium.

3.4   Applications of Machine Learning Models in Wireless Communication

The next generation of wireless communication will offer high speed supporting innovative applications. Specially, the next generation of wireless communication systems has to acquire different characteristics of users with their human behavior, in order to separately determine the optimal system configurations. These smart mobile terminals have to trust on sophisticated learning and decision-making algorithms. There are different machine learning techniques like yielding regression algorithms, instance-based algorithms, regularization algorithms, decision tree algorithms, Bayesian algorithms, clustering algorithms, association rule-based learning algorithms, artificial neural networks, deep learning algorithms, dimension reduction algorithms, and ensemble algorithms, and all are different from their structure and functionality.

This section covers how the machine learning models can help next generation wireless communication systems in order to improve the performance of the network. The current generation of the wireless network has several technical problems and these technical problems can be dealt with by applying different machine learning algorithms. The 5G Cellular network requires new technologies to provide predefined services to the intelligent wireless communication network. The 5G cellular network operators are in a tough condition to meet different service requirements and solve complex configurations as user and network are dynamic. Such a future requirement can be met by empowering machines and systems with intelligence. So it is vital to understand how the application of artificial intelligence is useful in the management of 5G communication network development [55–57].

3.4.1   Regression, KNN and SVM Models for Wireless

The relationship among the variables can be estimated using statistical analysis which will help regression models. The aim of regression model is to predict diverged values for a set of input variable with single or multi-dimensions. The linear regression model is linear in nature. The logistic regression model is sigmoid curve in nature. The support vector machine (SVM) and K-nearest neighbors (KNN) algorithms are based on object classification. In The K-nearest neighbors algorithm (KNN) object classification is based on k value of the object's neighbors and SVM algorithm relies on nonlinear mapping and transforming data into separable and searchable dimensions then it separates one class from another based on optimal linear separating hyper plane [56].

K-nearest neighbors algorithm (KNN) and support vector machine (SVM) models can be used to predict and estimate the radio parameters of a particular mobile user. The potential of addressing search problems by KNN and SVM models, the detection and channel estimation in massive MIMO systems were implemented using both of these machine learning techniques and MIMO-aided wireless used the hierarchical—support vector machine (H-SVM) for the same [58]. It also found the Gaussian channel's noise level between transmit antennas and receive antennas. The optimal solution for handover issues was using support vector machine (SVM) and K-nearest neighbors algorithm (KNN).The next generation wireless mobile user terminal's parameters like usage pattern can be used to train support vector machine (SVM) and K-NN. The K-nearest neighbor algorithms are used for the prediction of demand of energy. The user location and energy consumption rates can be used to train the machine learning models to predict energy demand [59]. The supervised machine learning models can interpret the patterns and learn from the user presence and usage to efficiently subdivide the signals into current system state for saving the energy and best user management.

3.4.2   Bayesian Learning for Cognitive Radio

The Bayesian learning model found the posteriori probability distribution of input signals. The special features of next generation wireless networks would be acquired and estimated by Bayesian learning. The main issue of the massive MIMO systems is that pilot contamination can be focused by estimating the channel parameters of both desired links in a target cell and interfering links of adjacent cells and the estimation of the channel parameters for addressing the pilot contamination issue can be made by applying Bayesian learning techniques. In this approach, Gaussians mixture model was defined based on received signal and channel parameters with weighted sum of Gaussian distribution and estimation carried by using expectation maximization [60].

Two-state hidden Markov model was applied to estimate the presence and absence of primary users. The expectation maximization algorithm was used to estimate the amount of time the available channels perform at optimized level [61]. The tomography model in Bayesian learning was used to estimate the prevalent parameters and interference patterns of data link and network layer in cognitive radio. The path delay and proportion of successful packer receptions in link layer and network layer of cogitative radio are estimated by tomography model [62].

3.4.3   Deep Learning in Wireless Network

It is widely acknowledged that the performance of traditional ML algorithms is low in the term of feature engineering [63]. The main advantage of deep learning is that it can automatically extract high-level features from data that has complex structure and inner correlations. The learning process is tremendously simplified due to prior feature handcrafting [64]. The importance of this in the context of mobile networks, as mobile data is usually generated by heterogeneous sources, is often noisy, and exhibits non-trivial spatial/temporal patterns [65], whose labeling would otherwise require outstanding human effort. Deep learning is capable of handling large amounts of data. Mobile networks generate high volumes of different types of data at fast pace. Training traditional ML algorithms (e.g. support vector machine (SVM) [66] and Gaussian process (GP) [67]) sometimes requires storing all the data in memory, which is computationally infeasible under big data scenarios. Furthermore, the performance of ML does not grow significantly with large volumes of data and plateaus relatively fast [68]. Deep neural networks further benefit as training with big data prevents model over-fitting. Traditional supervised learning is only effective when sufficient labeled data is available. However, most current mobile systems generate unlabeled or semi-labeled data [65]. Deep learning provides a variety of methods that allow exploiting unlabeled data to learn useful patterns in an unsupervised manner, e.g., restricted Boltzmann machine (RBM) [69], generative adversarial network (GAN)

[70]. Applications include clustering [68], data distributions approximation [71], un/semi-supervised learning [72, 73], and one/zero shot learning [74, 75], among others. Compressive representations learned by deep neural networks can be shared across different tasks, while this is limited or difficult to achieve in other ML paradigms (e.g., linear regression, random forest, etc.) [76]. Deep learning is effective in handing geometric mobile data [77], while this is a conundrum for other ML approaches. Geometric data refers to multivariate data represented by coordinates, topology, metrics and order [78]. Mobile data, such as mobile user location and network connectivity can be naturally represented by point clouds and graphs, which have important geometric properties. These data can be effectively modelled by dedicated deep learning architectures, such as PointNet++ [79] and Graph CNN [80]. Employing these architectures has great potential to revolutionize the geometric mobile data analysis [81].

3.4.4   Deep Reinforcement Learning in Wireless Network

Artificial intelligence (AI) including deep learning (DL) and deep reinforcement learning (DRL) approaches, well known from computer science (CS) disciplines is beginning to emerge in wireless communications. These AI approaches were first widely applied to the upper layers of wireless communication systems for various purposes like routing establishment, optimization and deployment of cognitive radio and communication network. These system models and algorithms designed with DL technology greatly improve the performance of communication systems based on traditional methods. New features of future communications, such as complex scenarios with unknown channel models, high speed and accurate processing requirements, make traditional methods no longer suitable, and provide many more potential applications of DL. DL technology has become a new hotspot in the research of physical-layer wireless communications and challenges conventional communication theories. Currently, DL-based 'black-box' methods show promising performance improvements but have certain limitations, such as the lack of solid analytical tools and the use of architectures specifically designed for communication and implementation research. With the development of DL technology, in addition to the traditional neural network-based data-driven model, the model-driven deep network model and the DRL model (i.e. DQN) which combined DL with reinforcement learning are more suitable for dealing with future complex communication systems. As in most cases of wireless resource allocation, there are no definite samples to train the model; hence DRL, which trains the model by maximizing the reward associated with different actions, can

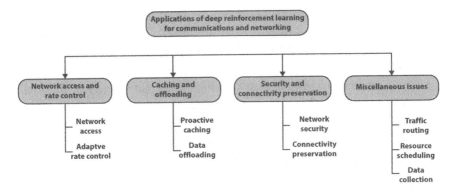

Figure 3.3 Taxonomy of the applications of deep reinforcement learning for communications and networking [82].

be adopted. Deep reinforcement is used to solve some issues in communications and networking. The issues include traffic engineering and routing, resource sharing and scheduling, and data collection. The Figure 3.3 shows how the deep reinforcement learning has been used in different areas of communications and networking.

3.4.5   Traffic Engineering and Routing

Traffic engineering and routing traffic engineering (TE) in communication networks refers to network utility maximization (NUM) by optimizing a path to forward the data traffic, given a set of network flows from source to destination nodes. Traditional NUM problems are mostly model-based. However, with the advances of wireless communication technologies, the network environment becomes more complicated and dynamic, which makes it hard to model, predict, and control. The recent development of DQL methods provides a feasible and efficient way to design experience-driven and model-free schemes that can learn and adapt to the dynamic wireless network from past observations. Routing optimization is one of the major control problems in traffic engineering. The authors in [83] present the first attempt to use the DQL for the routing optimization. Through the interaction with the network environment, the DQL agent at the network controller determines the paths for all source–destination pairs. The system state is represented by the bandwidth request between each source–destination pair, and the reward is a function of the mean network delay. The DQL agent leverages the actor–critic method for solving the routing problem that minimizes the network delay, by adapting routing configurations automatically to current traffic conditions. The DQL agent is trained using the traffic information generated by a gravity model [84]. The routing solution is then evaluated by OMNet+ discrete event simulator [85]. The well-trained DQL agent can produce a near-optimal routing configuration in a single step and thus the agent is agile for real-time network control. The proposed approach is attractive as the traditional optimization-based techniques require a large number of steps to produce a new configuration.

3.4.6   Resource Sharing and Scheduling

System capacity is one of the most important performance metrics in wireless communication networks. System capacity enhancements can be based on the optimization of resource sharing and scheduling among multiple wireless nodes. The integration of DRL into 5G systems would revolutionize the resource sharing and scheduling schemes from model-based to model-free approaches and meet various application demands by learning from the network environment. The authors in [86] study the user scheduling in a multi user massive MIMO system. User scheduling is responsible for allocating resource blocks to BSs and mobile users, taking into account the channel conditions and QoS requirements. Based on this user scheduling strategy, a DRL-based coverage and capacity optimization is proposed to obtain dynamically the scheduling parameters and a unified threshold of QoS metric. The performance indicators are calculated as the average spectrum efficiency of all the users. The system state is an indicator of the average spectrum efficiency. The action of the scheduler is a set of scheduling parameters to maximize the reward as a function of the average spectrum efficiency. The DRL scheme uses policy gradient method to learn a policy function (instead of a Q-function) directly from trajectories generated by the current policy. The policy network is trained with a variant of the REINFORCE algorithm [87]. The simulation results in [86] show that compared with the optimization-based algorithms that suffer from incomplete network information, the policy gradient method achieves much better performance in terms of network coverage and capacity.

3.4.7   Power Control and Data Collection

With the prevalence of IoT and smart mobile devices, mobile crowd sensing becomes a cost-effective solution for network information collection to support more intelligent operations of wireless systems. The authors in [88] leverage the DQL framework for sensing and control problems in a wireless sensor and actor network (WSAN), which is a group of wireless devices with the ability to sense events and to perform actions based on the sensed data shared by all sensors. The system state includes processing power, mobility abilities, and functionalities of the actors and sensors. The mobile actor can choose its moving direction, networking, sensing and actuation policies to maximize the number of connected actor nodes and the number of sensing events. The authors in [89] focus on mobile crowd sensing paradigm, where data inference is incorporated to reduce sensing costs while maintaining the quality of sensing. The target sensing area is split into a set of cells. The objective of a sensing task is to collect data (e.g., temperature, air quality) in all the cells. A DQL-based cell selection mechanism is proposed for the mobile sensors to decide which cell is a better choice to perform sensing tasks. The system state includes the selection matrices for a few past decision epochs. The reward function is determined by the sensing quality and cost in the chosen cells. To extract temporal correlations in learning, the authors propose the DRQN that uses LSTM layers in DQL to capture the hidden patterns in state transitions. Considering inter-data correlations, the authors use the transfer learning method to reduce the amount of data in training. That is, the cell selection strategy learned for one task can benefit another correlated task. Hence, the parameters of DRQN can be initialized by another DRQN with rich training data. Simulations are conducted based on two real-life datasets collected from sensor networks.

3.5   Conclusion

Machine learning is playing an increasingly important role in the mobile and wireless networking domain. In this chapter, the basic and advance concept of machine learning models was discussed. This chapter also includes their applications to mobile networks across different application scenarios. We also discussed how the deep reinforcement learning getting attention over other traditional machine learning models in wireless network. DRL can obtain the solution of sophisticated network optimizations. Thus, it enables network controllers. It also allows network entities to learn and build knowledge about the communication and networking environment including autonomous decision-making.

This chapter also discussed that the DRL accepted the advantage of deep neural networks (DNNs) to train the learning process, thereby improving the learning speed and the performance of reinforcement learning algorithms. As a result, DRL has been adopted in numerous applications of reinforcement learning in practice. In the areas of communications and networking, DRL has been recently used as an emerging tool to effectively address various problems and challenges. In particular, modern networks such as Internet of things (IoT), heterogeneous networks (HetNets), and unmanned aerial vehicle (UAV) network become more decentralized, *ad-hoc*, and autonomous in nature. Network entities such as IoT devices, mobile users, and UAVs need to make local and autonomous decisions, e.g., spectrum access, data rate selection, transmit power control, and base station association, to achieve the goals of different networks including, e.g., throughput maximization and energy consumption minimization.

References

1. Boccardi, F., Heath, R.W., Lozano, A., Marzetta, T.L., Popovski, P., Five disruptive technology directions for 5G. *IEEE Commun. Mag.*, 52, 2, 74–80, Feb. 2014.

2. Popovski, P., Ultra-reliable communication in 5G wireless systems. *International Conference on 5G for Ubiquitous Connectivity (5GU)*, Akaslompolo, Finland, Feb. 2014.

3. Johansson, N.A., Wang, Y.P.E., Eriksson, E., Hessler, M., Radio access for ultra-reliable and low-latency 5G communications. *IEEE International Conference on Communication Workshop (ICCW)*, London, UK, Sept. 2015.

4. Yilmaz, O.N.C., Wang, Y.P.E., Johansson, N.A., Brahmi, Ashraf, N., S.A., Sachs, J., Analysis of ultra-reliable and low-latency 5G communication for a factory automation use case. *Proc. of IEEE International Conference on Communication Workshop (ICCW)*, London, UK, Sept. 2015, pp. 1190–1195.

5. Gopal, D.G. and Kaushik, S., Emerging technologies and applications for cloud-based gaming: Review on cloud gaming. *Emerg. Technol. Appl. Cloud-Based Gaming*, 41, 07, 79–89, 2016.

6. Motlagh, N.H., Bagaa, M., Taleb, T., UAV selection for a UAV-based integrative IoT platform. *IEEE Global Communications Conference (GLOBECOM)*, Washington DC, USA, Dec. 2016.

7. Kawamoto, Y., Nishiyama, H., Kato, N., Yoshimura, N., Yamamoto, S., Internet of things (IoT): Present state and future prospects. *IEICE Trans. Inf. Syst.*, 97, 10, 2568–2575, Oct. 2014.

8. Motlagh, N.H., Bagaa, M., Taleb, T., UAV-based IoT platform: A crowd surveillance use case. *IEEE Commun. Mag.*, 55, 2, 128–134, Feb. 2017.

9. Zhou, J., Cao, X., Dong, Z., Vasilakos, A.V., Security and privacy for cloud-based IoT: Challenges. *IEEE Commun. Mag.*, 55, 1, 26–33, Jan. 2017.

10. LeCun, Y., Bengio, Y., Hinton, G., Deep learning. *Nature*, 521, 7553, 436–444, 2015.

11. Schmidhuber, J., Deep learning in neural networks: An overview. *Neural Netw.*, 61, 85–117, 2015.

12. Liu, W., Wang, Z., Liu, X., Zeng, N., Liu, Y., Alsaadi, F.E., A survey of deep neural network architectures and their applications. *Neurocomputing*, 234, 11–26, 2017.

13. Arulkumaran, K., Deisenroth, M.P., Brundage, M., Bharath, A.A., Deep reinforcement learning: A brief survey. *IEEE Signal Processing Mag.*, 34, 6, 26–38, 2017.

14. Li, Y., Deep reinforcement learning: An overview, http://arxiv.org/abs/1701.07274, 2017.

15. Zhang, S., Yao, L., Sun, A., Deep learning based recommender system: A survey and new perspectives, http://arxiv.org/abs/1707.07435, 2017.

16. Goodfellow, I., Bengio, Y., Courville, A., *Deep learning*, MIT press, Springer, 2016.

17. Jiang, C., Zhang, H., Ren, Y., Han, Z., Chen, K.C., Hanzo, L., Machine learning paradigms for nextgeneration wireless networks. *IEEE Wirel. Commun.*, 24, 2, 98–105, 2017.

18. Alsheikh, M.A., Lin, S., Niyato, D., Tan, H.P., Machine learning in wireless sensor networks: Algorithms, strategies, and applications. *IEEE Commun. Surv. Tut.*, 16, 4, 1996–2018, 2014.

19. Bkassiny, M., Li, Y., Jayaweera, S.K., A survey on machine-learning techniques in cognitive radios. *IEEE Commun. Surv. Tut.*, 15, 3, 1136–1159, 2013.

20. Buda, T.S., Assem, H., Xu, L., Raz, D., Margolin, U., Rosensweig, E., Lopez, D.R. *et al.*, Can machine learning aid in delivering new use cases and scenarios in 5G?, in: *IEEE/IFIP Network Operations and Management Symposium (NOMS)*, pp. 1279–1284, 2016.

21. Keshavamurthy, B. and Ashraf, M., Conceptual design of proactive SONs based on the big data framework for 5G cellular networks: A novel machine learning perspective facilitating a shift in the son paradigm. *IEEE International Conference on System Modeling & Advancement in Research Trends (SMART)*, pp. 298–304, 2016.

22. Klaine, P.V., Imran, M.A., Onireti, O., Souza, R.D., A survey of machine learning techniques applied to self organizing cellular networks. *IEEE Commun. Surv. Tut.*, 19, 4, 2392–2431, 2017.

23. Li, R., Zhao, Z., Zhou, X., Ding, G., Chen, Y., Wang, Z., Zhang, H., Intelligent 5G: When cellular networks meet artificial intelligence. *IEEE Wirel. Commun.*, 24, 5, 175–183, 2017.

24. Bui, N., Cesana, M., Hosseini, S.A., Liao, Q., Malanchini, I., Widmer, J., A survey of anticipatory mobile networking: Context-based classification, prediction methodologies, and optimization techniques. *IEEE Commun. Surv. Tut.*, 19, 3, 1790–1821, 2017.

25. Jiang, C., Zhang, H., Ren, Y., Han, Z., Chen, K.C., Hanzo, L., Machine learning paradigms for next generation wireless networks. *IEEE Wirel. Commun.*, 24, 2, 98–105, 2017.

26. Li, R., Zhao, Z., Zhou, X., Ding, G., Chen, Y., Wang, Z., Zhang, H., Intelligent 5G: When cellular networks meet artificial intelligence. *IEEE Wirel. Commun.*, 24, 5, 175–183, 2017.

27. Klaine, P.V., Imran, M.A., Onireti, O., Souza, R.D., A survey of machine learning techniques applied to self organizing cellular networks. *IEEE Commun. Surv. Tut.*, 19, 4, 2392–2431, 2017.

28. Jinsong, W., Song, G., Jie, L., Deze, Z., Big data meet green challenges: Big data toward green applications. *IEEE Syst. J.*, 10, 3, 888–900, 2016.

29. Xianfu, C., Jinsong, W., Yueming, C., Honggang, Z., Tao, C., Energy-efficiency oriented traffic offloading in wireless networks: A brief survey and a learning approach for heterogeneous cellular networks. *IEEE J. Sel. Areas. Commun.*, 33, 4, 627–640, 2015.

30. Fadlullah, Z., Tang, F., Mao, B., Kato, N., Akashi, O., Inoue, T., Mizutani, K., State-of-the-art deep learning: Evolving machine intelligence toward tomorrow's intelligent network traffic control systems. *IEEE Commun. Surv. Tut.*, 19, 4, 2432–2455, 2017.

31. Ahad, N., Qadir, J., Ahsan, N., Neural networks in wireless networks: Techniques, applications and guidelines. *J. Netw. Comput. Appl.*, 68, 1–27, 2016.

32. Lane, N.D. and Georgiev, P., Can deep learning revolutionize mobile sensing?, in: *Proc. 16th ACM International Workshop on Mobile Computing Systems and Applications*, pp. 117–122, 2015.

33. Mehdi, M., Ala, A., Sameh, S., Mohsen, G., Deep Learning for IoT Big Data and Streaming Analytics: A Survey. *IEEE Commun. Surv. Tut.*, 4, 2923–2960, 2018.

34. Mao, Q., Hu, F., Hao, Q., Deep learning for intelligent wireless networks: A comprehensive survey. *IEEE Commun. Surv. Tut.*, 20, 4, pp. 2595–2621, 2018.

35. Goodfellow, I., Bengio, Y., Courville, A., *Deep Learning*, MIT Press, *Cambridge*, MA, USA, 2016.

36. Moysen, J., Giupponi, L., From 4G to 5G: Self-organized Network Management meets Machine Learning, http://arxiv.org/abs/1707.09300, 2017.

37. Li, R., Zhao, Z., Zhou, X., Ding, G., Chen, Y., Wang, Z., Zhang, H., Intelligent 5G: When cellular networks meet artificial intelligence. *IEEE Wirel. Commun.*, 24, 175–183, 2017.

38. https://www.guru99.com/machine-learning-vs-deep-learning.html

39. McCulloch, W.S. and Pitts, W., A logical calculus of the ideas immanent in nervous activity. *Bull. Math. Biophys.*, 5, 115–133, 1943.

40. Rosenblatt, F., The perceptron: A probabilistic model for information storage and organization in the brain. *Psychol. Rev.*, 65, 386, 1958.

41. Hopfield, J.J., Neural networks and physical systems with emergent collective computational abilities. *Proc. Natl. Acad. Sci. U.S.A. 1982*, 79, 2554–2558, 1982.

42. Kohonen, T., Self-organized formation of topologically correct feature maps. *Biol. Cybern.*, 43, 59–69, 1982.

43. Ackley, D.H., Hinton, G.E., Sejnowski, T.J., A learning algorithm for Boltzmann machines, in: *Readings in Computer Vision*, pp. 522–533, Elsevier, Amsterdam, the Netherlands, 1987.

44. Rumelhart, D.E., Hinton, G.E., Williams, R.J., Learning representations by back-propagating errors. *Nature 1986*, 323, 533, 1986.

45. Broomhead, D.S. and Lowe, D., Radial Basis Functions, Multi-Variable Functional Interpolation and Adaptive Networks, in: *Technical Report*, Royal Signals and Radar Establishment, *Malvern*, UK, 1988.

46. Baldi, P. and Hornik, K., Neural networks and principal component analysis: Learning from examples without local minima. *Neural Netw.*, 2, 53–58, 1989.

47. Neal, R.M., Connectionist learning of belief networks. *Artif. Intell.*, 56, 71–113, 1992.

48. https://ailephant.com/overview-deep-reinforcement-learning/

49. Sutton, R. and Barto, A., *Reinforcement learning: An introduction*, MIT Press, Cambridge, MA, 1998.

50. Glorennec, P.Y., Fuzzy Q-learning and dynamical fuzzy Q-learning. *Proceedings of 1994 IEEE 3rd International Fuzzy Systems Conference*, Orlando, FL, USA, Jun. 1994, pp. 474–479.

51. Maghsudi, S. and Hossain, E., Distributed user association in energy harvesting dense small cell networks: A mean-field multi-armed bandit approach. *IEEE Access*, 5, 3513–3523, Mar. 2017.

52. Bubeck, S. and Cesa-Bianchi, N., Regret analysis of stochastic and nonstochastic multi-armed bandit problems. *Found. Trends Mach. Learn.*, 5, 1, 1–122, 2012.

53. Singh, S., Jaakkola Jaakkola, T., Littman, M., Szepesvri, C., Convergence results for single-step on-policy reinforcement-learning algorithms. *Mach. Learn.*, 38, 3, 287–308, Mar. 2000.

54. Perlaza, S., Tembine, M., H., Lasaulce, S., How can ignorant but patient cognitive terminals learn their strategy and utility? *Proceedings of SPAWC*, Marrakech, Morocco, pp. 1–5, Jun. 2010.

55. Li, R. *et al.*, Intelligent 5G: When Cellular Networks Meet Artificial Intelligence. *IEEE Wirel. Commun.*, 24, 5, 175–183, 2017.

56. Jiang, C., Zhang, H., Ren, Y., Han, Z., Chen, K.C., Hanzo, L., Machine Learning Paradigms for Next-Generation Wireless Networks. *IEEE Wirel. Commun.*, 24, 2, 98–105, Apr. 2017.

57. Alarcon, M.E. and Cabellos, A., A machine learning-based approach for virtual network function modeling, in: *2018 IEEE Wireless Communications and Networking Conference Workshops (WCNCW)*, pp. 237–242, 2018.

58. Feng, V. and Chang, S.Y., Determination of Wireless Networks Parameters through Parallel Hierarchical Support Vector Machines. *IEEE Trans. Parallel Distrib. Syst.*, 23, 3, 505–512, Mar. 2012.

59. Donohoo, K., Ohlsen, C., Pasricha, S., Xiang, Y., Anderson, C., Context-Aware Energy Enhancements for Smart Mobile Devices. *IEEE Trans. Mob. Comput.*, 13, 8, 1720–1732, Aug. 2014.

60. Choi, K.W. and Hossain, E., Estimation of Primary User Parameters in Cognitive Radio Systems via Hidden Markov Model. *IEEE Trans. Signal Process*, 61, 3, 782–795, Feb. 2013.

61. Yang, A., J., Champagne, B., An EM Approach for Cooperative Spectrum Sensing in Multiantenna CR Networks. *IEEE Trans. Veh. Technol.*, 65, 3, 1229–1243, Mar. 2016.

62. Yu, C.K., Chen, K.C., Cheng, S.M., Cognitive Radio Network Tomography. *IEEE Trans. Veh. Technol.*, 59, 4, 1980–1997, May 2010.

63. Domingos, P., A few useful things to know about machine learning. *Commun. ACM*, 55, 10, 78–87, 2012.

64. LeCun, Y., Bengio, Y., Hinton, G., Deep learning. *Nature*, 521, 7553, 436–444, 2015.

65. Alsheikh, M.A., Niyato, D., Lin, S., Tan, H.P., Han, Z., Mobile big data analytics using deep learning and Apache Spark. *IEEE Netw.*, 30, 3, 22–29, 2016.

67. Tsang, I.W., Kwok, J.T., Cheung, P.M., Core vector machines: Fast SVM training on very large data sets. *J. Mach. Learn. Res.* , 6, 363–392, 2005.

68. Rasmussen, C.E. and Williams, C.K., *Gaussian processes for machine learning*, vol. 1, MIT press, *Cambridge*, 2006.

69. Goodfellow, I., Bengio, Y., Courville, A., *Deep learning*, MIT press, Springer, 2016.

70. Goodfellow, I., Pouget-Abadie, J., Mirza, M., Xu, B., Warde-Farley, D., Ozair, S., Courville, A., Bengio, Y., Generative adversarial nets, in: *Advances in neural information processing systems*, pp. 2672–2680, 2014.

71. Schroff, F., Kalenichenko, D., Facenet, J.P., A unified embedding for face recognition and clustering, in: *Proc. IEEE Conference on Computer Vision and Pattern Recognition*, pp. 815– 823, 2015.

72. Kingma, D.P., Mohamed, S., Rezende, D.J., Welling, M., Semi-supervised learning with deep generative models, in: *Advances in Neural Information Processing Systems*, pp. 3581– 3589, 2014.

73. Stewart, R. and Ermon, S., Label-free supervision of neural networks with physics and domain knowledge, in: *Proc. National Conference on Artificial Intelligence (AAAI)*, pp. 2576–2582, 2017.

74. Rezende, D., Danihelka, I., Gregor, K., Wierstra, D. *et al.*, One-shot generalization in deep generative models, in: *Proc. International Conference on Machine Learning (ICML)*, pp. 1521–1529, 2016.

75. Socher, R., Ganjoo, M., Manning, C.D., Ng, A., Zero-shot learning through cross-modal transfer, in: *Advances in neural information processing systems*, pp. 935–943, 2013.

76. Georgiev, P., Bhattacharya, S., Lane, N.D., Mascolo, C., Low-resource multi-task audio sensing for mobile and embedded devices via shared deep neural

network representations. *Proc. ACM on Interactive, Mobile, Wearable and Ubiquitous Technologies (IMWUT)*, vol. 1, p. 50, 2017.

78. Monti, F., Boscaini, D., Masci, J., Rodola, E., Svoboda, J., Bronstein, M.M., Geometric deep learning on graphs and manifolds using mixture model CNNs, in: *Proc. IEEE Conference on Computer Vision and Pattern Recognition (CVPR)*, vol. 1, p. 3, 2017.

79. Roux, B.L. and Rouanet, H., *Geometric data analysis: from correspondence analysis to structured data analysis*, Springer Science & Business Media, New York, 2004.

80. Qi, C.R., Yi, L., Su, H., Guibas, L.J., PointNet++: Deep hierarchical feature learning on point sets in a metric space, in: *Advances in Neural Information Processing Systems*, pp. 5099–5108, 2017.

81. Kipf, T.N. and Welling, M., Semi-supervised classification with graph convolutional networks, in: *Proc. International Conference on Learning Representations (ICLR)*, 2017.

82. Luong, N.C., Hoang, D.T., Gong, S., Niyato, D., Wang, P., Liang, Y.C., Kim, D., *Applications of Deep Reinforcement Learning in Communications and Networking: A Survey*, 2018. https://ieeexplore.ieee.org/document/8714026.

83. Stampa, G., Arias, M., Sanchez-Charles, D., Muntes-Mulero, V., Cabellos, A., A deep-reinforcement learning approach for software-defined networking routing optimization, http://arxiv.org/abs/1709.07080, 2017.

84. Roughan, M., Simplifying the synthesis of internet traffic matrices. *ACM SIGCOMM Computer Communication Review*, 35, 5, 93–96, 2015. Online Available: http://arxiv.org/abs/1710.02913.

85. Varga, A. and Hornig, R., An overview of the OMNeT++ simulation environment, in: *proc. Int'l Conf. Simulation Tools and Techniques for Communications, Networks and Systems & Workshops*, 2008.

86. Yang, Y., Li, Y., Li, K., Zhao, S., Chen, R., Wang, J., Ci, S., Decco: Deep-learning enabled coverage and capacity optimization for massive mimo systems, *IEEE*, 2018, https://ieeexplore.ieee.org/document/8344405.

87. Sutton, R., McAllester, S., Singh, D.S., Mansour, Y., Policy gradient methods for reinforcement learning with function approximation. *12th International Neural Inform. Process. Syst*, pp. 1057–1063, 1999.

88. Oda, T., Obukata, R., Ikeda, Barolli, M., L., Takizawa, M., Design and implementation of a simulation system based on deep q-network for mobile actor node control in wireless sensor and actor networks. *International Conference on Advanced Information Networking and Applications Workshops (WAINA)*, pp. 195–200, 2017.

89. Wang, L., Liu, W., Zhang, D., Wang, Y., Wang, E., Yang, Y., Cell selection with deep reinforcement learning in sparse mobile crowd sensing, http://arxiv.org/abs/1804.07047, 2018.

4

Cognitive Computing for Smart Communication

Poonam Sharma[1]*, Akansha Singh[2] and Aman Jatain[1]

[1]Department of Computer Science, Amity University, Gurgaon, India
[2]Department of Computer Science and Engineering, Amity University Uttar Pradesh, Noida, India

Abstract

With a lot of development in network technologies and artificial intelligence techniques smart information applications and services are growing worldwide. Cloud-based communication has also added on to this by providing powerful communication services. But simply providing cloud based environment and intensive data processing techniques is not sufficient because we have limited capacity and require low latency, high reliability and improved user experience. Cognitive computing is the science which aims to mimic human thought processes. Thus the capabilities of cognitive science if integrated with communications can improve the traditional systems and provide better accuracy and low latency. In this paper, we have discussed in detail cognition-based communications, which combines both AI-based intelligent computing and advanced communication technologies. First an overview of cognitive computing and its evolution is provided. Then a systematic and detailed architecture for applying cognition in communication is described which combines networking with analytics and cloud computing. Finally some applications are also discussed on which these techniques may be applied.

Keywords: Cognitive computing, cloud computing, deep learning, AI wireless communication, physical layer

*Corresponding author: poonamsharma.2289@gmail.com

Krishna Kant Singh, Akansha Singh, Korhan Cengiz and Dac-Nhuong Le (eds.) Machine Learning and Cognitive Computing for Mobile Communications and Wireless Networks, (73–90) © 2020 Scrivener Publishing LLC

4.1   Introduction

Computing has always been a real game changer and area of interest for researchers since early 1990s. The initial inventions in computing started with tabulating devices like calculators which reduced the complexity involved with manual computing. Then came the era of programming in which everything was processed and controlled with the help of devices containing microprocessors. Today is the era of cognitive computing where we do not talk about numbers, rather we talk about data and making sense out of that data. Also with inventions in big data and artificial intelligence, systems designed using the power of cognitive computing can be used to extract meaningful and useful information from data and use it as experience to make systems which are useful in unknown or newer situations.

With a lot of growth and development in wireless technologies and communication over the network there is a big scope and requirement in enhancing user's quality of experience in terms of wide-range coverage, hot-spot with high capacity, huge connections using low power, low latency and higher reliability in communication networks. In recent years massive research has been going on integrating computing and communication to achieve the goal of designing such smart communication systems which can support optimization in management, fast response time in servicing and dynamic configurations. A lot of work has been done and architectures have been proposed in the literature which focuses on such networks. The basic idea used behind these systems was of cognitive radios [1, 2]. These are the radios which comprises of sensors, radio, database which contains knowledge about all the communications, learning component and an engine which can do reasoning based on existing factors. The various architectures proposed using these systems includes green communication [3], D2D (device to device) communication [4] etc. In this paper we will be discussing cognition based communication and its various characteristics. In summary the main contribution of the chapter includes:

1) A brief overview of cognitive computing and its evolution.
2) A cloud based communication network architecture which used both cloud computing, cognition and analytics.
3) Some typical technologies where this communication system can be integrated and used are also discussed.

4.2 Cognitive Computing Evolution

Cognitive computing is basically development of computer systems which can mimic human intelligence. Such systems should be capable of processing natural language, learnable and able to make decisions in every kind of situations [5]. The humans show the cognition process in two stages. In the first stage they perceive about the ambience and take input from the external environment with the help of organs like skin, eyes and ear etc. In the second stage the input is transmitted to neurons for further storage, analysis, processing and decision making. The decision made is again transmitted to the organ which initiated the input and the reaction comes as the output. As this process gets repeated many a times in a day, humans keep on learning from their experiences side by side and update their knowledge also establishing their own cognition system. Since cognition is a combination of data, communication and learning, many subjects needs to be understood and combined for designing such systems. The basic evolution process of the cognitive computing is shown in Figure 4.1.

The concept of big data brought in a huge acceleration in data handling and knowledge discovery paradigms. The reason behind this was not only increase in size but also in speed and heterogeneity of the data. Most of the data generated on the web nowadays is unstructured in nature as it

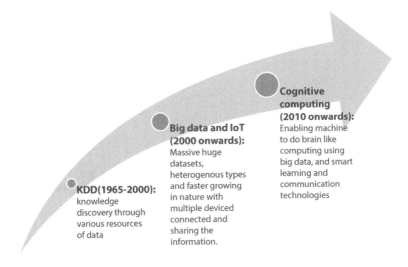

Figure 4.1 Evolution of cognitive computing.

may contain video, images, symbols and natural language. To handle such data a new computing model is required which can sense information out of this data, and enhance and extend the expertise of humans. Therefore cognitive computing makes use of this data with learning techniques from artificial intelligence to write the algorithms and advanced communication with the help of edge computing and cognitive radios to completely make systems smart and able to make decisions same as humans do.

4.3   Characteristics of Cognitive Computing

The main characteristics of cognitive computing are summarized in Figure 4.2. As we are able to integrate a lot of heterogeneous data it is information debt. The system keeps on learning and updating itself as soon as it received some new information and therefore is dynamic in training. It is highly integrated and probabilistic in nature as it combines too many modules with it and gives decision on the bases of previous historical information. They are able to analyze the context before giving any solution and also in case there are multiple situations the systems are able to give weight age to every possible solution and find the best among them. They must be made highly attractive with tools and techniques to effective communication

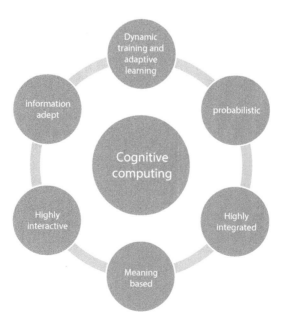

Figure 4.2 Characteristics of cognitive computing.

may be built in them so that users can easily put their queries and get solution for the same.

4.4 Basic Architecture

The basic architecture of a cognitive computing frame work is shown in Figure 4.3. The bottom layer shows the basic infrastructure like 5G networks [6, 7], deep learning and AI, big data and IoT services which are used to design the framework involving human computer interactions. The framework may be basically designed with the help of different libraries of python like tensorflow, Theano etc. The upper layer applications supported by this framework may be smart city, smart healthcare, smart homes, smart agriculture etc. The data and libraries used will be specific to the applications.

4.4.1 Cognitive Computing and Communication

Rapid development of information services and smart applications has raised the need to improve user's quality of experience in terms of usage of wireless technologies or mobile phones. The wireless technologies nowadays require decision making capabilities, intelligent and dynamic network management,

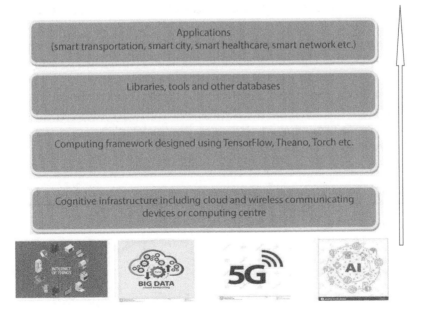

Figure 4.3 Basic architecture of cognitive computing framework.

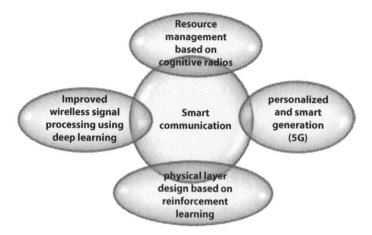

Figure 4.4 Integration of various technologies for smart communication.

and knowledge discovery capabilities in complex environmental situations. There has been vast research going on integrating all the latest technologies and designing such smart communicating networks. The various components in which work is going on are summarized in Figure 4.4.

In the sections below all the components are discussed in detail.

4.5 Resource Management Based on Cognitive Radios

Spectrum allocation and utilization is major concern in wireless communication systems. One of the solutions to have such balanced communication is to use the functionalities provided by cognitive radios. The basic idea behind the concept of cognitive radios is to combine the information available with local radios with the available capability knowledge base to make decisions on parameter changes. The major phases of a cognitive radio are shown in Figure 4.5.

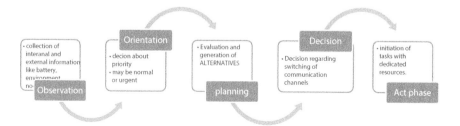

Figure 4.5 Cognitive radio cycle.

As a number of hot-spots are increasing, WLANs are also deployed accordingly even in a small locality. Also the operators which provide this WLAN functionality may be different. To have an efficient communication in such environments a multi-agent based system based on the concept of cognition radios is required in which there is no central coordinator which is making decisions. This system should be able to perform efficient information sharing and decision making in abnormal conditions. The basic framework for such a system is shown in Figure 4.6.

The major working components in this architecture are WLANs and WPANs. Each of the mobile station works within a cluster which collects information from the dynamic RF environment created with the help of cognitive radios and performs resource management. The RF environment sensing component plays a very important role as it collects statistics from both, mobile stations within that cluster and other external and operational environment factors as well. The standardization for the same is provided by IEEE 802.11k protocol. The various statistical parameters used for predictive modeling includes

- Quality of link between the mobile agent and access points
- The rate of change of mobility
- Energy requirement for the transmission of packet between access points and mobile stations
- Throughput in terms of traffic
- Expected delay in time

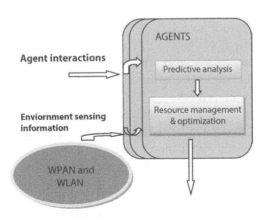

Figure 4.6 Framework of a multi agent based system.

Finally the resource management and optimization component takes the information from predictive model and make the decisions regarding routing and load balancing for increasing and optimizing the performance of WLAN. The various types of decisions that may be taken include:

- Transmission of power to access points
- Association requests between neighborhoods
- Load balancing
- Maximum allowable throughput at each access point

In this way the concept of cognitive radios is best utilized by dynamically optimizing all the resources of the wireless network and a cognitive communication environment may be created.

4.6   Designing 5G Smart Communication with Cognitive Computing and AI

Design and implementation of 5G smart networks are very challenging as these require complex decision making and resource optimization [8]. Cognitive computing when combined with AI and cloud computing can very easily handle the wireless system application and services. The various domains in which this technology combination may be used are summarized in Table 4.1.

All these applications may be implemented with the help of deep learning and AI techniques. The basic architecture for designing such communications is shown in Figure 4.7.

The architecture is composed of two different layers namely cognition layer and communication layer. The cognition layer consists of three different modules namely data cognition module, resource cognition module and resource allocation module.

The data cognition modules collects real world data related to network capabilities and infrastructure using techniques of data mining. The data will be specific to the application as well as network. For example if the application is a smart mobile application the data may include real time behavior information of user, the quality of communication, environmental specifications, number of active mobile stations and so on. From this collected data the interesting patterns are identified and analyzed by applying deep learning and AI based techniques. The resulting patterns are then passed to resource cognition module.

Table 4.1 Applications of cognitive computing in wireless networks.

Domain	Applications
Wireless communication	Channel modeling
	Beamforming
	Codebook design
	Channel state estimation
Wireless transmission	Coordination in multiple point transmission
	Multi-hop relay
Wireless applications and services	Mobility management
	Resource management
	Overhead and collision management

The resource cognition module does the optimization of resources based on the gathered patterns from data cognition module. In the first it handles the flow of admissions to the network and does load balancing. After that it performs scheduling and sends the requests to resource allocation

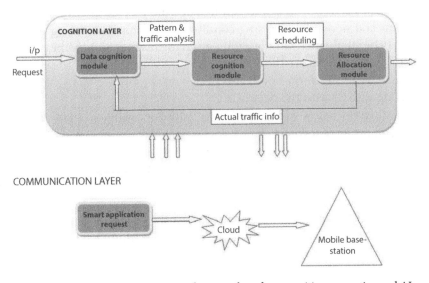

Figure 4.7 Wireless communication architecture based on cognitive computing and AI.

module for further assignment and analysis. The result is also fed back to data cognition module for further learning and quality enhancement of the network.

The communication layer consists of various smart devices which may include smart vehicles, smart homes, sensors devices and mobile devices making IoT environment. Any request raised by user specific to application is send to the cloud followed by to nearest base station. The base station in communication with cognitive layer environment handles the overall communication intelligently.

With this architecture there is a great feasibility of having enhanced user experience, dynamic and intelligent allocation of resources and energy optimization of resources.

4.6.1   Physical Layer Design Based on Reinforcement Learning

Reinforcement learning is very much similar to learning process of humans. It is a kind of supervised learning with some rewards. Let's take the example of designing a chess game. With each step the system learns the new techniques and plans for winning the game. In this way the machine is not only learning from past experiences but also tries to learn new paths for winning and getting the maximum reward points. Reinforcement learning when combined with cognition can be greatly used to design the automatic network management agents which can adapt to the environment conditions, can self learn from past experiences and present network status and can manage themselves in adverse environment and network collapsing conditions. For this the routing protocols may be augmented with learning mechanisms to maintain the packet delivery rates and ensure the service level agreements (SLAs). The overall overhead of the network should also not increase as we are applying additional algorithms with the network.

The different issues which need to be addressed while designing such intelligent protocol include:

- The type and context of information to be exchanged by different layers of communication
- The network parameters required for re-configuring the network in adverse conditions
- At what intervals and time the results of learning have to be used to re-configure the network
- How to maintain the quality of service

The form of reinforcement learning which is used in network management is termed as Q-learning F. The reward point at each activity in such networks is calculated as

$$O(S', A') = (1 - \mu)O(S, A) + \mu.r \qquad (4.1)$$

Here $O(S', A')$ = reward point calculated based on State S and
  Action A
μ = *learning rate of the network*
r = *current reward value based on environment statictics and policy*

The various metrics which may be used for calculating the reward points include:

- Hop count ($H(S, A)$): calculated as difference between *S and S'* to the destination
- Residual energy ($E(S,A)$): energy of node S'
- Number of paths ($P(S,A)$): number of routing paths at S'
- Link reliability ($L(S,A)$): calculated between node S and S'
- Expected number of transmission (ETS)
- Effective number of transmission (ENS)

The overall function for decision making becomes:

$$\partial(S, A) = \{H(S, A), E(S, A), P(S, A), L(S, A), ETS, ENS\} \quad (4.2)$$

All of the values are normalized in the range of [-1, 1] to implement this cross layer learning based protocol. Various protocols have been proposed in the literature which uses this approach for designing intelligent cross layer adaptive protocols like AdaR [9]. The basic architecture behind designing such protocols is shown in Figure 4.8. The various steps are summarized below.

Step 1: Middleware collects requirements from applications and set the demands.
Step 2: Learning agent available at middleware receives the demand and apply reinforcement learning techniques using different metrics valued from previous SLA database.

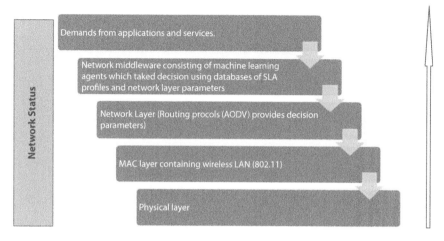

Figure 4.8 Architecture of protocol design using reinforcement learning.

Step 3: The various parameters' current value is made available to middleware using network layer protocol like AODV.

Step 4: The learning agent finally takes decision about reconfiguration of the network and various parameters are reset according to the requirement.

This general architecture can be used as a basic building block for designing the learning based protocols for better QoE and network utilization.

4.7   Advanced Wireless Signal Processing Based on Deep Learning

Machine learning has shown a great impact on handling signals in wireless communications in terms of modulation handling [10], encoding and decoding [11], channel equalization [12] and channel modeling [13]. But as commercial machine learning algorithms were having limitations as a huge amount of data is generated in wireless communications, the learning techniques were conceptual only and have not been used very much. With the advent in deep learning technologies which can handle large amounts of data, researchers started working on designing algorithms using deep learning which can also be used for wireless communication. Also deep learning based communications can ensure end to end delivery, therefore not only enhancing the local performance of network but achieving global rise in the performance.

The basic areas of the communication which can be improved with deep learning technologies include modulation recognition [14], channel encoding and decoding [15] and using auto encoders to completely change the overall architecture of the communication. The basic architecture of a communication system is shown in Figure 4.9.

Deep learning can be applied at modulation, channel decoding and detection phases. Applications of deep learning for each one of them has been discussed below.

4.7.1   Modulation

The traditional schemes for modulation were purely decision theoretic and pattern recognition based approaches [16]. These schemes were having a problem of limited memory capacity and feature extraction was also not learning based and automatic. To overcome these limitations a CNN based deep learning model may be used [17]. This technique learns modulation techniques by taking the input in the form of time series data that is taken in the radio frequency range. As a result the performance is not degraded with increasing signal to noise ratio up to a certain extent. But as the life of the input signals is very less and they are generated at a very fast rate sometimes it may become difficult for CNN to take the decisions due to ambiguity in data. So there is a great scope to extend the possibilities of usage of CNN for modulation purpose.

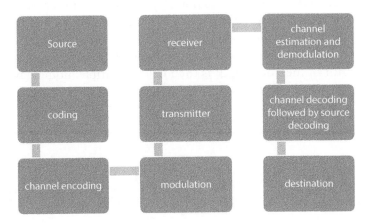

Figure 4.9 Basic communication building blocks.

4.7.2   Deep Learning for Channel Decoding

Neural networks were used at a very large extent for channel decoding as the input which is in the form of log likelihood ratios of the different codeword generated during the communication and output is a mathematical model which can simply convert those inputs to another form which can be easily handled using some hidden layer on NNs [18]. But these algorithms were having a disadvantage that they can only be used with limited block length. As we will increase the size of the block that needs to be decoded the complexity of the network will grow exponentially which may result in slow performance of the decoding phase.

As deep learning can very well address the concept of dimensionality, they can result in a very good solution to such problem. Many decoders have been proposed in the literature which is based on deep learning. One of them is algorithm which is based on belief propagation [19]. This algorithm was able to handle simple parity checks but could not handle high density checks. To overcome the limitation recurrent neural network based decoders have also been used in the literature [20]. These networks take the knowledge from previous inputs and also from the current and also feedbacks the output of the parity layers to other variable layers in the network. The basic DNN based decoding architecture has been shown in Figure 4.10.

The basic steps of the procedure may be summarized as

> Step 1: Take input of length k and convert into a codeword of length N and pass the same to modulation layer.
> Step 2: Modulation layer and noise layer represents the communication channel affects which may be reducing the performance of the network.
> Step 3: The log likelihood (LLR) generated by the LLR generator of the noisy input is then fed to multiple hidden layers which are trained to give decoded message of length k as a result.

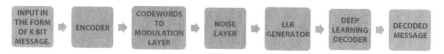

Figure 4.10 Basic deep learning architecture for channel decoding.

4.7.3   Detection Using Deep Learning

The deep learning model which is best suited for detection purpose is LSTM (long short term memory) network [20]. These networks can very well work with time series data which is changed at a very fast rate and also keeps the results of last outputs for getting the result from current input. That's why they are considered to be best suitable for detection purpose. The network can be combined with inter symbol interference (ISI) to give best results. The basic architecture form the same has been shown in Figure 4.11.

The detector will take Y as input and convert it into original transmitted value X taking input channel matrix H as shown in Figure 4.11.

The simulations done with these proposals have shown a great potential in applying deep learning models in future communication systems. Just a suitable deep learning model needs to be decided which can very well reflect the characteristics of channel at physical layer of the communication.

4.8   Applications of Cognition-Based Wireless Communication

Wireless communications are used by almost everyone nowadays. Therefore if it is possible to enhance the quality of experience of the user in terms of low latency and smart responses there may be a dramatic change

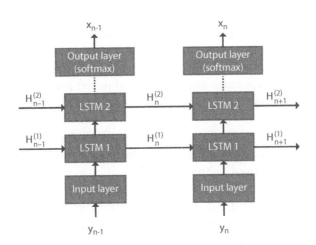

Figure 4.11   LSTM based detectors.

in the community. Some applications of designing such networks are discussed below.

4.8.1 Smart Surveillance Networks for Public Safety

As public safety workers such as police, firemen or ambulance operators are fully equipped with smart devices like mobiles and laptops nowadays smart communication can easily handle the adverse situations. Also with the availability of surveillance cameras and sensors, live streaming of the data can be made easily available for the analysis of current situations. But sometimes the radio frequencies which are allocated for this purpose may become so congested due to high use or high degree of data generation. Therefore there is a need to design a smart network which can take smart decisions in such situations or even may not give rise to such conditions. Cognitive radios can play a very good role for handling these situations. With these a public safety worker may obtain additional spectrum other than the one which is allocated to him in adverse conditions. There may be sharing of the spectrum possible with the usage of such cognitive radio networks.

4.8.2 Cognitive Health Care Systems

The health status of the driver is very important as he/she is not only responsible for his/her safety but also for the safety of the passengers. In case the health of the driver is poor or fatigue of he/she may not be able to drive attentively which may result in accidents or even casualties as the response time of the driver is increased in such scenarios. Therefore, monitoring of physical health of the driver is very important. It was nearly impossible in the traditional driving systems. To remedy such a situation, the cognitive intra-vehicle network can apply emotion analysis or behavior analysis using different features of face.

The camera can detect the eyelid state and micro-nod of the driver for analyzing the behavior and give necessary warnings in case of adverse situations.

Other applications in health care may involve smart cloth operations. These cloths can easily sense the body signals like temperature, humidity, heart rate etc. By using any AI based techniques available on the cloud the user may be classified into one of the categories, whether he/she is at high risk, medium risk, low risk or no risk at all. The same information may be immediately supplied to the base station and if the patient is at high risk his doctor may be immediately contacted by the base station for video conferencing or other medical services which may again demand for immediate bandwidth allocation intelligently. The basic scheme of the application is shown in Figure 4.12.

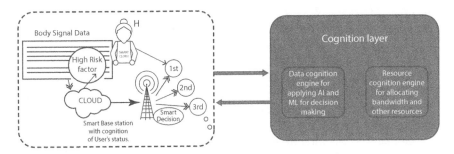

Figure 4.12 Smart healthcare application.

4.9 Conclusion

In this chapter we have first discussed about the concept of cognitive computing and its evolution. Then we have discussed the possibilities for the applications of cognitive computing in handling wireless communications and to better enhance the quality of experience. Four major areas where the computing may be applied include resource management, physical layer designing, coding and detection at physical layer with deep learning and 5G generations of communications. The applications and available architecture in all of the four areas are discussed. Then some applications are also discussed where these communications can be used.

References

1. Modha, S.D., Ananthanarayanan, K.R., Esser, S., Nadirango, A., Sherbondy, J.A., Singh, R., Cognitive computing. *Commun. ACM*, 54, 8, 62–71, 2011.
2. Berlemann, L., Mangold, S., Walke, B.H., Policy-based reasoning for spectrum sharing in cognitive radio networks, in: *Proc. IEEE International Symposium on New Frontiers in Dynamic Spectrum Access Networks*, Baltimore, USA, pp. 1–10, 2005.
3. Luo, Y., Gao, L., Huang, J., An integrated spectrum and information market for greencognitive communications. *IEEE J. Sel. Areas Commun.*, 34, 12, 3326–3338, 2016.
4. Karunakaran, P. and Gerstacker, W., Sensing algorithms and protocol for simultaneoussensing and reception-based cognitive D2D communications in LTE-a systems. *IEEE Trans. Cognit. Commun. Networking*, 4, 1, 93–107, 2018.
5. Kelly, E.J. and Hamm, S., *Smart machines: IBM's Watson and the era of cognitive computing*, pp. 55–80, Columbia University Press, Columbia Business School, 2013.

6. Chen, M., Zhang, Y., Li, Y., Mao, S., Leung, V.C., *EMC: Emotion-aware mobile cloud computing in 5G*, 29, 2, pp. 32–38, IEEE Network, 2015.

7. Iwamura, M., NGMN View on 5G Architecture, in: *Proc. of 81ˢᵗIEEE Conference on Vehicular Technology (VTC Spring)*, Glasgow, UK, pp. 1–5, 2015.

8. Pozna, C. and Precup, R.E., Novel design of cognitive system strategies, in: *Proc. of 4th IEEE International Symposium on Logistics and Industrial Informatics*, Smolenice, Slovakia, pp. 205–214, 2012.

9. Fang, M., Wang, J., Xu, X., A pre-emptive distributed address assignment mechanism for wireless sensor networks, in: *Proc. of 4th International Conference on Wireless Communications, Networking and Mobil Computing, (WICOM'08)*, Dalian, China, pp. 1–5, 2008.

10. Fehske, A., Gaeddert, J., Reed, J.H., A new approach to signal classification using spectral correlation and neural networks, in: *Proc. of IEEE International Symposium on New Frontiers in Dynamic Spectrum Access Networks (DYSPAN)*, Baltimore, USA, pp. 144–150, 2005.

11. Sjoberg, J., Zhang, Q., Ljung, L., Benveniste, A., Delyon, B., Glorennec, Y.P., Hjalmarsson, H., Juditsky, H., Nonlinear black-box modelling in system identification: a unified overview. *Automatica*, 31, 12, 1691–1724, 1995.

12. Wen, C.K., Jin, S., Wong, K.K., Chen, J.C., Ting, P., Channel estimation for massive mimo using gaussian-mixture bayesian learning. *IEEE Trans. Wireless Commun.*, 14, 3, 1356–1368, 2015.

13. Ibukahla, M., Sombria, J., Castanie, F., Bershad, N.J., Neural networks for modelling non - linear memoryless communication channels. *IEEE Trans. Commun.*, 45, 7, 768–771, 1997.

14. Ibnkahla, M., Applications of neural networks to digital communications–a survey. *Signal Process.*, 80, 7, 1185–1215, 2000.

15. Jiang, C., Zhang, H., Ren, Y., Han, Z., Chen, K.C., Hanzo, L., Machine learning paradigms for next-generation wireless networks. *IEEE Trans. Wireless Commun.*, 24, 2, 98–105, 2017.

16. Nandi, A.K. and Azzouz, E.E., Algorithms for automatic modulation recognition of communication signals. *IEEE Trans. Commun.*, 46, 4, 431–436, 1998.

17. OShea, T. and Hoydis, J., An introduction to deep learning for the physical layer. *IEEE Trans. Cognit. Commun. Networking*, 3, 4, 563–575, 2017.

18. Wang, X.A. and Wicker, S.B., An artificial neural net Viterbi decoder. *IEEE Trans. Commun.*, 44, 2, 165–171, 1996.

19. Nachmani, E., Beery, Y., Burshtein, D., Learning to decode linear codes using deep learning, in: *Proc. International Conference on Communication, Control, and Computing (Allerton)*, Monticello, USA, pp. 341–346, 2016.

20. Gruber, T., Cammerer, S., Hoydis, J., Brink, S.T., On deep learning-based channel decoding, in: *Proc. of 51st Annual Conference on Information Sciences and Systems (CISS)*, Baltimore, USA, pp. 1–6, 2017.

5

Spectrum Sensing and Allocation Schemes for Cognitive Radio

Amrita Rai[1]*, Amit Sehgal[1], T.L. Singal[2] and Rajeev Agrawal[1]

[1]ECE Dept., G. L. Bajaj Institute of Technology and Management,
Greater Noida, India
[2]Chitkara University, Rajpura, India

Abstract

In wireless communication system, the radio spectrum is one of the biggest resource constraints with limited availability in nature. To regulate the use of this limited resource, Fixed Spectrum Access policy (FSA) was adopted by spectrum regulators. To overcome the limitation due to scarcity of spectrum and optimize spectrum utilization, Dynamic Spectrum Access (DSA) was proposed. In DSA, users are categorized as Primary Users (PUs) and Secondary Users (SUs). Incorporation of cognizance about the available spectrum into radio communication devices lead to the evolution of Cognitive Radio Networks (CRN) and radio devices with this capability are called Cognitive Radios (CR). To access radio spectrum using cognitive intelligence, several access models have been proposed for the CRs such as Concurrent Spectrum Access (CSA), Opportunistic Spectrum Access (OSA) and Hybrid Spectrum Access (HAS). In most cases, the CR user needs to frequently observe the spectrum to identify the spectrum holes. Such mechanism is known as Spectrum Sensing. Several techniques of spectrum sensing have been developed, broadly categorized into Direct Sensing and Indirect Sensing. The implementation of these techniques along with challenges faced in their implementation have been briefly discussed in the chapter along with the related research issues.

Keywords: Dynamic spectrum access, cognitive radio spectrum, spectrum sensing, spectrum allocation, spectrum detection

------

*Corresponding author: amritaskrai@gmail.com

Krishna Kant Singh, Akansha Singh, Korhan Cengiz and Dac-Nhuong Le (eds.) *Machine Learning and Cognitive Computing for Mobile Communications and Wireless Networks,* (91–130) © 2020 Scrivener Publishing LLC

5.1   Foundation and Principle of Cognitive Radio

For any wireless communication system, the radio spectrum is one of the crucial resource constraints and forms the basis for energy-bandwidth tradeoff in wireless systems. It is also a resource with limited availability and restricted access for any specific application or service. To regulate the use of this limited resource, fixed spectrum access policy (FSA) was adopted by spectrum regulators. Under this policy, a fixed piece of spectrum is assigned for a dedicated purpose which is further distributed to the users for access to wireless services. This assigned piece of spectrum with a limited bandwidth is called licensed spectrum and no other user is allowed to use it even though the user with allocation is not using its part. The first decade of the 21st century experienced an exponential increase in services and applications based on wireless communication which resulted in the allocated spectrum occupying almost an entire range of available radio spectrum and not enough bands were available for upcoming technologies such as Internet of things (IoT) and low power wide area network (LP-WAN). On the other hand, it was reported that a large portion of allocated spectrum was under-utilized whereas some other portions were heavily congested due to allocation with very narrow band gaps, thus resulting in severe adjacent channel interference and drop in quality of service and user experience. The unutilized portions of spectrum are called 'spectrum holes' or 'white spaces'. It can, therefore, be concluded that the scarcity of spectrum is, primarily, due to the lack of flexibility in spectrum allocation and weak optimization in utilization of allocated spectrum.

To overcome the limitation due to scarcity of spectrum and optimize spectrum utilization, techniques based on dynamic spectrum access (DSA), also known as opportunistic spectrum access (OSA), were developed [1, 2]. In DSA, users are categorized as primary users (PUs) and secondary users (SUs). PUs, also known as legacy owners of spectrum, are those users to whom the spectrum is allocated and they have higher priority of using it. SUs are allowed to use the spectrum allocated to PUs when it is not in use. The dynamic allocation of spectrum bands is shown in Figure 5.1. Provision for sharing of the spectrum between PUs and SUs was also introduced in DSA.

To implement DSA, some kind of intelligence is required to sense the utilization of spectrum and identify the not-in-use band. Incorporation of such cognizance about the available spectrum into radio communication devices leads to the evolution of cognitive radio networks (CRNs) and SUs having radio devices with this capability are called cognitive radios (CR). Several surveys and studies on DSA and CR have been

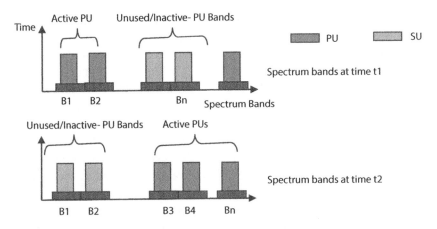

Figure 5.1 Dynamic spectrum allocation between PUs and SUs.

conducted in the first decade of the 21st century [3–5]. In general, CR is a technology which allows for dynamic spectrum utilization based on the need and availability of radio resources, thus optimizing its use with enhanced efficiency [6]. CRs consist of analog RF front end and digital processors which may be dedicated digital signal processors or field programmable gate arrays (FPGAs) customized to function as digital processors. General purpose processors can also be programmed for digital processing of signals received by the front-end. These digital processors are responsible for spectrum sensing. When the spectrum hole available for use by an SU is identified, the software tools running in these digital processors perform all the required changes in parameters of SU such as center frequency and bandwidth of channel to be used, transmit power, wave shape etc. For spectrum sharing between PUs and SUs, three spectrum allocation models are commonly followed—interweave, underlay and overlay [7]. Figure 5.1 shows the interweave model of DSA. In case of underlay model, SUs share the spectrum simultaneously with PUs but at a much lower power level so that there is no or little interference and desired signal can be filtered at the corresponding receiver. In case of overlay, SUs transmit at a much higher power level using the same band even when the PU is active.

Despite the improved spectrum utilization, several limitations and challenges are faced by DSA models which limit their use and deployment for commercial applications. For example, in case of interweave DSA, the SU cannot access a particular band until an active PU exists in that band. This detection of active PU needs to be very accurate to avoid any chances of interference or denial of service. Another challenge is to decide the rate of sensing the spectrum i.e. how recent the sensed data about availability of a spectrum is. Coordination among various PUs and SUs and exchange of control information regarding allocation of spectrum further increase the complexity of the system. Threats by malicious PUs include blocking spectrum bands of inactive PUs, thus causing denial or service to SUs. Similarly, malicious SUs may occupy the available bands and not release it, thus causing severe interference or denial of service for legacy owners or PUs. An SU must release the spectrum band immediately when a signal for its legacy owner PU appears, even though there is an ongoing transmission. This reduces the stability and reliability of the DSA based systems. The techniques to shift to another available band without disrupting the ongoing transmission must be developed to improve these quality of service parameters. In addition to these and many other similar technical challenges, there are several other policies based challenges due to the required coordination and cooperation required between various stakeholders of the overall system. To overcome all these challenges and deployment issues, several techniques and modified forms of DSA are being developed and tested by researchers and industries. These, primarily, include efficient and reliable techniques to sense the spectrum availability in real time and methods to allocate spectrum bands between PUs and SUs maintaining seamless transmission of data and minimizing delay or denial of service. Further sections of this chapter explore such spectrum sensing and allocation techniques.

5.2   Spectrum Sensing for Cognitive Radio Networks

As introduced in section 5.1, several access models have been proposed for the CRs to access radio spectrum using cognitive intelligence. Through these models, spectrum holes are identified by the SUs and used for transmission. For some networks, the SUs may get this information about spectrum holes through broadcasting due to their predetermined availability. However, in most cases, the CR user needs to frequently observe the spectrum to identify the spectrum holes to acquire the spectrum when needed and also to release the in-use spectrum whenever it is demanded by the PU to which it is allocated originally. Such mechanism is known as spectrum sensing [8–10]. To increase the chances of getting access to the vacant spectrum, the CR needs the capability to sense a much wider band of spectrum that it actually requires for communication. This can be implemented by using either an ultra-wideband frontend or multiple frontends sensing different smaller bands. Both these cases will result in an increase in processing time, complexity and hardware cost. Several sensing techniques have been proposed and tested to minimize the effect of these limiting factors with increased efficiency in terms of spectrum sensing capability. The process of spectrum sensing can be described mathematically as shown in equation (5.1).

$$S(n) = \begin{cases} Gc * P(n) + W(n) & H_1 : PU \text{ is detected} \\ W(n) & H_0 : PU \text{ is not detected} \end{cases} \tag{5.1}$$

where S(n) is the signal received at the SU which is a CR user, Gc is the gain of sensing channel, P(n) is the signal from PU and W(n) is the white additive Gaussian noise (AWGN). The two hypotheses corresponding to detection and absence of PU signal are represented by H_1 and H_0 respectively. The signal detected by the frontend of a CR node i.e. S(n) is compared to a threshold (δ) and decision is made using the rule given in equation (5.2).

$$\begin{cases} S(n) \geq \delta & H_1 \\ S(n) < \delta & H_0 \end{cases} \tag{5.2}$$

Based on the hypothesis result, the SU can utilize a particular band at the instant of time if no PU is detected in that band i.e. in the case of H_0. This process of spectrum sensing is shown in Figure 5.2. Several techniques of spectrum sensing have been developed to detect the presence of a PU and vacant spectrum holes.

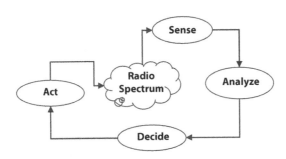

Figure 5.2 Spectrum sensing cycle.

5.3 Classification of Spectrum Sensing Techniques

Depending upon the source of which is being tested to detect the presence of PU, sensing techniques can be broadly categorized into direct sensing and indirect sensing [8]. Figure 5.3 shows various sensing techniques grouped into direct and indirect sensing.

In case of direct sensing, the CT transmitter searches for the presence of an active primary receiver within its coverage area. Such detection will ensure that the particular frequency band is in use by a PU and thus cannot be used by SU. Techniques such as local oscillator detection, proactive sensing, and interference temperature management have been used for direct sensing. These are also called interference based sensing techniques. The major challenge faced by direct sensing is that the receivers, generally, do not share signals with other users which can be used to identify their active

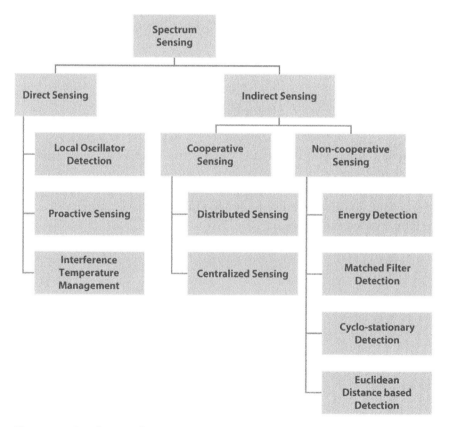

Figure 5.3 Classification of spectrum sensing techniques.

state and spectrum in use. Thus, the task of detecting an active primary transmitter is the preferred approach for spectrum sensing and termed as indirect sensing. In this case, the CR transmitter detects for the presence of an active PU transmitter at a distance which is the sum of its own coverage radius and that of the PU transmitter. Such detection will ensure that the CR transmitter can use the band of detected PU without any interference since chances of active primary receiver within its coverage area will be minimal.

Indirect sensing is further classified into two categories—cooperative sensing and non-cooperative sensing. In non-cooperative sensing, there is no collaboration or co-operation between different SUs and each one takes its own decision regarding presence of PUs. The commonly used non-cooperative sensing techniques are based on various detection mechanisms such as energy detection, matched filter detection, cyclo-stationary detection, Euclidean distance based detection etc. These techniques are easy to implement and benefitted by low processing time and hardware cost. However, these benefits are available at the cost of increase in error rate due to high noise uncertainty, interference and fading. The implementation of these techniques has been briefly discussed in the chapter along with the related research issues.

In case of cooperative sensing, SUs coordinate among themselves while making decision regarding the presence of a PU and availability of spectrum hole [11]. Cooperative sensing is categorized into three types: distributed, centralized and relay assisted. Though drawbacks of non-cooperative sensing are removed using these techniques, they have their own limitations. The succeeding section in this chapter explores non-cooperative sensing techniques.

5.4   Energy Detection

Energy detection is the simplest among all non-cooperative sensing techniques. It does not require any a priori information about the signal of PUs. The sensed energy is used to detect the presence of a PU by comparing it with a pre-decided threshold value which depends upon the noise level. If the received signal is higher than the threshold, the presence of PU signal is concluded. Figure 5.4 shows a basic block diagram of energy detection model. It being a narrow band sensing technique, band pass filter is used to band limit the received signal before it is analyzed for presence of PU signal so that a single frequency channel is tested at a time. The corresponding hypothesis is represented as H_1. The absence of PU signal is represented by hypothesis H_0 [12]. These hypotheses are given in equation (5.3).

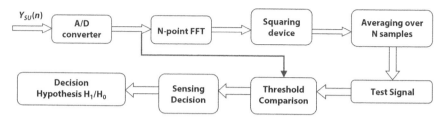

Figure 5.4 Block diagram of energy detection model.

$$H_1: y_{SU}(n) = x_{PU}(n) + \eta(n) > \lambda, \text{ PU signal is present}$$

$$H_0: y_{SU}(n) = \eta(n) < \lambda, \text{ PUs signal is absent} \tag{5.3}$$

where $y_{SU}(n)$ is the received signal at SU at the output of detector, $x_{SU}(n)$ is the PU transmitted signal, $\eta(n)$ is white Gaussian noise and λ is the threshold value.

Before hypothesis testing, the analog signal received $(Y_{SU}(n))$ at SU is converted to digital form using digital to analog (D/A) converter and then its fast Fourier transform (FFT) is obtained. The magnitude of FFT is squared and averaged over N samples to obtain $y_{SU}(n)$ which can be written as shown in equation (5.4). This sampled average is compared with threshold for hypothesis testing [13].

$$y_{SU}\left(n\right) = \frac{1}{N}\sum_{n=1}^{N}\left(Y_{SU}\left(n\right)\right)^2 \tag{5.4}$$

The received signal $Y_{SU}(n)$ is approximated as a Gaussian random signal and test signal $y_{SU}(n)$ has central chi-square distribution for H_0 hypothesis and non-central chi-square distribution for H_1 with N degrees of freedom for $N > 250$ based on the central limit theorem. The Gaussian approximation of SU test signal can be written as shown in equation (5.5).

$$\begin{cases} H_0: y_{SU}(n) \sim \mathbb{N}\left(N\delta_w^2, 2N\delta_w^4\right) \\ H_1: y_{SU}(n) \sim \mathbb{N}\left(N\left(\delta_w^2 + \delta_s^2\right), 2N\left(\delta_w^2 + \delta_s^2\right)^2\right) \end{cases} \tag{5.5}$$

where $\mathbb{N}$ represents normal distribution function, δ_w^2 is noise variance and δ_s^2 is variance of PU signal. For a channel with additive white Gaussian noise (AWGN), the accuracy of energy detection based sensing technique is measured in terms of its accuracy to detect presence of PU and probability of generating a false alarm regarding presence of a PU signal which may force an SU to release the spectrum resource even though it is available. The probabilities of detection and false alarm can be obtained as given in equations (5.6) and (5.7).

$$P_d = Q\left(\frac{\lambda - \left(N\left(\delta_w^2 + \delta_s^2\right) \right)}{\sqrt{2N\left(\delta_w^2 + \delta_s^2\right)^2}\,)} \right) \tag{5.6}$$

$$P_{fd} = Q\left(\frac{\lambda - N\delta_w^2}{\sqrt{2N\delta_w^4}} \right) \tag{5.7}$$

where Q(.) represents Q-function and λ is sensing threshold.

Although energy detection scheme is easy to implement due to it being independent of any prior knowledge of PU signal, its inability to differentiate between signal and noise for low power signals restricts its use in locations which experience strong signal losses or come under deep faded region. The threshold value used for decision making is critical performance parameter for energy detection based sensing schemes. Several schemes have been proposed to dynamically select the threshold in real time and also the decision algorithms [14–18]. These include techniques such as reduction of error in noise power estimation by using dynamic noise estimation [19]. With SINR based linear adaptation for threshold control [20, 21] improvement in SU throughput was achieved but at the cost of increased chances of false alarm. In another adaptive threshold technique based on noise power estimation, the false alarm rate was kept within acceptable limits by using a dedicated noise estimation channel in [22]. Techniques based on wideband spectrum sensing [23], double-threshold [24], filter bank using discrete Fourier transform (DFT) [25] and image binarization [26] have also been used with the objective to reduce false alarm and increase accuracy and probability of detection of PU signal.

5.5   Matched Filter Detection

A linear coherent filter that maximizes the output signal-to-noise ratio (SNR) in the presence of additive noise for a given input signal can be regarded as a matched filter. Let the impulse response of the matched filter be $h(n - k)$ which is the folded time-shifted version of the primary user signal. For the received signal $x(k)$, the basic operation of the matched filter is given by

$$Y(n) = \sum_{k=-\infty}^{\infty} h(n-k)x(k) \tag{5.8}$$

Matched filter detection is applicable for spectrum sensing in cognitive radio networks only when the a priori knowledge about the center frequency, the bandwidth, the modulation scheme, and other related parameters of the primary user signal as well as the response of the wireless channel are well known. This technique involves the comparison of the received signal with pilot sample signals (or, synchronization codes in some communication systems) received from the same radio transmitter. The test statistic for the matched filter is computed using these saved pilot signals [27, 28].

Let $y(n)$ represent the vector of received signals $y(t)$, and let $x_p(n)$ represent the pilot samples. For N number of samples, the test statistic for matched filter detection technique is given by:

$$T_{MFD} = \frac{1}{N} \sum_{n=1}^{N} y(n)x_p^*(n) \tag{5.9}$$

The computed test statistic is then compared with a pre-defined threshold level, δ_{MFD}. If the computed test statistic is higher than this threshold level, then hypothesis H_1 is valid (i.e., the primary user is present). If the computed test statistic is lower than this threshold level, then hypothesis H_0 is valid (i.e., the primary user is not present). Mathematically, this can be written as:

$$T_{MFD} > \delta_{MFD};\ H_1\ \text{(Primary user is present)} \tag{5.10}$$

$$T_{MFD} > \delta_{MFD};\ H_0\ \text{(Primary user is not present)} \tag{5.11}$$

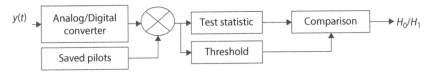

Figure 5.5 A simplified block diagram of matched filter detection technique for spectrum sensing.

The value of the pre-defined threshold level, δ_{MFD} is usually chosen depending on the noise signal level within the incoming received signal. As noise level is quite uncertain, this may result into inaccurate results [29, 30]. Figure 5.5 illustrates a typical block schematic of matched filter detection technique for spectrum sensing [31, 32].

Let us now consider the main performance metrics of spectrum sensing techniques. These are probability of detection (P_d), probability of false detection (P_{fd}), and probability of miss detection (P_{md}). The sum of all these performance metrics is unity which determines the overall efficiency of the spectrum sensing techniques. That is,

$$P_d + P_{fd} + P_{md} = 1 \qquad (5.12)$$

The probability of detection, P_d signifies that the secondary consumer declares the occurrence of the primary consumer signal when the spectrum is actually busy or occupied. In terms of hypothesis H_1 and H_0 (as defined earlier), these metrics can be stated as:

$$P_d = \text{Prob}\,(H_1/H_1) \qquad (5.13)$$

Higher value of P_d will ensure that there will not be any interference to the primary user signal by the secondary user.

The probability of false alarm detection, P_{fd} signifies that the secondary user declares the presence of the primary user signal as soon as the spectrum is actually idle or free. In terms of hypothesis H_1 and H_0, these metrics can be expressed as:

$$P_{fd} = \text{Prob}\,(H_1/H_0) \qquad (5.14)$$

Lower value of P_{fd} will ensure that the secondary users are more likely to access the spectrum, and its higher value may result into interference to the primary user.

The probability of miss detection, P_{md} signifies that the secondary user declares the non-presence (absence) of the primary user signal when the spectrum is actually busy or occupied. In terms of hypothesis H_1 and H_0, these metrics can be expressed as:

$$P_{md} = \text{Prob}\ (H_0/H_1) \tag{5.15}$$

It may be noted that there is always a trade-off between P_{fd} and P_{md}, that is, if one is higher, then the other will be lower, or vice versa. A good spectrum sensing technique has to consider the constraints posed by both these metrics. If E_{PU} represents the primary user signal energy, then the probability of detection, P_d in terms of primary user signal energy, the sensing threshold level and the noise is given by:

$$P_d = Q\left(\frac{\delta_{MFD} - E_{PU}}{\sqrt{E_{PU}\sigma_N^2}}\right) \tag{5.16}$$

where $Q(\text{-})$ is the Q-function, δ_{MFD} represents the sensing threshold level, and σ_N^2 signifies the noise variance. Similarly, the probability of false alarm detection, P_{fd} is given by:

$$P_{fd} = Q\left(\frac{\delta_{MFD}}{\sqrt{E_{PU}\sigma_N^2}}\right) \tag{5.17}$$

Alternatively, the sensing threshold level, δ_{MFD} can be expressed as a function of the primary user signal energy and the noise variance, that is,

$$\delta_{MFD} = Q^{-1}\left(P_{fd}\right)\sqrt{E_{PU}\sigma_N^2} \tag{5.18}$$

In order to enhance the performance of spectrum sensing using matched filter detection technique, dynamic selection of the threshold can be exploited [33]. Although this technique requires a few number of pilot signal samples to obtain good detection performance, it may be impractical sometimes due to non-availability of prior information about the primary user signal. In addition, when the response of the wireless channel changes rapidly (i.e., fading), its performance degrades significantly. This technique may also become unreliable due to presence of primary user emulation security concerns in which a malicious sensor node mimics the primary user signal.

The computational complexity of the matched filter detection is quite high because perfect timing synchronization is needed at both layers—physical as well as medium access control. The detection accuracy can be affected adversely for sensing the spectrum hole in the presence of several primary user signals over the same bandwidth. However, a dedicated matched filter can be used for each primary user signal which, in turn, will increase the complexity of implementing this technique for opportunistic and dynamic spectrum sensing [34–36].

Matched filter detection technique exhibits a good alternative for applications where the transmitted signal is well-known a priori like radar signal processing. To overcome the frequency offset sensitivity, a combination of parallel and segmented matched filter can be used [37]. This arrangement enables the required criteria for sensing time with moderate hardware complexity.

5.6   Cyclo-Stationary Detection

If autocorrelation function of a signal is periodic in nature, then it is termed as a cyclo-stationary signal. The autocorrelation function depends on frequency only in Fourier series expansion. In cyclo-stationary process, different spectral components are not correlated to each other. Almost all communication signals exhibit a statistical property, known as cyclo-stationarity. This can be exploited to determine desired signals and to discriminate against undesired signals, noise signals, and interference in various signal processing techniques without requiring much prior knowledge.

The cyclo-stationary detection technique is primarily based upon the analysis of features of the cyclic autocorrelation function of received periodic data signal and aperiodic noise signals which are regarded as wide-sense stationary signals without any correlation [38]. It is observed that a modulated signal is generally cyclo-stationary, which distinguishes it from noise signals. Some of the statistics such as the mean and autocorrelation function of the modulated signals are periodic in nature [39]. The detection process essentially involves a test on the presence of the cyclo-stationary characteristics of the received primary user signal.

The primary user signal has the periodicity properties which are embedded in its cyclic prefixes, the carrier frequency, modulation rate, pulse trains, hopping sequence, or spreading codes [40]. These are considered to possess cyclo-stationary features whereas the noise is stationary without any correlation. Therefore, this technique is capable of discriminating various primary user signals, the secondary user signals, or the interfering signals (assumed to be either stationary, or, cyclo-stationary with different time periods). Thus, the cyclo-stationary properties are extracted by using either the spectral correlation between the input and output signals, or the cyclic spectrum [41]. The detection of cyclo-stationary signals over multiple cyclic frequencies can be made possible by utilizing generalized likelihood ratio test [42].

The mean, $m_y(t)$ of a cyclo-stationary received signal $y(t)$ is periodic with T_0 as the period of the signal. Mathematically,

$$m_y(t) = m_y(t + T_0)$$

(5.19)

Similarly, the autocorrelation function, $R_y(t, T_0)$ of a cyclo-stationary received signal $y(t)$ is periodic with T_0 as the period of the signal. This is expressed mathematically as:

$$R_y(t,u) = R_y(t + T_0, u + T_0)$$

(5.20)

By replacing t with $(t + \tau/2)$, and u with $(t - \tau/2)$, we write auto-correlation function in terms of cyclic autocorrelation function (CAF), R_y^α which represents the Fourier series expansion of a cyclo-stationary signal. That is,

$$R_y\left(t + \tau/2, t - \tau/2\right) = \sum R_y^\alpha\left(\tau\right) e^{j2\pi\alpha t}$$

(5.21)

Here α represents the cyclic frequency, which is known to the receiver. The value $\alpha = 0$ results in the standard autocorrelation function of the signal $y(t)$. In fact, a nonzero cyclic frequency (i.e., $\alpha \neq 0$) exists for a cyclo-stationary signal such that $R_y^\alpha \neq 0$.

Or, the Fourier coefficient,

$$R_y^\alpha\left(\tau\right) = \frac{1}{T_0} \int_{-1/T_0}^{1/T_0} R_y\left(t + \tau/2, t - \tau/2\right) e^{-j2\pi\alpha t} dt$$

(5.22)

The cyclic spectral density (CSD), $S_y^\alpha(f)$ signifies Fourier transform of CAF. It is given by:

$$S_y^\alpha(f) = \int_{-\infty}^{\infty} R_y^\alpha(\tau) e^{-j2\pi f\tau} d\tau \qquad (5.23)$$

The CSD signifies the correlation density between two spectral components. The difference between them is the cyclic frequency. When cyclic spectral density for primary user signals having cyclo-stationary features is computed, the periodicity of their statistics is highlighted. This is quite useful to discriminate the noise signal from the primary user signal. Fast Fourier transform of the correlated signals helps in determining the peak frequencies, indicating the primary user signals even in the presence of noise signals which does not exhibit any periodicities [43, 44]. This means that the CSD has peaks at cyclic frequencies that are multiples of $1/T_0$, which happens to be the fundamental frequency of the received primary user signal.

In cyclo-stationary detection, the frequency-domain test statistic for at a specified value of α is given by:

$$Y = \int_{-f_s/2}^{f_s/2} \hat{S}_y^\alpha(f) \left[S_y^\alpha(f) \right]^* df \qquad (5.24)$$

Here the term $\hat{S}_y^\alpha(f)$ represents an estimate of the spectral correlation function, and f_s denotes the sampling frequency of the received primary user signal.

In cyclo-stationary detection technique, an analog-to-digital converter is used to convert the received analog signal into digital signal. Fast Fourier transform is then computed using N-point FFT. These values are auto correlated, averaged over number of samples, and then subjected to feature detection. The output of feature detection determines the presence of the primary user (that is, the hypothesis H_1) in case the received signal $y(t)$ is cyclo-stationary (that means the spectrum is occupied), or the absence of the primary user (that is, the hypothesis H_0) in case the received signal $y(t)$ is stationary (that means the spectrum is free). Figure 5.6 illustrates a typical block schematic of cyclo-stationary detection technique.

In cyclo-stationary detection technique, it is assumed that the period T_0 of the received primary user signal is known a priori. If this assumption is

Figure 5.6 A typical block schematic of cyclo-stationary detection technique.

not true, then this technique requires either the extraction of, or the search for, the cyclic frequencies. However, this increases the computational complexity. In such case, the Fourier coefficient can be estimated as:

$$\hat{R}_y^\alpha(\tau) = R_y^\alpha(\tau) + \varepsilon_y^\alpha(\tau) \tag{5.25}$$

Here $\varepsilon_y^\alpha(\tau)$ signifies the estimation error. It diminishes asymptotically in case of consistent estimator as the observation length tends to approach infinity.

Since the observation length is finite practically, i.e., $\hat{R}_y^\alpha(\tau) \neq 0$, then the following hypothesis conditions are checked:

- If $\hat{R}_y^\alpha(\tau) = \varepsilon_y^\alpha(\tau)$; then hypothesis H_0
- If $\hat{R}_y^\alpha(\tau) = R_y^\alpha(\tau) + \varepsilon_y^\alpha(\tau)$; then hypothesis H_1

This is possible if autocorrelation functions are transformed into N-vectors by choosing a set of $\{\tau_1, \tau_2, \ldots\ldots\ldots, \tau_N\}$. The performance of cyclo-stationary detector is analyzed asymptotically [45].

Cyclo-stationary detection is quite robust against noise level uncertainties. It works well even in very low signal-to-noise ratio regions. Due to this, this technique has much less probability of false detection. By increasing the count of samples, the performance of detection can be further enhanced. But this also increases the length of the received signal which, in turn, results in higher sensing time and complexity of implementation. Moreover, sample timing errors and frequency offset may weaken the spectral correlation density [46, 47]. This technique is not robust against fading statistics uncertainties. In a nut-shell, there is a trade-off among performance, complexity, and practicability.

The orthogonal frequency-division multiplexing (OFDM) signals are a typical example of cyclo-stationary signals. Modern wireless communication systems including LTE, WiMAX, Wi-Fi, and DVB-T use spectrum sensing technique with OFDM, and hence use spectrum sensors exploiting cyclo-stationary feature detection [48].

5.7   Euclidean Distance-Based Detection

This technique is an improved version of cyclo-stationary detection technique in terms of reducing noise uncertainty [49]. The shortest path between two active user nodes in a cognitive radio network is referred to as Euclidean distance (ED). Euclidean distance-based detection technique is a robust and simple method for spectrum sensing. The minimum value of Euclidean distance (ED) determines the shortest possible distance between two active secondary user nodes [50]. This technique is primarily based on autocorrelation of signals received by the secondary user. The autocorrelation error of the power spectra of the wireless communication channel is measured at different instants of time [51]. The autocorrelation error computes the probability that the primary users are present. The autocorrelation of the received signal can be expressed as:

$$R_{y,y}(\tau) = \sum_{n=1}^{N} y(n) y^*(n-\tau)$$

(5.26)

Here the term $R_{y,y}(\tau)$ represents the autocorrelation function at *lag* τ (τ being the lag in time required to generate the time-shifted version of received signal $y(n)$), N represents number of samples, and $*$ denotes complex conjugate of the function.

When adjacent autocorrelation function values of the received signal happen to be quite close, then the received signal is said to be highly correlated. In order to estimate the degree of correlation, the Euclidean distance is computed between the autocorrelation function of a reference vector and the received signal. The autocorrelation function reference vector, ACF_{REF} consists of the auto-correlated values of a strong received signal. Its equation is given by:

$$ACF_{REF} = \left(\frac{2}{M}\right) t + 1$$

(5.27)

where $M \left(0 \le t \le \dfrac{M}{2}\right)$ is the number of lags that autocorrelation has which includes both positive and negative values.

Mathematically, the Euclidean distance (D) is expressed as:

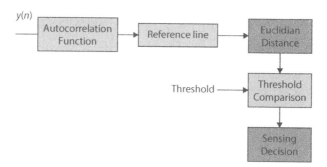

Figure 5.7 A typical block schematic of Euclidean distance-based detection technique.

$$D = \sqrt{\sum \left(R_{y,y}\left(\tau\right) - ACF_{REF}\right)^2} \qquad (5.28)$$

The hypothesis is determined on comparing the Euclidean distance, D with a pre-determined sensing threshold value, δ as:

- If $D < \delta$, then hypothesis H_1
- If $D \geq \delta$, then hypothesis H_0

Figure 5.7 depicts a typical block schematic of implementing Euclidean distance-based detection technique [52, 53].

Euclidean distance-based detection technique has a higher success rate of the primary user signal detection as compared to that of the autocorrelation-based detection technique [54–57].

5.8   Spectrum Allocation for Cognitive Radio Networks

In the present day, network development is suffering the enormous spectrum inadequacy problem due to the fixed assignment policy; due to this technique, a great quantity of spectrum remains unused [58]. To overcome this limitation of spectrum allocation, different authors proposed different methods of allocation which concern mainly network coverage with simplified communication, Channel availability and network throughput must be considered in a dynamic manner. Generally, spectrum allocation in CRNs is required two ways [59]: first, one step allocation in which the spectrum regulator instantaneously allocates spectrum to primary and secondary users in a single allocation and second, two-step allocation in which the spectrum regulator first allocates spectrum to primary users, then allocates vacant portions on their channels to secondary users. For improvement in spectrum utilization of unused spectrum in cognitive radio, many researchers proposed spectrum allocation methods based on genetic algorithm (GA), quantum genetic algorithm (QGA), and particle swarm optimization (PSO), which decreases the search space [60]. Spectrum allocation is based on both spectrum mobility and sharing. *Spectrum mobility* is a process by which a cognitive-radio user changes its frequency of operation to use the spectrum in a dynamic manner by allowing radio terminals to operate in the best available frequency band, maintaining seamless communication requirements during transitions to better spectrum. On the other hand *spectrum sharing* allows cognitive radio users to share the spectrum bands of the licensed-band users [61, 62]. CRNs have a high bandwidth for mobile users due to heterogeneous wireless architecture and dynamic spectrum techniques, imposing some challenges in spectrum allocation like spectrum sensing, spectrum decision, spectrum sharing and spectrum mobility [61]. The main focus of spectrum allocation in cognitive radio network is to provide unutilized spectrum leftover by registered licensed or primary user to the secondary or unregistered user without interference from and to the licensed user. Hidden Markov models (HMM) and Markov based channel prediction algorithm (MCPA) are also used for dynamic spectrum allocation and prediction [62]. Another author presented fragmented spectrum synchronous PFDM-CDMA modulation and allocation techniques which provide more efficient use of available spectrum holes for secondary users. This allocation method for cognitive radio network is excellent even if the primary user occupied bandwidth is more than 50% of the total [63]. In the fragmented spectrum allocation, spectrum allocation is assigned at the cognitive base station (CBS) causing channel switching cost and channel capacity for allocating and scheduling frequency for every frame. For fair allocation and scheduling, an energy efficient heuristic scheduler (EEHS) was proposed by Kokkali V. with less energy consumption [64].

Optimized allocation scheme of cognitive radio network also required to offer fairness across frequency distribution between devices and users [65]. Many algorithms have been developed, based on game theory, pricing and auction mechanisms, and local bargaining [67, 68] for spectrum allocation in CRN. The article in [69] proposed an optimizing channel and power scheduler for a multi-channel model established on the probabilities of channel availability, where an NP-hard graph coloring problem (GCP) and a color sensitive graph coloring (CSGC) mechanism were established for spectrum allocations. Similarly graph coloring theory based algorithm for spectrum utilization was presented in [70]. Graph coloring and bidding theory techniques are utilized in a novel conveyed intrigue component in [71] for channel allocation in the spectrum pool.

Dynamic spectrum allocation required distance statistics of transmission and reception in CRN system. New adaptive modulation and coding were employed for better control of information from statistic distance, mitigating the interference or fading and fast adaptation process [72]. In a CRN system, spectrum allocation is a process of maximizing the network utilization without any interference and power disturbance of network; solving such problem [73] addresses many different algorithms based on differential evolution (DE) algorithm for reducing time complexity with practicable swarm optimization (PSO) and firefly algorithm. All those proposed interface with a Xilinx Virtex-5 FPGA and are simulated for performance check. The processes of spectrum allocation become more complex when cognitive radio network users increase i.e. multiple CR users are available. Such type of situation needed continuous sensing and monitoring of unutilized spectrum by the licensed user and allocation of a suitable band for the secondary user. In [74] periodic sensing and transmission method is used to increase collaboration between users and utilize maximum spectrum, improving the overall performance of CRNs and hence enhancing dynamic spectrum access capabilities. Effective consumption of frequency spectrum is possible using dynamic spectrum allocation. To fulfill the quality of service (QoS) need of the users, many optimization methods such as genetic algorithm (GA), ant colony optimization (ACO) and mutated ant colony optimization (MACO) were well defined for cognitive radio [75]. All cognitive radio parameters like transmission, allocation and sensing were compared, and every optimization method has some pros and cons.

The proposed chapter briefs about dynamic spectrum allocation (DSA) techniques such as artificial neural network, game theory, the genetic algorithm (GA), graph coloring problem (GCP), ant colony system (ACS) used for cognitive radio networks. The general DSA techniques offered include independent reflection of radio spectrum by a responsive radio receiver (typically a "secondary" component), that are used for continuous adaptation of the free frequency band to minimize interference. The DSA strategy notice above was prescribed for rapid information systems encased by the IEEE 802.22 standard which utilizes TV void area as allowed by the FCC [76]. However, considerable improvement is needed on an Internet-scale dispersion of spectrum services and/or spectrum coordination protocols that empower improved coordination, an Internet-scale dispersion of range administrations and, additionally, range coordination conventions that empower improved coordination.

Artificial Neural Network: Dynamic spectrum allocation in CRN required different learning models for spectrum sensing, spectrum selection and performance analysis such as machine learning, adaptive filtering, Markova model, artificial neural network (ANN) and deep neural network (DNN) etc. Neural network is mostly used in pattern recognition and probabilistic problem, so that ANN and DNN are mostly used for transmission rate, signal prediction and decision making in CRN [18]. Self-learning ability of neural network easily detects the surrounding spectrum. Different learning methods of CRN are summarized in Table 5.1 [77]. Artificial neural network (ANN), an intelligent learning technique, is used and works by improving wireless communication for cognitive radio mobile terminal, reducing the optimization complexity and improving the decision quality [78]. The criteria for the spectrum allocation and sensing can be an analyzed using ANN, because some of the properties and characteristics of CRN and ANN, especially in intelligence toward the sensing or tracking, are similar [79]. ANNs have the ability to self-learn which is useful in spectrum sensing and allocation of CRN. ANNs are applied for transmission rate, signal prediction, and decision making in CRN. Two types of ANN are applied for spectrum allocation: The first one is feed forward neural network (FFNN) [80, 81] which is powerful mapping techniques for excellent approximation and faster learning. The second is the back propagation (BP) algorithm for effective learning. For multichannel cognitive radios networks, deep neural network (DNN) and artificial neural network (ANN) are utilized for resource allocation due to fast sensing and less interference between secondary user and primary user [82–84].

The ANN structure is a set of nonlinear functions with an adaptive parameter which produces different output in different situations using neurons exactly simulated as human brain learning. The core element of ANN is neurons which process information in the cognitive sense [81]. Various ANN working models are available for different applications and their network configurations; we focus only on the cognitive radio network based applications and utilization for spectrum allocation, like radial based function networks (RBFNs), multi-layer perceptron networks (MPNS) and multilayer nonlinear perceptron networks (MNPNs) etc. [78]. The basic model of ANN is depicted in Figure 5.8, which consists of three layers: an input layer, one or more hidden layers and an output layer. There is no transfer function required between input and output layers in such model; there are only biological sensors known as neuron sensing surrounding environment that are fed to higher layers until they reach the final output. Such type of neural network model is known as feedforward network [79]. Neural network learning is achieved by iteration of weight functions until

Table 5.1 Learning techniques of cognitive radio networks.

Learning techniques	Models used for	Advantages	Limitations
Markov model	Dynamic spectrum access	Boost throughput	Gives some unfortunate arrangements
Q-learning	Modeling cognitive cycle	Better performance rate	Acceptable for local parameter
Game theory	Channel selection	Better utilization area	Execution to be oppressed upon specific parameter determination
Fuzzy logic	Prediction of transmission rate	Minimize complexity	Need some worldwide data moreover
Genetic algorithms	Optimization	Excellent for parameter optimization	Execution to be oppressed upon specific parameter choice
Neural network	Dynamic channel selection, cognitive engine	Learn in absence of previous information	Execution to be oppressed upon specific parameter choice.

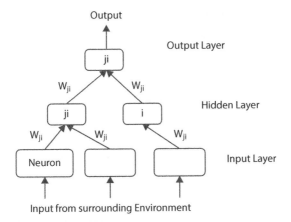

Figure 5.8 A basic neural network model [79].

the network achieves a certain task. ANNs follow certain rules for updating of connection weights, for the learning and allocation of network optimality [79–84].

Artificial neural network has been a model on artificial neuron, which consists of the following components: a group of input signals, a group of output signals and an activation value assigned to each neuron that means the potential membrane in the biological neuron [81, 82]. Each neuron adapts its states from its neighbors to achieve the output for which it has been designed. The processing element produces a single output on the basis of information it has received. For the target of frequency allocation in CRN network topology can be modeled as graph G = [N(t), C(t), L(t)], where N(t), C(t) and L(t) refer to a set of vertices, edge and availability of frequency respectively [81–84]. Each vertex is connected with neuron characteristics by weight (W_{jk}) and input signal (X_{jk}), and mathematically an artificial neuron j can be modeled as given in equation (5.1) [81]:

$$o_j\left(w_j,\ b_j,\ x_j\right)=f\left(b_j+\sum_{i=K}^{N}x_{jk}.w_{jk}\right) \qquad (5.29)$$

where $x_j = [x_{j1}, x_{j2}, x_{j3}\ldots\ldots x_{jN}]$ is the input vector of neuron j, x_{jk} is the vector of input signal from neuron j to neuron i, w_{jk} is the weight vector of neuron j to neuron i, and $w_j = [w_{j1}, w_{j2}, w_{j3}\ldots\ldots\ldots\ldots w_{jN}]$ is the vector of weight fuction of neuron j. The out signal o_j is dependent upon the nonlinear activation function of neuron $f(.)$ which is defined in equation (29), and b_j is

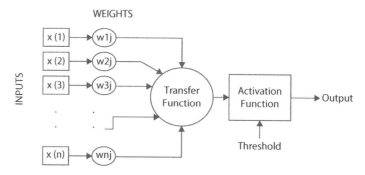

Figure 5.9 Scheme of ANN.

the bias of neurons. The bias function changes the value of activation function of neuron which can reflect the success of the learning process [81–84]. Figure 5.9 shows the basic schemes of ANN on which it can model the spectrum allocation.

In the above figure every neuron is initialized with an accepted frequency and the network work in serial mode which updated neuron after every iteration, which is use for changing the activation parameter to fulfill target output. ANN used tentative values during the search of channel frequency through the insertion and selection technology directed by learning algorithms. The middle layer connecting weight function adaptation in the ANN is defined as the neuron state adaptation in its neighbors. This is controlled by neuron state change and defines fitness function evaluation for expected values. In essence, an ANN is a structure of several neurons associated in different ways and operating using different activation functions [81–84].

Game Theory: The game theory is also applicable to spectrum allocation in cognitive radio network; similarly, players (network node) interact with each other and formulate the competition among primaries and secondary users. Cognitive radio network system is a depiction of one primary system with several cognitive users which is shared with game theory to compensate the detection cost through detection probability and allocation on the basis of availability. Game theory gazes at the connections between contributors in a specific model and predicts their optimal decisions [30, 85].

Dynamic spectrum allocation is also based on detection probability of CRN which is mutually connected with game theory to adjust the detection cost using Nash equilibrium (NE). The author discussed about a cognitive user effectiveness function associated with game theory that includes a wireless network with one primary user system and several cognitive users, which reflects non-interference spectrum allocation in CRN [85]. The basic parameter of spectrum allocation algorithm is based on the following steps to satisfy various conditions and optimize certain system performance [86].

(a) The number of spectrum users (primary users) was initialized.
(b) The number of secondary users was initialized.
(c) The punishment counter is created.
(d) Structure of users either primary and secondary is required a unique identification so that ID is created. User utilization frequency, counter for punishment period, sensed channels and demand channels are also created.
(e) Allocation is done after comparison of demand and supply matrix.
(f) Secondary user always on high demand is punished.
(g) Normalization of all the parameters is done in case the primary user comes back or after a certain number of timeslots which is unknown to secondary users [86].

CRN's main goal is to improve spectrum utilization using different spectrum allocation methods and algorithms. Spectrum sensing and allocation have an essential job of finding the accessible frequency band and then making the decision to assign a secondary user based on various parameters like fairness, quality of service requirement, throughput, spectrum efficiency etc. There are different procedures of spectrum allocation, like centralized, distributed, clustered and inclusion of primary user [87]. Another system model and the problem of spectrum allocation in CRN is figured as spectrum allotment in time domain for one frame, it can be solved and allocated only just by making association with game theory. In this optimal allotment scheme of cognitive radio access another algorithm for spectrum allocation in time domain was proposed, which is also combined with non-cooperative game theoretic load balancing problem [88], known as spectrum load balancing (SLB) algorithm.

The special characteristic of dynamic spectrum allocation of CRN is to offer a viable scheme for the sharing of spectrum resources between the primary user and secondary users, which solves the current spectrum resource inadequacy problem. The spectrum allocation models for CRN are based on the game theory from cooperative game and non-cooperative game, providing a detailed overview and analysis on the state of the art of spectrum allocation. The game theory based allocation gives a wide range of flexible and efficient spectrum allocation in wireless networks. Different game models have some pros and cons; Table 5.2 summarizes the different

Table 5.2 Summary of game theory models for spectrum allocation.

Game theory model	Advantages	Disadvantages
Matching game model	Efficiency, fairness, pareto optimum	Augmentation of joined advantage, however not the specific interests; restricted extent of utilizations
Cournot game model	Modest model of two oligarchs, explains the problem associated with spectrum allocation through two authorized users and multiple cognitive users	Numerous limitations, static game model, poor adaptability, restricted application scope
Bertrand game model	Takes care of the range assignment issue with two approved clients and different subjective clients; suitable for the game among the approved clients	Static game model. poor adaptability; constrained application scope; non ideal harmony
Stackelberg game model	Improves the tenemental proportion of range, reduces the tenemental expenses of range, high use	Too much constrained condition
Repeated game	Maximizes the gross income; minimizes total interference level	High complexity
Super modular game model	Boosts throughput, reduces the obstruction of cognitive users to primary users	Rigorous application
Potential game model	Expands throughput, diminishes the obstruction issue of cognitive users to primary users, reasonable for collaboration clients	Convergence is easier for the simple model.
Evolutionary game model	Accurately predicts the dynamic behavior	High complexity
Auction game model	Impacts the game with various band use rate	Limited application scope

game models for spectrum allocation with their advantages and disadvantages [89].

The Genetic Algorithm (GA): A genetic algorithm (GA) is an optimization experiential process or algorithm for examining very large spaces that parodist the process of natural selection. The GA sets three main types of rules to create the next generation from the current situations which are selection rules, crossover rules, and mutation rules. Genetic algorithm first optimizes the transmitting power for controlling interference between primary and secondary users after that combing ant clone algorithm it also optimized spectrum allocation in CRN. GA is well matched for multi-objective performance and non-mathematical optimization problems in cognitive radio networks as it can search for multiple sets of solutions over a large search space and can enforce constraints. GA also offers efficient way to access the availability of spectrum for primary user and secondary user [90–93]. A method was proposed by Kamal [90] using a binary genetic algorithm (BGA) based soft fusion (SF) scheme for better bandwidth utilization and maximized detection. For changing environment where spectrum change using primary and secondary users, BGA perform better resource allocation algorithms to adapt CRN parameters [90]. Other spectrum allocation parameter like fairness, quality of service requirement, throughput, spectrum efficiency is also optimized and improved using adaptive and demand based genetic algorithms. The CRN system as time varying nature of spectrum hole is measured and having capability of adaption with the varying nature of spectrum holes [90]. Genetic algorithm (GA) is a type of algorithm that replicates biological progression mechanism to search universal optimal solution to target problem. Other dynamic genetic algorithm based on the new sophisticated crossover and mutation operators are used for spectrum allocation in a dynamic environment [91]. To overcome probability of crossover and mutation in genetic algorithm it required adaptively adjustable crossover and mutation to keep it always in appropriate state. A new improved genetic algorithm with more equal individual competition opportunity by hierarchical measures for improvement in all parameter of spectrum allocation [91]. In context of spectrum allocation for CRN a centralized approach is used for adaptation and channel assignment decisions. This brought together methodology considers the elements of channel accessibility of SUs and relegates the directs in a consecutive way [92].

There are different conditions for allocating the spectrum to the secondary users in CRN. The main condition of decide the spectrum allocation algorithm is interference power and temperature. Interference temperature plays a vital role in limiting the ratio of power at the receiver end to RF bandwidth and Boltzmann constant which can limit by power control [93]. Second condition is to maximize the number of secondary user channels known as maximize spectrum utilization. The throughput should be maximized and another condition for selection of algorithm of spectrum assignment leads to fairness. Because maximization of throughput does not guarantee the fairness in the network i.e. maximization of each and every secondary user's throughput. Lastly delay is one of the qualities of service condition and is switching delay and end to end delay experience by the network [94].

5.9   Challenges in Spectrum Allocation

As described in previous sections, the CR nodes need to follow a cognitive cycle which is a series of spectrum aware operations such as spectrum sensing and decision, spectrum allocation and sharing, spectrum mobility etc. For interoperability with primary network, it is required to incorporate each of these functions into the protocols operating at various levels of the classical layered network architecture. Most of these operations are performed at physical and link layer with spectrum decision and mobility spread across all the layers. The benefits targeted through deployment these network operations at various layers are [95–102]:

a) Increased information carrying capacity and data rate of CRN.
b) Enhanced security of the CR nodes by addressing threats and vulnerability related issues across the entire layered architecture.
c) Spectrum sensing algorithms providing continuous and accurate information regarding available bands, presence of PU signal in a band or demand for spectrum resource by a PU.
d) Efficient resource allocation schemes competent enough to operate in heterogeneous spectrum i.e. bands licensed to PU and unlicensed bands.
e) The transceiver device design with cognitive ability at physical layer while maintaining desired QoS levels.
f) Protocols for medium access control (MAC) for efficient resource sharing between CR nodes.

5.9.1 Spectrum and Network Heterogeneity

The spectrum used by CR nodes may spread over widely separated bands which differ in channel characteristics such as coverage area, error rate, path loss, end-to-end delay. This variation accounts for the spectrum heterogeneity and affects the performance of spectrum sharing schemes. Such heterogeneity was introduced in [97] static SUs and fixed channel allocation. Similar approach for both static and mobile users was suggested in [98]. SUs under CRN are being developed with ability to connect using both licensed spectrum bands owned by PUs and unlicensed bands available through various wideband access technologies. Multiple network access modes by different users of a CRN lead to network heterogeneity [99]. Three different access modes are commonly used by CR nodes:

(a) Access to primary network: CR users can access the primary cellular network under licensed bands through their access points of base stations. To enable network heterogeneity, MAC protocols are required which can support mobility with horizontal or vertical handover for point of access.

(b) Access to CRN: CR users can connect to the CRN using its own CR base station or access points operating on both licensed and unlicensed bands. The spectrum sharing policy in case of communication within the CR need not depend upon primary access techniques.

(c) Ad hoc access to CRN: Peer-to-peer or multi-hop communication between various CR nodes can be done in ad hoc mode using licensed or unlicensed spectrum.

This heterogeneity in terms of spectrum and network access raises several challenges and issues in spectrum management for CRN including spectrum sensing, sharing, decision and optimum utilization. Some of these are:

- Common control channel: What radio control parameters must be uncovered and what are the base common interfaces expected to permit interoperability in a heterogeneous situation.
- Control necessities as far as inertness and data move between collaborating hubs.

- Dynamic radio range: Particular of range server information base and convention interfaces and assessment of execution in dense radio situations.
- Spectrum unit: This is commonly a two-advance procedure: radios need to figure out what recurrence groups are accessible, given the proper FCC rules, and the radios at that point need to choose what band is the most appropriate.
- Location information: Specifically, the wireless devices will need to agree on how to realize various physical, link, and network layer functions in a way that makes best use of the available spectrum, while also satisfying the policy constraints that apply in the selected band.

Issues related to various network operations and actions of CR cycle are discussed further in this section.

5.9.2 Issues and Challenges

The coexistence of primary and CR networks and diverse nature of spectrum utilization by PUs increases the challenges faced by spectrum sensing techniques used in SUs. The CR nodes must adapt to variations in presence of spectrum holes across a wide band of frequencies and remain aware about the spectrum usage by PUs. The spectrum sensing in CR nodes is, generally implemented by exploiting one or more of the three characteristics of spectrum - time, frequency and space. Several aspects of CRN such as intelligence in CR nodes for sensing and decision, overheads in MAC protocols, cross layer implementation of spectrum decision and mobility schemes and flexibility required in CR receiver design contribute to their challenges in design and implementation. Some of these design challenges faced while developing spectrum management algorithms for CRNs are as follows:

- Avoid interference with primary network and its active users.
- Communication with desired QoS levels through dynamic channel with random characteristics and spectrum and network heterogeneity.
- Seamless spectrum and network handoff irrespective of availability or shift of spectrum holes and presence of primary users.
- Efficient MAC protocol for optimization of transmit power and frequency band allocation adaptable to dynamic network conditions.

- Interference due to coexisting primary and secondary CR users is a challenge to opportunistic communication required for sharing of spectrum.
- Hidden nodes continue to exist and remain undetected by CR nodes due to their low signal strength within the coverage area of SU. This results in additional noise at the SU front end receiver.
- Prediction of spectrum usage by PUs is required for efficient allocation of radio resources to SUs which requires minimum shift from one band to another during an ongoing communication, thus making the link more reliable.
- The complexity involved in implementing spectrum sensing, deciding and allocating schemes for CR needs to be justified in terms of its outcome and benefits achieved. The adoption of CR schemes within the existing regulatory constraints including application domains which restrict the dynamic spectrum allocation is a challenge to be resolved through strategies which are a composite of CR and primary radio schemes [95–100].

The existence of CRNs depends on the ability of CR nodes to decide sense and decide the available spectrum spaces. The placement of such channel sensing, selection/decision and other related performance optimization algorithms is a challenge for researchers. Centralized and distributed are two modes of operation for CR systems. Several sensing and allocation/decision algorithms have been discussed in this chapter. However, their customized or modified forms are being developed to resolve the issues related to performance improvement and implementation in unexplored application areas. The extensive growth of machine learning has helped the CR nodes in various aspects of cognitive cycle. The choice of supervised or unsupervised learning is the first challenge faced while making a suitable decision for adopting machine learning algorithms. The design and implementation of such algorithms may further increase the complexity of CR systems. Another challenge is associated with implementing geo-location technology which is by CR systems to find and track the location of mobile PUs and SUs, thus contributing to estimation of resource requirement and availability of spectrum holes or chances of a PU entering the coverage area of an SU. The challenges are related to implementation and use of database along with acquiring accurate location of CR nodes. It becomes more challenging in case of the nodes which are not equipped with GPS.

Security of devices and users (identity and data) are the foremost requirements for any network based system. This also includes compliance of regulations. The related challenges include device access authorization, attempts of violation and potential threats, security certifications of software resources and presence of malicious software in the device. Front-end of CR nodes is another major source of challenges faced by CR designers. This includes frequency agile transceivers with wide-band operation, low noise amplifier (LNA) with high linearity in wide band and impedance matching for a variety of device outputs. The ADC and DAC are integral parts of CR systems since processing within the CR devices is conducted in digital domain whereas the RF signal at the front-end is analog. The need to operate these ADC and DAC over a wide spectrum and at several power levels is a challenge for researchers. Other related challenges are calibration of channel mismatch for difference spectrum bands occupied by CR nodes at different times and skew error correction in sensing and front-end tuning [101]. Techniques such as post-linearization in digital domain and interleaving time and frequency multiplexing using set-pass sampling filter are being used to reduce complexity, increase sensitivity with less imperfections. The design issues at baseband level architecture include flexible operation with optimized tradeoff between power consumption and performance. This demands for reconfigurable resources, efficient power management schemes and dynamic task management.

The issues and challenges highlighted are crucial for effective deployment of CRNs for real-time communication systems. The challenges are multiple depend upon the usage scenarios and bounds of physical systems. Further research is required to develop algorithms, protocols and schemes which can resolve the issues and challenges faced by the current implementation of CRN and future technologies.

5.10   Future Scope in Spectrum Allocation

The problem of assisted multicast scheduling in CRN can be further examined using the multicast data. In future network coding will also help as another assistance technique that further reduced the total multicast time in CRN allocation for multilevel network. Research may be done on more impactful solutions for ad hoc cognitive radio networks. The ad hoc case is of course more challenging due to the lack of a central entity, where decision to improve performance can be made.

References

1. Zhang, Y., Dynamic Spectrum Access in Cognitive Radio Wireless Networks. *2008 IEEE International Conference on Communications*, Beijing, pp. 4927–4932, 2008.
2. Song, M., Chunsheng, X., Yanxiao, Z., Xiuzhen, C., Dynamic spectrum access: From cognitive radio to network radio. *IEEE Wirel. Commun.*, 19, 23–29, 2012.
3. Akyildiz, I.F., Lee, W.Y., Vuran, M.C., Mohantly, S., Next generation/dynamic spectrum access/cognitive radio wireless network: A survey. *Elsevier Comput. Netw.*, 50, 2127–2159, 2006.
4. Raychaudhuri, D. *et al.*, Cognet: An Architectural Foundation For Experimental Cognitive Radio Networks Within the Future Internet. *Proc. Mobi. Arch.*, 11–16, 2006.
5. Cormio, C. and Chowdhury, K.R., A survey on MAC protocols for cognitive radio networks. *Ad Hoc Netw.*, 7, 7, 1315–1329, 2009.
6. Mitola, J. and Maguire, G.Q., Cognitive radio: Making software radios more personal. *IEEE Pers. Commun.*, 6, 4, 13–18, 1999.
7. Goldsmith, *et al.*, Breaking Spectrum Gridlock with Cognitive Radios: An Information Theoretic Perspective. *Proc. IEEE*, 97, 5, 894–914, 2009.
8. Kaabouch, N. and Hu, W.-C., Handbook of Research on Software-Defined and Cognitive Radio Technologies for Dynamic Spectrum Management. *IGI Glob. J.*, 2014.
9. Salahdine, F., Kaabouch, N., El Ghazi, H., A Real Time Spectrum Scanning Technique based on Compressive Sensing for Cognitive Radio Networks. *The 8th IEEE Annual Ubiquitous Computing, Electronics & Mobile Commun. Conf.*, pp. 1–6, 2017.
10. Yucek, T. and Arslam, H., A Survey of Spectrum Sensing Algorithms for Cognitive Radio Applications. *IEEE Commun. Surv. Tutorials* 11, 1, 116–130, 2009.
11. Ben Letaief, K. and Zhang, W., Cooperative Spectrum Sensing. *Cogn. Wirel. Commun. Netw.*, 115–138, 2007.
12. Cabric, D., Mishra, S.M., Brodersen, R.W., Implementation issues in spectrum sening for cognitive radios. *Proceedings of the Thirty-Eighth Asilomar Conference on Signals*, vol. 1, pp. 772–776, 2004.
13. Manesh, M.R., Apu, S., Kaabouch, N., Hu, W., Performance Evaluation of Spectrum Sensing Techniques for Cognitive Radio Systems. *Ubiquit. Comput. Electron. Mobile Commun. Conf. IEEE Annu.*, 19, 1–6, 2016.
14. Rawat, P., Singh, K.D., Bonnin, J.M., Cognitive radio forM2Mand Internet of Things: A survey. *Comput. Commun.*, 94, 1–29, 2016.
15. Plata, D.M.M. and Reátiga, Á.G.A., Evaluation of energy detection for spectrum sensing based on the dynamic selection of detection-threshold. *J. Procedia Eng.*, 35, 135–143, 2012.

16. Joshi, D.R., Popescu, D.C., Dobre, O.A., Adaptive spectrum sensing with noise variance estimation for dynamic cognitive radio systems. *Proceedings of the Conference on Information Sciences and Systems*, Princeton, NJ, USA, 17–19 March, pp. 1–5, 2010.

17. Muralidharan, A., Venkateswaran, P., Ajay, S.G., Prakash, D.A., Arora, M., Kirthiga, S., An adaptive threshold method for energy-based spectrum sensing in Cognitive Radio Networks. *Proceedings of the International Conference on Control, Instrumentation, Communication, and Computational Technologies*, Kumaracoil, India, 18–19 December, pp. 8–11, 2015.

18. Sarker, M., Energy detector based spectrum sensing by adaptive threshold for low SNR in CR networks. *Proceedings of the Wireless and Optical Communication Conference*, Taipei, Taiwan, 23–24 October, pp. 118–122, 2015.

19. Khan, A.A., Rehmani, M.H., Reisslein, M., Cognitive radio for smart grids: Survey of architectures, spectrum sensing mechanisms, and networking protocols. *IEEE Commun. Surv. Tutorials*, 18, 1, 860–898, 2016.

20. Vartiainen, J., Sarvanko, H., Lehtomaki, J., Juntti, M., Latva-Aho, M., Spectrum Sensing with LAD-Based Methods. *IEEE 18th Int. Sym.*, 1–5, 2007.

21. Manesh, M.R., Kaabouch, N., Reyes, H., A Bayesian Approach to Estimate and Model SINR in Wireless Networks. *Int. J. Commun. Syst. Wiley*, 1–11, 2016.

22. Gong, S., Wang, P., Liu, W., Spectrum sensing under distribution uncertainty in cognitive radio networks. *IEEE Int. Conf. Commun.*, 1512–1516, 2012.

23. Lim, C.H., Adaptive energy detection for spectrum sensing in unknown white Gaussian noise. *IET Commun.*, 6, 1884–1889, 2012.

24. Xiang, L., Bin, W., Hong, W., Pin-Han, H., Zhiqiang, B., Lili, P., Adaptive Threshold Control for Energy Detection Based Spectrum Sensing in Cognitive Radios. *IEEE Wirel. Commun. Lett.*, 1, 448–451, 2012.

25. Joshi, D.R., Popescu, D.C., Dobre, O.A., Adaptive spectrum sensing with noise variance estimation for dynamic cognitive radio systems. *Proceedings of the Conference on Information Sciences and Systems*, Princeton, NJ, USA, 17–19 March, 2010.

26. Muralidharan, A., Venkateswaran, P., Ajay, S.G., Prakash, D.A., Arora, M., Kirthiga, S., An adaptive threshold method for energy-based spectrum sensing in Cognitive Radio Networks. *Proceedings of the International Conference on Control, Instrumentation, Communication, and Computational Technologies*, Kumaracoil, India, 18–19 December, pp. 8–11, 2015.

27. Salahdine, F., El Ghazi, H., Kaabouch, N., Fihri, W.F., Matched filter detection with dynamic threshold for cognitive radio networks. *2015 International Conference on Wireless Networks and Mobile Communications (WINCOM)*, IEEE, pp. 1–6, 2015.

28. Zhang, X., Chai, R., Gao, F., Matched filter based spectrum sensing and power level detection for cognitive radio network. *2014 IEEE global conference on signal and information processing (GlobalSIP)*, IEEE, pp. 1267–1270, 2014.

29. Jiang, C., Li, Y., Bai, W., Yang, Y., Hu, J., Statistical matched filter based robust spectrum sensing in noise uncertainty environment. *2012 IEEE 14th International Conference on Communication Technology*, IEEE, pp. 1209–1213, 2012.

30. Lv, Q. and Gao, F., Matched filter based spectrum sensing and power level recognition with multiple antennas. *2015 IEEE China Summit and International Conference on Signal and Information Processing (ChinaSIP)*, IEEE, pp. 305–309, 2015.

31. Manesh, M.R., Subramaniam, S., Reyes, H., Kaabouch, N., Real-time spectrum occupancy monitoring using a probabilistic model. *Comput. Netw.*, 124, 87–96, 2017.

32. Avinash, P., Gandhiraj, R., Soman, K.P., Spectrum sensing using compressed sensing techniques for sparse multiband signals. *Int. J. Sci. Eng. Res.*, 3, 5, 2012.

33. Sharma, S.K., Bogale, T.E., Chatzinotas, S., Le, L.B., Wang, X., Ottersten, B., Improving robustness of cyclostationary detectors to cyclic frequency mismatch using Slepian basis. *2015 IEEE 26th Annual International Symposium on Personal, Indoor, and Mobile Radio Communications (PIMRC)*, IEEE, pp. 456–460, 2015.

34. Cabric, D., Mishra, S.M., Brodersen, R.W., Implementation issues in spectrum sensing for cognitive radios. *Conference Record of the Thirty-Eighth Asilomar Conference on Signals, Systems and Computers*, vol. 1, pp. 772–776, 2004.

35. Chen, H.-S., Gao, Wen, Daut, D.G., Signature based spectrum sensing algorithms for IEEE 802.22 WRAN. *2007 IEEE International Conference on Communications*, IEEE, pp. 6487–6492, 2007.

36. Sahai, A., Hoven, N., Tandra, R., Some fundamental limits on cognitive radio. *Allerton Conference on Communication, Control, and Computing*, pp. 1662–1671, 2004.

37. Zhang, Z., Yang, Q., Wang, L., Zhou, X., A novel hybrid matched filter structure for IEEE 802.22 standard. *2010 IEEE Asia Pacific Conference on Circuits and Systems*, IEEE, pp. 652–655, 2010.

38. Gardner, W.A., Exploitation of spectral redundancy in cyclostationary signals. *IEEE Signal Process. Mag.*, 8, 2, 1991.

39. Gardner, W.A., An introduction to cyclostationary signals, in: *Cyclostationarity in communications and signal processing*, pp. 1–90, IEEE press, New York, 1994.

40. Akyildiz, I.F., Lo, B.F., Balakrishnan, R., Cooperative spectrum sensing in cognitive radio networks: A survey. *Phys. Commun.*, 4, 1, 2011.

41. Atapattu, S., Tellambura, C., Jiang, H., *Energy detection for spectrum sensing in cognitive radio*, Springer, New York, NY, USA, 2014.

42. Lundén, J., Koivunen, V., Huttunen, A., Poor, H.V., Collaborative cyclostationary spectrum sensing for cognitive radio systems. *IEEE Trans. Signal Process.*, 57, 11, 2009.

43. Gardner, W.A., *An Introduction to Cyclostationary Signals, Chapter 1, Cyclostationarity in Communications and Signal Processing*, IEEE Press, Piscataway, NJ, 1993.

44. Cabric, D., Mishra, S.M., Brodersen, R.W., Implementation issues in spectrum sensing for cognitive radios, in: *Conference Record of the Thirty-Eight Asilomar Conference on Signals, Systems and Computers*, vol. 1, pp. 772–776, 2004.

45. Dandawate, A.V. and Giannakos, G.B., Statistical tests for presence of cyclostationarity. *IEEE Trans. Signal Process.*, 42, 9, 2355–2369, 1994.

46. Fan, R. and Jiang, H., Optimal multi-channel cooperative sensing in cognitive radio networks. *IEEE Trans. Wirel. Comm.*, 9, 3, 1128–1138, 2010.

47. Zeng, Y., Liang, Y.-C., Hoang, A.T., Zhang, R., A review on spectrum sensing for cognitive radio: Challenges and solutions. *EURASIP J. Adv. Signal Process.*, 1, 2010.

48. Goldsmith, A., *Wireless communications, Chapter 12*, Cambridge University Press, Stanford University, California, 2005.

49. Mitola, J. and Maguire, G.Q., Cognitive radio: Making software radios more personal. *IEEE Pers. Commun.*, 6, 4, 13–18, 1999.

50. Hu, H., Zhang, H., Yu, H., Delay QoS guaranteed cooperative spectrum sening in cognitive radio networks. *AEU-Int. J. Electron. Commun.*, 67, 9, 804–807, 2013.

51. Mukherjee, A., Choudhury, S., Goswami, P., Bayessa, G.A., Tyagi, S.K.S., A novel approach of power allocation for secondary users in cognitive radio networks. *Comput. Electr. Eng.*, 75, 301–308, 2019.

52. Salahdine, F., El Ghazi, H., Kaabouch, N., Fihri, W.F., Matched filter detection with dynamic threshold for cognitive radio networks. *2015 International Conference on Wireless Networks and Mobile Communications (WINCOM)*, IEEE, pp. 1–6, 2015.

53. Khan, A.A., Rehmani, M.H., Reisslein, M., Cognitive radio for smart grids: Survey of architectures, spectrum sensing mechanisms, and networking protocols. *IEEE Commun. Surv. Tutorials*, 18, 1, 860–898, 2015.

54. Manesh, M.R., Quadri, A., Subramaniam, S., Kaabouch, N., An optimized SNR estimation technique using particle swarm optimization algorithm. *2017 IEEE 7th Annual Computing and Communication Workshop and Conference (CCWC)*, IEEE, pp. 1–6, 2017.

55. Quan, Z., Cui, S., Sayed, A.H., Poor, H.V., Wideband spectrum sensing in cognitive radio networks, *Proceedings of the 2008 IEEE International Conference on Communications*, Beijing, May 19–23, 2008. arXiv preprint arXiv:0802.4130.

56. Subramaniam, S., Reyes, H., Kaabouch, N., Spectrum occupancy measurement: An autocorrelation based scanning technique using USRP. *2015 IEEE 16th Annual Wireless and Microwave Technology Conference (WAMICON)*, IEEE, pp. 1–5, 2015.

57. Naraghi-Pour, M. and Ikuma, T., Autocorrelation-based spectrum sensing for cognitive radios. *IEEE Trans. Veh. Technol.*, 59, 2, 718–733, 2009.
58. Almasaeid, H.M., *Spectrum Allocation Algorithms for Cognitive Radio Mesh Networks*, Graduate Theses and Dissertations, p. 10383, 2011.
59. Kasbekar, G.S., *Economics of Spectrum Allocation in Cognitive Radio Networks*, Publicly Accessible Penn Dissertations, p. 446, 2011.
60. Zhao, Z., Peng, Z., Zheng, S., Shang, J., Cognitive radio spectrum allocation using evolutionary algorithms. *IEEE Trans. Wirel. Comm.*, 8, 9, 4421–4425, 2009.
61. Akyildiz, I.F., Lee, W., Vuran, M.C., Mohanty, S., A survey on spectrum management in cognitive radio networks. *IEEE Commun. Mag.*, 46, 4, 40–48, 2008.
62. Akbar, I.A. and Tranter, W.H., Dynamic spectrum allocation in cognitive radio using hidden Markov models: Poisson distributed case. *Proceedings 2007 IEEE South east Con*, Richmond, pp. 196–201, 2007.
63. Akhoondi, F., Poursaeed, O., Salehi, J.A., Resource allocation using fragmented-spectrum synchronous OFDM-CDMA in cognitive radio networks. *2014 Iran Workshop on Communication and Information Theory (IWCIT)*, Tehran, 2014.
64. Kokila, V. and Bharathi, A.J., Fragmented Spectrum Allocation in Cognitive Radio Networks for Energy Efficiency and Improved Throughput. *J. Eng. Technol.*, 9–15, 2015.
65. Koroupi, F., Talebi, S., Salehinejadb, H., Cognitive radio networks spectrum allocation: An ACS perspective. *Sci. Iran.*, 19, 3, 767–773, 2012.
66. Zhao, Z., Peng, Z., Zheng, S., Shang, J., Cognitive radio spectrum allocation using evolutionary algorithms. *IEEE Trans. Wirel. Comm.*, 8, 4421–4425, 2009.
67. Zhou, X., Li, G., Li, D., Wang, D., Soong, K., Probabilistic resource allocation for opportunistic spectrum access". *IEEE Trans. Wirel. Comm.*, 99, 1–10, 2010.
68. Wang, J., Huang, Y., Jiang, H., Improved algorithm of spectrum allocation based on graph coloring model in cognitive radio. *Int. Conf. Commun. Mobile Comput.*, 353–357, 2009.
69. Liu, Y., Xu, G., Tan, X., A novel spectrum allocation mechanism based on graph coloring and bidding theory. *Int. Conf. Comput. Intell. Nat. Comput.*, 155–158, 2009.
70. Borkotoky, S.S., Kottapalli, S.L., Pursley, M.B., Analytical Methods for Performance Evaluations of Adaptive Modulation and Coding in Cognitive Radio Systems That Employ Distance Statistics. *IEEE Trans. Cogn. Commun. Netw.*, 5, 1, 2019.
71. Anumandla, K.K., Peesapati, R., Sabat, S.L., Field programmable gate array implementation of spectrum allocation technique for cognitive radio networks. *Comput. Electr. Eng.*, 178–192, 2015.

72. Bin Shahid, M.I., Kamruzzaman, J., Hassan, Md. R., Modeling multiuser spectrum allocation for cognitive radio networks. *Comput. Electr. Eng.*, 2015.
73. Sandeep, A Comparative Analysis of Optimization Techniques in Cognitive Radio (QoS). *Int. J. Eng. Adv. Technol.*, 6, 3, 2017.
74. Steenkiste, P., Sicker, D., Minden, G., Raychaudhuri, D., *Future Directions in Cognitive Radio Network Research*, 2009, NSF Workshop Report.
75. Kirar, V.P.S., Artificial Neural Networks for Cognitive Radio Network: A Survey. *Int. J. Electron. Commun. Eng.*, 9, 1, 2015.
76. Salau, H.B. *et al.*, An Examination of Application of Artificial Neural Network in Cognitive Radios. *IOP Conf. Ser.: Mater. Sci. Eng.*, 53, 012036, 2013.
77. Jamal, E., Dynamic Spectrum Allocation in Cognitive Radio Cellular Networks. *WSEAS Trans. Commun.*, 16, 2017.
78. Zhou, F., Zhang, X., Hu, R.Q., Papathanassiou, A., Meng, W., Resource Allocation Based on Deep Neural Networks for Cognitive Radio Networks. *2018 IEEE/CIC International Conference on Communications in China (ICCC)*, Beijing, China, pp. 40–45, 2018.
79. Tuberquia-David, L.M., Cruz, L., Hernández, C., Spectral Prediction: Approaches in Cognitive Radio Networks. *Int. J. Appl. Eng. Res.*, 13, 10, 2018.
80. Tan, X., Huang, H., Ma, L., Frequency allocation with Artificial Neural Networks in cognitive radio system. *IEEE 2013 Tencon - Spring*, Sydney, NSW, pp. 366–370, 2013.
81. Lee, W., Resource Allocation for Multi-Channel Underlay Cognitive Radio Network Based on Deep Neural Network. *IEEE Commun. Lett.*, 22, 9, 1942–1945, 2018.
82. Chen, M., Challita, U., Saad, W., Yin, C., Debbah, M., *Machine Learning for Wireless Networks with Artificial Intelligence: A Tutorial on Neural Networks*, 2017.
83. Anghuwo, A.A., Liu, Y., Tan, X., Liu, S., Spectrum Allocation Based on Game Theory in Cognitive Radio Networks, in: *Information and Automation. ISIA 2010. Communications in Computer and Information Science*, vol. 86, L. Qi (Ed.), Springer, Berlin, Heidelberg, 2011.
84. Pai, V., Prabhu, A., Menon, A., Game Theoretic optimization of spectrum allocation in cognitive radio. *International Conference on Computing Communication Control and automation (ICCUBEA)*, Pune, pp. 1–5, 2016.
85. Musku, M.R. and Cote, P., Time Domain Spectrum Allocation using Game Theory for Cognitive Radios. *Proceedings of the 9th International Conference on Mobile and Wireless Communications Networks*, Cork, Ireland, September 19-21, 2007.
86. Ni, Q., Zhu, R., Wu, Z., Sun, Y., Zhou, L., Zhou, B., Spectrum Allocation Based on Game Theory in Cognitive Radio Networks. *J. Netw.*, 8, 3, 2013.
87. Hossain, K., El-Saleh, Md. A., Ayman, Cognitive Radio Engine Model Utilizing Soft Fusion Based Genetic Algorithm For Cooperative Spectrum Optimization. *Int. J. Comput. Netw. Commun.*, 2013.

88. Chatterjee, S., Dutta, S., Bhattacharya, P., Roy, J., Optimization of Spectrum Sensing Parameters in Cognitive Radio Using Adaptive Genetic Algorithm. *J. Telecommun. Inf. Technol.*, 1, 21–27, 2017.

89. Elhachmi, J. and Guennoun, Z., Cognitive radio spectrum allocation using genetic algorithm. *Elhachmi and Guennoun EURASIP J. Wirel. Commun. Netw.*, 2016.

90. Hou, B., Zu, Y., Li, W., Liu, G., Ding, J., Cognitive Radio Spectrum Allocation Strategy Based on Improved Genetic Algorithm. *Commun. Netw.*, 2013.

91. Devi, M., Sarma, N., Deka, S.K., Spectrum Allocation in Cognitive Radio Networks—A Centralized Approach, in: *Advanced Computational and Communication Paradigms. Lecture Notes in Electrical Engineering*, vol. 475, Springer, Singapore, 2018.

92. Singh, W.J. and Marchang, N., A Review on Spectrum Allocation in Cognitive Radio Network. *Int. J. Commun. Netw. Distr. Syst.*, 2018.

93. Thomas, A.T., Vergados, D.D., Siakavara, K., Nikolaidis, S., Goudos, S.K., Sarigiannidis, P., Obaidat, M., Spectrum allocation in cognitive radio networks using chaotic biogeography-based optimization. *IET Netw.*, 2018.

94. Rahama, Y.A., Hassan, M.S., Ismail, M.H., A Stochastic-Based Rate Control Approach for Video Streaming Over Cognitive Radio Networks. *IEEE Trans. Cogn. Commun. Netw.*, 5, 1, 2019.

95. Wang, D. and Song, Y., ECCO: A Novel End-to-End Congestion Control Scheme in Multi-Hop Cognitive Radio Ad Hoc Networks. *IEEE Trans. Cogn. Commun. Netw.*, 5, 1, 2019.

96. Ning, G., Cao, X., Duan, J., Chowdhury, K.R., A Spectrum Sharing Algorithm Based on Spectrum Heterogeneity for Centralized Cognitive Radio Networks. *2011 IEEE 73rd Vehicular Technology Conference (VTC Spring)*, Yokohama, pp. 1–5, 2011.

97. Miao, M. and Tsang, D.H.K., Impact of Channel Heterogeneity on Spectrum Sharing in Cognitive Radio Networks. *Proc. IEEE ICC*, 2377–2382, 2008.

98. Qiu, R.C., Hu, Z., Li, H., Wicks, M.C., *Cognitive Radio Communications and Networks Principles and Practice*, John Wiley & Sons Ltd, Wiley Online Library, 2012.

99. Akyildiz, F., Lee, W., Chowdhury, K.R., Spectrum management in cognitive radio ad hoc networks. *IEEE Netw.*, 23, 4, 6–12, 2009.

100. Kamil, A.S. and Khider, I., Open Research issues in Cognitive Radio. *16th Telecommunications Forum TELFOR*, Serbia, Belgrade, 25-27 Nov, 2008.

101. Gruget, M.R., Nguyen, V.T., Lelandais-Perrault, C., Bénabès, P., Loumeau, P., Wide-band multipath A to D converter for cognitive radio applications. *Proceedings of the IEEE International Microwave Workshop Series on RF Front-Ends for Software Defined and Cognitive Radio Solutions (IMWS '10)*, Aveiro, Portugal, pp. 73–76, 2010.

102 Garg, P.K., Dua, T.R., Chandra, A., Spectrum Challenges for Modern Mobile Services, *J. ICT Standardization*, 1, 137–158, 2013.

6

Significance of Wireless Technology in Internet of Things (IoT)

Ashish Tripathi[1]*, Arun Kumar Singh[1], Pushpa Choudhary[1], Prem Chand Vashist[1] and K. K. Mishra[2]

[1]Department of Information Technology, G. L. Bajaj Institute of Technology and Management, Greater Noida, India
[2]Department of Computer Science & Engineering, Motilal Nehru National Institute of Technology Allahabad, India

Abstract

In recent years, it is found that wireless technology has played a significant role in the evolution of the Internet of Things (IoT) to make the society smarter in all aspects of people's lives. IoT is applicable in domains such as education, transportation, retail, smart farming, healthcare, smart wearable devices, smart homes, transportation, retail, and security. According to Cisco, in India by 2020, more than 50 billion devices will be connected to the Internet, including smartphones, computers, and any electronic devices/things. Although the IoT is expanding rapidly and industries are investing money and effort to create new IoT applications, still it faces some issues such as the selection of appropriate wireless protocols, interoperability among wireless standards, security issues, inference among wireless devices, and trade-off among power consumption, rate of data transfer, and coverage range. So choosing the right wireless technology addresses the issues outlined above, for developing IoT applications can be very challenging. This chapter presents an overview of the key issues related to the selection of different wireless technologies in the development of IoT services. A number of research challenges have been identified as a major research trends in the IoT environment. Details of the hardware components are discussed. Also, the chapter discusses the significance of wireless technology in IoT followed by a complete overview of the various wireless-enabled IoT networks, connections, and protocols. Finally, concluding remarks are given.

Keywords: Internet of Things (IoT), wireless technology, RFID, Arduino, Raspberry Pi, sensors, actuators, IoT networks

Corresponding author: ashish.mnnit44@gmail.com

Krishna Kant Singh, Akansha Singh, Korhan Cengiz and Dac-Nhuong Le (eds.) Machine Learning and Cognitive Computing for Mobile Communications and Wireless Networks, (131–154) © 2020 Scrivener Publishing LLC

6.1   Introduction

The Internet of Things (IoT) is a well-known and fast-growing paradigm which comprises different physical entities having the ability to gather and share information through wireless technologies [5]. IoT devices use sensors, actuators, radio-frequency identification (RFID) [15], and Global Positioning System (GPS) [49] to collect and compute data and interact with one another using different communication protocols. These devices follow the request and response authentication strategy for data transfer and could be operated and managed from remote locations by using the Internet [17].

In recent years, IoT has emerged as a major domain to work in for academic institutions, research communities, and industries. In IoT, lots of research works have been done in the last few years to provide a sustainable growth in the people's quality of life as well as reducing the operational cost of the services provided by public authorities and industries. Several IoT applications have been identified in different domains, such as healthcare, agriculture, transportation, education, and security, and new applications are still appearing every day that have required research and innovations to overcome these challenges [12].

IoT and wireless technologies together have many existing and novel opportunities to work with. However, some major challenges have been identified in the selection of appropriate wireless technology for IoT devices. In this context, several wireless standards are available in the market which employs various communication protocols and frequency bands. So the selection of the best among all available standards is quite challenging [4].

The first challenge of wireless technology is the frequency bands, which are categorized into spectrums and differ from country to country. The generation of spectrum defines the throughput/data transfer of the channels, e.g., 2G, 3G, 4G, and 5G [22]. Higher generation of spectrum can offer a broader bandwidth and handle huge data throughput. In contrast to this, lower-frequency bands (e.g., radio waves) can propagate more smoothly than higher-frequency bands in small premises such as schools and hotels.

The second challenge is the wireless communication protocol due to the availability of different protocols for specific operations. Wireless communication is based on the network range, which is categorized into four types, namely, wireless personal area network (WPAN: 10 m), wireless local area network (WLAN: 100 m), neighborhood area network (NAN: 1600 m), and wireless wide area network (WWAN: several miles) [39].

Geometrical representation of these networks is based on the rules defined in the topologies [48].

The third challenge is to maintain interoperability among IoT devices due to the availability of different specifications and testing methods provided by several vendors [47].

In the above context, IoT infrastructure needs common wireless communication system standards to provide two-way communication among IoT devices for collecting data and message delivery in a controlled manner. To ensure highest-quality services through the designing of IoT devices, a proper understanding of various wireless communication protocols and standards and different modules is required to provide wireless communications in a variety of usage conditions.

6.1.1   Internet of Things: A Historical Background

The term *Internet of Things* (IoT) was officially coined for the first time by Kevin Ashton, executive director and co-founder of "Auto-ID Center" at the Massachusetts Institute of Technology (MIT), during his presentation in 1999. To make the presentation more effective in front of the senior management of Procter & Gamble on the existing technology called radio-frequency identification (RFID), he named his presentation "Internet of Things," which was inspired by the term *Internet*. In the summer of 2010, the IoT concept was becoming very popular due to its applicability. In the same year, IoT was also included at the highest priority in the five-year strategic plan by the Chinese government. In 2011, a market research company named Gartner recognized IoT as a new emerging technology. In 2012, the "Internet of Things" was used as a conference theme for Europe's biggest conference. In 2013, IoT evolved itself as a system having various technologies to provide support in different applications [45].

From 2000 to 2010, IoT-related concepts and activities found rapid growth due to the successful completion of few projects and availability of some applications in practical. During this period, many projects were completed that were applicable to smart cities, self-driving cars, automatic home/office security systems, etc. [24].

6.1.2   Internet of Things: Overview, Definition, and Understanding

The word *Things* in *Internet of Things* refers to the combination of software, hardware, data, connection protocols, and services [34]. The working of IoT is based on the collection of useful and valid data and sharing of the data among other devices without human intervention. A very practical example of IoT is the home automation system, where the system uses Bluetooth/Wi-Fi to exchange data among various devices available at home [46].

The IoT is a collection of physical entities that use Internet to establish a connection and exchange data through routers/network devices. In IoT, devices are controlled remotely using the existing networking technology, which reduces human effort and provides easy and smooth accessibility to physical devices [1].

The term *Internet of Things* (IoT) includes various devices which use inbuilt wireless technology and are connected with the same using the Internet. It encompasses not only mobile phones, tablets, and personal computers but also different machines, devices, and communication protocols which have not been previously linked with the Internet.

The idea of this concept is to understand how the IoT is enabling our life very easily and smoothly through the application of various IoT devices surrounding us. This uses unique addressing schemes for the devices to establish communication and cooperation to achieve a common goal [13].

There are multiple definitions of IoT that have been proposed, but all follows the same concept. Some of the definitions are as follows:

The IoT encompasses networks of various physical devices equipped with software, sensors, actuators, electronics, and networking for collecting and exchanging data among them.

It can be defined as a system which consists of sensors, actuators, and other smart devices which collectively establish a connection in such a way to make them interact with humans and each other.

To make a feasible information society, IoT provides a global infrastructure that enables the services to be accessible through the interconnection of different devices for sharing information through reliable communication [41].

The scope of the IoT is very vast. It deals with connecting different physical objects (such as different machines, electronic devices, and household appliances) to the Internet and also provides a platform to establish communication and exchange of data among the objects. The collected data are then processed to attain a common goal (i.e., user/machine goal) [38].

The strength of the IoT can be seen everywhere from smart homes to transportation, industrial automation, healthcare, agriculture, drug discovery, and quick response in the case of disasters (natural/manmade). In such domains, making appropriate and smart decisions by a human being is very difficult. The fundamental architecture of IoT is shown in Figure 6.1.

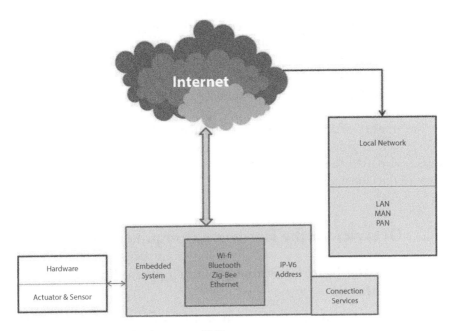

Figure 6.1 Fundamental architecture of IoT.

6.1.3   Internet of Things: Existing and Future Scopes

In recent years, IoT-enabled devices have recorded an immense growth in manufacturing due to their growing demand and applicability in different domains. This has also provided a potential opportunity and a market for manufacturers, application developers, and Internet service providers, which are expanding day by day. As per a survey, it is estimated that 212 billion units of IoT smart devices will be deployed globally by the end of 2020 [11]. According to the report of McKinsey Global Institute, the contribution of IoT businesses in revenues will increase by $6.2 trillion by 2025 [1].

An information technology research and advisory firm named "Gartner" estimated that in the consumer sector, 2.9 billion connected devices would be used by 2015 and it would be expected to increase to more than 13 billion by 2020 [1].

Nearly 8.4 billion IoT-enabled devices were available in the year 2017 in the whole world. In the year 2018, the quantity the devices increased by 9.2 billion. As per the current scenario of the usage of IoT-enabled devices in different sectors, the expected quantity of the same would reach 20.8 billion worldwide [46].

According to the report published on forbes.com, the combined markets of the IoT will reach $520 billion in 2021. This expenditure will be actually double of the overall expenditure in year 2017, i.e., $235 billion. Due to the fastest growth rate in data center and data analytics in the IoT segment, till 2021 the compound annual growth rate (CAGR) will reach up to 50% [23].

The market of IoT-based services related to healthcare applications is expected to grow annually from $1.1 to $2.5 trillion globally by 2025, whereas by 2025, the impact of annual economic growth of IoT-based services in the global market will be from $2.7 to $6.2 trillion [11, 26].

6.2   Overview of the Hardware Components of IoT

6.2.1   IoT Hardware Components: Development Boards/ Platforms

In IoT, a wide range of devices are used, such as sensors, actuators, routers, and servers. These devices are involved in handling various key tasks and functions, which include security-related activity, communication among the entities, action specifications and timely activation of system, and detection of goals and actions [25].

Different development boards/platforms are available in the market, but in this section, mainly three components are taken, which are as follows.

6.2.1.1   Arduino

Arduino is a very much familiar name for those who have been working in the IoT space from a very long time. Audrino boards were generally being used for different purposes for a long time. But nowadays, these are generally used in making different IoT products from the entry level to the advance level due to ease of programming and ease of use.

Due to its simplicity and plug-and-play nature, the Arduino board has become very popular among IoT working people [32]. The open-source nature allows us to easily program, reprogram, and erase the Arduino microcontroller at any instant of time. It was designed by Interaction Design Institute Ivrea in 2005 especially for students and hobbyists to create devices using sensors and actuators. The open-source computing platform of Arduino allows constructing and programming electronic products. It acts like a mini computer that takes inputs and gives outputs applicable for various types of electronic devices.

There are different types of Arduino boards, such as Arduino Uno (R3), LilyPad Arduino, Red Board, Arduino Mega (R3) [42], and Arduino Leonardo [30] applicable for specific purposes.

Initially, when the Arduino came in the market, it was generally introduced as a general-purpose microcontroller connected to the Internet via the modules of GSM and Wi-Fi. But as soon as the IoT started to progress, special features were added to the board to support the IoT. Some IoT-supported boards such as Arduino 101, MKR1000, Arduino WiFi Rev 2, and MKR Vider 4000 are very much applicable in the market. These boards were specially designed for IoT to solve specific problems and to develop products for IoT [33].

6.2.1.2   Raspberry Pi

Raspberry Pi is a product of Raspberry Pi Foundation, which is very handy, small in size, affordable, and very popular among the students, educators, hobbyists, and experimenters. It is applicable not only for the development of sensors and actuators but also for use as hubs, data aggregators, and gateways in several IoT projects. This board makes it feel like a small computer that has USB ports for connecting the keyboard and mouse, wired Internet connectivity through an Ethernet port, an HDMI port to display on the screen, and Wi-Fi adapters for wireless connectivity. Raspberry Pi has a huge community support worldwide that helps develop IoT-related projects. This community provides technical support whenever we are stuck in a problem [25].

6.2.1.3   BeagleBone

This device was developed by the joint effort of Texas Instruments, Network Element14, and DigiKey. It is a single-board device which provides an open-source platform for the development of embedded designs with high performance and accuracy [28].

Its simplicity and smallness like a debit card makes it popular among IoT developers. It takes low power to perform a task and allows doing experimental work with various operating systems such as Android, Linux, and Ubuntu. A Universal Serial Bus (USB) port on the BeagleBone allows attaching via Bluetooth, Wi-Fi, or any radio-frequency (RF) USB adapter.

6.2.2 IoT Hardware Components: Transducer

6.2.2.1 Sensors

Sensors are the most significant part of IoT to collect data regarding the activities happening in the environment. These consist of different modules such as radio-frequency, sensing, power management, and energy modules to collect and process data. Sensors are the backbone of digital data to provide smart solutions for a given task. Sensors uses electric pulses to measure any activity sensed from different entities such as moisture, light, motion, heat, sound, and other similar entities. The sensor converts the physical parameters into electrical signals which are useful for other components in the system. For example, a microphone senses the sound waves and converts these into electrical signals in a meaningful way to be used by other devices in the system. Hence, sensors are significant IoT devices which are required to be precise and accurate to make feasible decisions [14].

More than a hundred different sensors are available in the environment, used in different IoT projects such as smart homes, wearable electronic devices, and smart traffic systems.

Different kinds of sensors have been used for a long time by industries, organizations, and individuals in a conventional manner. But the IoT has completely changed the application of sensors at different levels. The IoT platform uses sensors to collect and share data with connected devices in the network. Further, these collected data are used by the devices to function autonomously to make the system smarter every day [37].

6.2.2.2 Actuators

Actuators are another kind of transducers like sensors. But actuators are used to act upon the signals received in the form of energy. Actuators actually receive electrical signals as input and convert these into physical action, i.e., into motion. In other words, we can say that actuators are used to transform energy into motion. There are different types of actuators, such as a hydraulic system taking liquid to produce motion; an electric motor using external power as a source to produce motion, i.e., battery; thermal actuators employing heat to generate motion; and pneumatic actuators applying heat as a source to produce motion [9].

In IoT, actuators are utilized whenever it is required to start or stop any device or machine by applying some force in the form of electrical signals. It is well known that IoT is not only fetching and processing the data, but it also involved in triggering various devices to be in action to perform the given tasks based on the nature of the data. IoT uses sensors and actuators together to perform automation without human intervention, and this makes the IoT very much popular in various applications.

There are various fields where actuators are very much useful in ensuring the accuracy of the task. The use of actuators is generally found in robotics and assembling and manufacturing processes.

6.3 Wireless Technology in IoT

Wireless technology is the basis of IoT infrastructure, which uses radio frequency (RF), Bluetooth, light, and sound to establish communication in dual direction for message delivery and data collection in a controlled manner without physical interaction [20]. This way of communication between devices makes the IoT feasible in reality. Wireless technology is useful for various IoT applications, including critical industrial missions such as automation of power grids, controlling oil and gas fields, and various activities in our daily routine life such as smart cities, home automation, smart farming, industrial Internet, and many more [16].

IoT can be seen as a broad term which includes not only small computing devices such as smartphones and tablets but also millions of wirelessly connected devices and machines surrounding us. As we know, all IoT devices send and receive information through a wireless medium, and for this wireless communication, various options are available which are applicable as per the severity of the application.

In the selection of appropriate wireless technology for a given application, different factors are required to be considered, such as battery life, power consumption, signal strength, and bandwidth [2].

Thus, it is very significant to choose the appropriate wireless technology while designing IoT devices to deliver high quality in terms of accuracy and reliability to the end users [21].

In this section, details about wireless technologies including topology, networks, connections, and protocols are given that play a significant role in the IoT infrastructure.

6.3.1 Topology

The term *topology* in IoT refers to the set of rules that help establish healthy and smooth communication among IoT components such as sensors, actuators, gateways, and other devices. The selection of topology is based on the domain of the application. So for that, the pros and cons of each

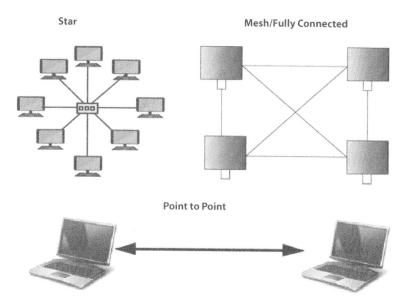

Figure 6.2 IoT topologies.

topology are required to be known [51]. There are several topologies are available for networking in IoT, but mainly three topologies, namely, mesh, star, and point-to-point, are best suited for IoT. The details of the topologies are as follows, and a respective picture is shown in Figure 6.2.

6.3.1.1 Mesh Topology

In mesh topology, a particular channel is used to connect all nodes and they work together to share data in a network. In a wireless mesh network, nodes are associated with each other via extending a radio signal to route a message to/from the client [31]. The application of this topology can be seen in developing smart cities, in healthcare equipment to quickly locate and monitor medical devices, in ensuring the feasibility of smart homes using different sensors and mesh-enabled nodes for capturing real-time data and response accordingly, in sustainable farming, and in industrial Internet. Industry standards such as Z-Wave and ZigBee use this topology [7].

There are mainly three types of nodes such as gateway node, sensor node, and router node are available in the mesh topology. The gateway node is used to allow passing data between different networks, the sensor node is used to sense the data from sensing devices and the router node is used to provide the optimized route to the networks [27].

This topology is robust and provides high-level security and privacy to the data. This topology uses dedicated links/channels to transfer data among the devices and through this ensures the reliability of the data.

This topology has some limitations. Configuration and installation of this topology is very complex as compared to that of other topologies.

Due to the requirement of a huge amount of wiring, the cost of cables becomes high, and hence, it is not feasible for large networks. Hence, it is useful for only a limited number of devices [44].

6.3.1.2 Star Topology

Star topology consists of nodes connected to a central hub via a link. Here, the central hub works as a gateway node to connect to the outside world and other nodes work as sensor nodes to sense the data. A common connection point is provided for all other nodes to connect with the central hub. Communication among all peripheral nodes is done by sending message to, and receiving from, the central hub.

In other words, the star network can be defined as a group of nodes consisting of a middle node that works as an access point/router for other nodes to establish a connection and distributing data among them.

Star topology has different advantages. First, it provides a fast and consistent network; i.e., it gives high throughput and maintains low latency. Second, setting up of the entire network is very simple; only one port is required by each device to connect to the central hub (node). Third, it provides high quality of a reliable network because in this topology, detection of faults is very easy as compared to that in the mesh topology. Isolation of devices and faults is very simple in the star topology [27].

This topology has some limitations/disadvantages. It is well known that the star topology depends on the central hub; if the central hub fails, the entire system will fail. The installation cost of a star-topology-based network is very high. The range of the network is equal to the transmission range of a node.

Energy consumption in this topology is high to relay a message to the end node due to long radio link between the central node and the end node. Also, there is no facility to handle radio-frequency obstacles [7].

6.3.1.3 Point-to-Point Topology

Unlike mesh and star topologies, point-to-point topology is used to connect two nodes in a network together. In other words, this type of network establishes a connection only between two nodes/devices [27].

The major advantage of this topology is its minimum cost and easy installation in comparison to those of mesh and star network topologies. This topology uses either a unidirectional or a bidirectional mode to stream data between two nodes.

The limitation of this topology is its communication only between two nodes. The main problem of this topology is its inability to extend beyond two nodes. Thus, the network range is limited by one hop and the transmission range of one node is used for defining this range [7].

6.3.2   IoT Networks

There are different categories of IoT networks, and these categories are based on the range they cover and their application. A brief of the IoT networks is as follows, and a respective figure is shown as Figure 6.3.

6.3.2.1   Nano Network

A group of few small devices (usually sized a few micrometers) is used to form this network. This network is used to perform tasks which are very simple in nature, such as sensing, actuation, storage, and computing. Such type of network is applicable for some specific purposes such as in military

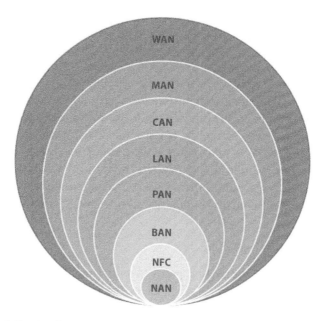

Figure 6.3 IoT networks.

operations, biometric activities, and nanoscience. Due to its different nature of working, it is not a suitable choice for residential use [29].

6.3.2.2 Near-Field Communication (NFC) Network

The speed of this network is low. Due to this, only devices that come within the range of 4 cm can be connected with the network. Such type of network is useful for identity cards (ID card), contactless payment systems, and keycards [24].

6.3.2.3 Body Area Network (BAN)

This type of device is very much useful for patients to provide real-time alert messages about the nature of their body organs. It gives information on whether the symptoms are positive or negative and also takes appropriate action accordingly. Such devices are either wearable at different places of the human body or implants inside the body.

For example, a pacemaker is an example of inside implantation which helps keep the heart beating by producing electrical impulses, and HeartGuide is the first wearable blood-pressure-monitoring device for tracking heart data and for learning the effect of the patient behavior on the heart health [52].

6.3.2.4 Personal Area Network (PAN)

PAN is used to connect devices within the range of hardly 10 meters or within a radius of 10-20 feet approximately. For this, only some forms of Wi-Fi technology are needed rather than plugging any physical device or using wires to connect with the Internet or any other networks [18].

6.3.2.5 Local Area Network (LAN)

The name implies that this category of network is used in a localized area which covers an entire building, i.e., a home or an office. Interaction between LAN users can be feasible via email or chatting software.

6.3.2.6 Campus/Corporate Area Network (CAN)

A limited geographical area such as a university or an enterprise comes under this network [8, 35]. It is also known as residential network or ResNet. Its speed is higher than that of the Internet.

6.3.2.7 Metropolitan Area Network (MAN)

MAN covers a specific portion of the metropolitan area. A large portion of the geographical area, including various smaller networks (i.e., LANs, CANs, and MANs) comes under MAN. It uses the microwave transmission technique to establish communication among devices.

6.3.2.8 Wide Area Network (WAN)

A large portion of a geographical area comes under WAN, which covers small networks such as LANs, PANs, CANs, and MANs [36]. WAN uses TCP/IP for connecting devices such as switches, modems, routers, and firewalls. This network is used for wired and wireless communication.

6.3.3 IoT Connections

A three-level architecture such as devices, gateways, and data systems are used in the IoT system. Four types of transmission channels are used to move the data between these levels, which are as follows, and a respective figure is shown as Figure 6.4.

6.3.3.1 Device-to-Device (D2D)/Machine-to-Machine (M2M)

In this connection, information sharing is done through direct interaction of two devices instantly without using any intermediaries. For example, sensors and industrial robots may establish a direct connection together to

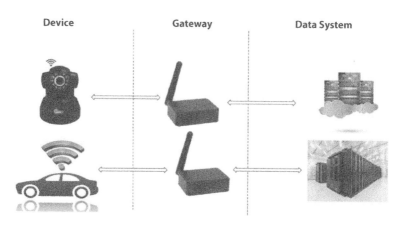

Figure 6.4 IoT networks.

coordinate the actions of various devices. But, in the real-scenario, seeing such type of connection is very less due to the distinct nature of the devices.

6.3.3.2 Machine-to-Gateway/Router (M2G/R)

Such type of connection is established between gateway and sensor nodes using telecommunication. It is well known that the computing power of the gateway is much better than that of a sensor node. The gateway is leveraged with two functions. The first one deals with the collection of data from the sensors and delivering these to the appropriate data system. The second one deals with the analysis of data and, if any problem occurs, returns these back to the relevant device [6].

6.3.3.3 Gateway/Router-to-Data System (G/R2DS)

This connection deals with the transmission of data from the gateway to the appropriate data system. For this, the traffic of the data is analyzed to select the relevant protocol [53].

6.3.3.4 Data System to Data System (DS2DS)

This connection is used between clouds/datacenters for transferring information. This connection provides such type of protocols for existing applications to easily integrate and deploy with high availability and disaster recovery with reliability.

6.3.4 IoT Protocols/Standards

IoT protocols are used to establish secure communication and exchange of data among various IoT devices as per need. The connection of IoT devices to the Internet is established through Internet Protocol (IP) addresses. However, these IoT devices use Bluetooth and RFID to connect locally. But the coverage range, power consumption, and memory usage are different between IP and non-IP networks [50]. Non-IP networks require less memory and less power with range limitation as compared to IP networks.

A large number of IoT protocols are available as per their usage. Some of them are more popular and well known than others. There are various connectivity options available for IoT infrastructure, but for simplicity, the concerned standards and protocols are categorized into two parts [19]. The details are as follows.

6.3.4.1   Network Protocols for IoT

Protocols that come under this category are used for connecting devices over the network. These protocols are specially built for using over the Internet and allow data communication in end-to-end mode [3]. Various network protocols are mentioned below.

Bluetooth

It is the most popular wireless protocol which is widely used to connect IoT devices for exchanging data. This protocol is secure and suitable for low-power, short-range, and low-cost wireless communication for IoT devices. A version of Bluetooth technology named Bluetooth Low Energy (BLE) is used to consume less power to connect IoT devices.

The Bluetooth protocol is mostly applied where data are required to be exchanged in small fragments with less memory and low power. Due to its ease of use and cost-effective nature, Bluetooth is top ranked among IoT protocols. Bluetooth 4.2 is the latest version, which helps accessing the Internet in fast-forward mode via 6LoAPAN. Bluetooth 5, a newly developed version, provides a high-coverage range and easy communication between two Bluetooth-enabled IoT devices within the same time-span as compared to its previous versions.

Hypertext Transfer Protocol (HTTP)

It is the most commonly used network protocol that deals with communicating and transferring data over the web. When a huge amount of data is to be published, HTTP provides feasibility to IoT devices. The best use case of HTTP is 3D printing, where it helps in connecting 3D printers to the computer and provides the printing of 3D objects.

But due to its high cost, high energy consumption, short battery life, and many other constraints, it is not the preferred protocol for IoT devices.

Wi-Fi

Processing a large quantity of data and quick data transfer at a high rate is offered by the Wi-Fi technology. The Institute of Electrical and Electronics Engineers (IEEE) has assigned a standard 802.11 to Wi-Fi technology. This standard allows transferring 100 Mb data in a second and performs operation at a frequency of 2.4 GHz/5 GHz.

Many IoT devices use Wi-Fi for easy, smooth, and fast data transfer. One limitation of the Wi-Fi protocol is that for some IoT applications, it takes a huge amount of power consumption.

ZigBee

Like Bluetooth, ZigBee has a strong user base and it enables smart devices to work together in a collaborative environment. ZigBee is not a general-purpose protocol; i.e., it is generally applicable for industries and less applicable for consumers. In home automation, this protocol is mostly useful. It supports data transfer at a low rate for short distances usually in a building or at home. It takes 2.4 GHz frequency to do the operational task. This frequency is very much ideal for industrial purposes.

ZigBee Remote Control is a version of ZigBee which is known as a security protocol for IoT to provide scalable solutions with high security and low power consumption.

ZigBee 3.0 is another version of ZigBee which provides wireless network at a low data rate and low power. ZigBee 3.0 is mainly useful for industrial sites.

The wireless standard IEEE 802.15.4 is generally used in industrial application and in some home automation. Usually the range of ZigBee is 100 meters, but by using a mesh network, this range can be increased. The ZigBee protocol provides high scalability and high-level secure connection through 128-bit encryption.

Z-Wave

Z-Wave is a MAC protocol which takes low power for communication between devices. Its communication is based on radio frequency (RF). This protocol is specially used in smart commercial and home automation.

Z-Wave works at a frequency of 900 MHz, and it is used for point-to-point communication that covers about 30-100 meters.

The rate of data transfer of this protocol is 40-100 Kbits/s. This protocol is specially used for sending small messages for IoT applications.

The application domain of this protocol may be in energy control, light control, healthcare control through wearable devices, and many more.

Long-Range Wide Area Network (LoRaWAN)

LoRaWAN is specially developed to cover a wide area network for IoT applications. This topology connects a centralized network server with IoT devices to provide communication in a low-power wide area network at low bit rates.

This protocol is mainly applicable for those devices that take less memory and low power for their functioning; for example, this type of protocol is specially used in smart cities.

The frequency of this protocol may vary, and it depends on the type of network. Generally, the rate of data transfer of this protocol varies between 0.3 and 50 kbps. This range may vary from 2 to 5 km in urban areas and about 15 km in sub-urban areas. LoRaWAN (IEEE 802.15.4g) has a data rate of 0.3-0.5 kbps and works in an unlicensed spectrum which is less than 1 GHz.

6.3.4.2   Data Protocols for IoT

Those IoT devices having low power are connected through these protocols for point-to-point communication in the absence of the Internet. Some of these protocols are mentioned as follows.

Message Queue Telemetry Transport (MQTT)

MQTT is the most preferable protocol for devices used in the IoT environment. It is developed by Arlen Nipper and Andy Stanford Clark in 1999. Monitoring of the devices from remote locations is supported by this protocol. It is also used for collecting data from various electronic devices. It uses wireless network for event-driven message exchange [40].

The functioning of this protocol happens on top of the transmission control protocol/Internet protocol (TCP/IP). The three core components of this protocol are the subscriber, publisher, and broker. The role of the publisher is to generate and transmit the data to the subscriber, and this task is completed with the help of the broker. The broker also ensures the security of the data by checking the subscribers and the publishers for their authorization credentials for the communication.

It is a kind of lightweight protocol used for devices which take less memory and power to collect data from various electronic devices and monitoring IoT from remote locations. These devices may include sensors used in car and heavy vehicles, smart watches, fire detectors, and text-based messaging applications.

Secure Message Queue Telemetry Transport (SMQTT)

It is an extended version of MQTT which offers encryption based on lightweight attributes. The encryption applies the features of multicast for message encryption in which one encrypted message is delivered to multiple nodes except the sender node. The algorithm used for this operation has four stages, namely, setup, encryption, publishing, and decryption.

The setup phase provides a platform for publishers and subscribers to receive a master secret key by registering themselves to the concerned broker.

After that, the broker encrypts and publishes the data and sends these to the subscriber. At the subscriber side, the message is decrypted by using the same master key [43].

Advanced Message Queuing Protocol (AMQP)

An application layer protocol, AMQP is basically used for messaging in a middleware environment. It is internationally approved as a standard protocol. It has three significant components, namely, exchange, message queue, and binding. The exchange component is used to get the messages and put them in the queues.

The work of the message queue is to store messages until the client application successfully processes these messages safely. The binding component is responsible for managing the connection between exchange and message queue components.

AMQP provides point-to-point reliable connection. For the exchange of data, AMQP gives a secure, reliable, and seamless platform between the cloud and the devices. Mainly the banking industry is using this protocol. When a bank server sends a message, the tracking of message is done by the protocol to ensure that all the messages are delivered to the intended destination without any failure.

Constrained Application Protocol (CoAP)

CoAP provides services as a utility protocol, and it is used only for some specific smart devices/gadgets. This protocol supports the hypertext transfer protocol (HTTP), through which a request can be sent by the client to the server and a response can be received from the server to the client.

The protocol supports the user datagram protocol (UDP) for lightweight data implementation and also minimizes the use of storage space. The data format used by the protocol is in binary format named Efficient Extensible Markup Language Interchanges (EXL). The protocol also supports restful architecture. CoAP uses strategies of HTTP such as get, put, delete, and places to remove ambiguity. Application of CoAP is found especially in mobiles, automation, and microcontrollers [10].

6.4 Conclusion

Due to the wide presence of IoT devices in different domains like education, health care, home automation, farming, and many more, various wireless technologies are available to get the desired solution. Each technology has some pros and cons. But here the question arises as to which technology is more appropriate and has fewer flaws in comparison to other existing technologies.

There are several issues remaining, due to the specific requirements of different applications related to the coverage range, throughput, topologies, and power consumption. Further, other factors such as security, cost of implementation and maintenance, and coupling of devices are also a challenging task.

The chapter focuses on various wireless technologies and their significance in the Internet of Things (IoT). It discusses the existing and future scopes of the IoT in different applications followed by the details of different hardware components.

After that, the importance of wireless technology for IoT is explained. It also includes IoT-specific wireless topologies, networks, connections, and protocols.

References

1. Aayush, Internet of Things(IoT): Introduction, Applications and Future Scope, 2017, Source: https://www.gkmit.co/blog/internet-of-things-iot-introduction-applications-and-future-scope.
2. Rathore, A., Wireless Technologies for IoT, 2018, source: https://iot.electron-icsforu.com/expert-opinion/wireless-technologies-iot/.
3. Al-Sarawi, S., Anbar, M., Alieyan, K., Alzubaidi, M., Internet of Things (IoT) communication protocols, in: *2017 8th International conference on information technology (ICIT)*, IEEE, pp. 685–690, 2017.
4. Al-Turjman, F. and Radwan, A., Data delivery in wireless multimedia sensor networks: Challenging and defying in the IoT era. *IEEE Wireless Commun.*, 24, 5, 126–131, 2017.
5. Amarilli, F., Amigoni, F., Fugini, M.G., Zarri, G.P., A semantic-rich approach to IoT using the generalized world entities paradigm, in: *Managing the Web of Things*, pp. 105–147, Morgan Kaufmann, Edinburgh, London, 2017.
6. Andreev, S., Galinina, O., Pyattaev, A., Gerasimenko, M., Tirronen, T., Torsner, J., Sachs, J., Dohler, M., Koucheryavy, Y., Understanding the IoT connectivity landscape: a contemporary M2M radio technology roadmap. *IEEE Commun. Mag.*, 53, 9, 32–40, 2015.
7. Ray, B., Comparing Mesh, Star & Point-To-Point Topology In IoT Networking, January 09, 2018, source: https://www.link-labs.com/blog/iot-topology.

8. Cardei, I., Wu, Y., Junco, J., Backup Wi-Fi Ad-hoc Network for Emergency Response in Scenarios with Sporadic Connectivity and Primary Users, in: *2014 10th International Conference on Mobile Ad-hoc and Sensor Networks*, IEEE, pp. 66–73, 2014.

9. Casado-Vara, R., Martin-del Rey, A., Affes, S., Prieto, J., Corchado, J.M., IoT network slicing on virtual layers of homogeneous data for improved algorithm operation in smart buildings. *Future Gener. Comput. Syst.*, 102, 965–977, 2020.

10. Colitti, W., Steenhaut, K., De Caro, N., Buta, B., Dobrota, V., Evaluation of constrained application protocol for wireless sensor networks, in: *2011 18th IEEE Workshop on Local & Metropolitan Area Networks (LANMAN)*, IEEE, pp. 1–6, 2011.

11. Gantz, J. and Reinsel, D., The digital universe in 2020: Big data, bigger digital shadows, and biggest growth in the far east. *IDC iView: IDC Analyze the future*, 2007, 2012, 1–16, 2012.

12. Gazis, V., Görtz, M., Huber, M., Leonardi, A., Mathioudakis, K., Wiesmaier, A., Zeiger, F., Vasilomanolakis, E., A survey of technologies for the internet of things, in: *2015 International Wireless Communications and Mobile Computing Conference (IWCMC)*, IEEE, pp. 1090–1095, 2015.

13. Giusto, D., Iera, A., Morabito, G., Atzori, L. (Eds.), *The internet of things: 20th Tyrrhenian workshop on digital communications*, Springer Science & Business Media, Springer-Verlag New York, 2010.

14. IoT technology stack from IoT devices, sensors, actuators and gateways to IoT platforms, i-SCOOP, 2016 - 2020, source: https://www.i-scoop.eu/internet-of-things-guide/iot-technology-stack-devices-gateways-platforms/.

15. Jia, X., Feng, Q., Fan, T., Lei, Q., RFID technology and its applications in Internet of Things (IoT), in: *2012 2nd international conference on consumer electronics, communications and networks (CECNet)*, IEEE, pp. 1282–1285, 2012.

16. Tang, J., Wireless Communication for IoT (Internet of Things), 2012, (Source: https://researcher.watson.ibm.com/researcher/view_group.php?id=4343).

17. Kalra, S. and Sood, S.K., Secure authentication scheme for IoT and cloud servers. *Pervasive Mob. Comput.*, 24, 210–223, 2015.

18. Karimi, K. and Atkinson, G., What the Internet of Things (IoT) needs to become a reality. pp. 1–16, White Paper, FreeScale and ARM, Austin, Texas, United States, 2013.

19. Uppalapati, K., How IoT Protocols and Standards Support Secure Data Exchange in the IoT Ecosystem, May 2019, source: https://www.kelltontech.com/kellton-tech-blog/internet-of-things-protocols-standards.

20. Kogias, D.G., Michailidis, E.T., Tuna, G., Gungor, V.C., Realizing the Wireless Technology in Internet of Things (IoT), in: *Emerging Wireless Communication and Network Technologies*, pp. 173–192, Springer, Singapore, 2018.

21. Kong, L., Khan, M.K., Wu, F., Chen, G., Zeng, P., Millimeter-wave wireless communications for IoT-cloud supported autonomous vehicles: Overview, design, and challenges. *IEEE Commun. Mag.*, 55, 1, 62–68, 2017.

22. Li, S., Da Xu, L., Zhao, S., 5G Internet of Things: A survey. *J. Ind. Inf. Integr.*, 10, 1–9, 2018.

23. Columbus, L., IoT Market Predicted To Double By 2021, Reaching $520B, 2018, Source: https://www.forbes.com/sites/louiscolumbus/2018/08/16/iot-market-predicted-to-double-by-2021-reaching-520b/#13b37a401f94.

24. Lueth, K.L., IoT basics: Getting started with the Internet of Things. White paper, 2015. Madakam, S., Ramaswamy, R., Tripathi, S., Internet of Things (IoT): A literature review. *J. Comput. Commun.*, Hamburg, Germany, 3, 05, 164, 2015.

25. Maksimović, M., Vujović, V., Davidović, N., Milošević, V., Perišić, B., Raspberry Pi as Internet of things hardware: performances and constraints. *Des. Issues*, 3, 8, 136, 137, 2014.

26. Manyika, J., Chui, M., Bughin, J., Dobbs, R., Bisson, P., Marrs, A., *Disruptive technologies: Advances that will transform life, business, and the global economy*, vol. 180, McKinsey Global Institute, San Francisco, CA, 2013.

27. Pacelle, M., The importance of network architecture on the Internet of Things, April 4, 2014, source: http://radar.oreilly.com/2014/04/3-topologies-driving-iot-networking-standards.html.

28. McPherson, A. and Zappi, V., An environment for submillisecond-latency audio and sensor processing on BeagleBone Black, in: *Audio Engineering Society Convention 138*, Audio Engineering Society, Warsaw, Poland, 2015.

29. Miraz, M.H., Ali, M., Excell, P.S., Picking, R., A review on Internet of Things (IoT), Internet of everything (IoE) and Internet of nano things (IoNT), in: *2015 Internet Technologies and Applications (ITA)*, pp. 219–224, IEEE, Wrexham, UK, 2015.

30. Monk, S., *Programming Arduino next steps: going further with sketches*, McGraw-Hill Education, New York, USA, 2018.

31. Nair, K., Kulkarni, J., Warde, M., Dave, Z., Rawalgaonkar, V., Gore, G., Joshi, J., Optimizing power consumption in iot based wireless sensor networks using Bluetooth Low Energy, in: *2015 International Conference on Green Computing and Internet of Things (ICGCIoT)*, IEEE, pp. 589–593, 2015.

32. Nayyar, A. and Puri, V., A review of Arduino board's, Lilypad's & Arduino shields, in: *2016 3rd International Conference on Computing for Sustainable Global Development (INDIACom)*, IEEE, pp. 1485–1492, 2016.

33. Emmanuel, O., Top Hardware Platforms for Internet of Things (IoT), 2018, (https://circuitdigest.com/article/top-hardware-platforms-for-internet-of-things-iot).

34. Patel, K.K. and Patel, S.M., Internet of things-IOT: definition, characteristics, architecture, enabling technologies, application & future challenges. *Int. J. Eng. Sci. Comput.*, 6, 5, 133, 2016.

35. Rathod, N., Jain, P., Subramanian, R., Yawalkar, S., Sunkenapally, M., Amrutur, B., Sundaresan, R., Performance analysis of wireless devices for a campus-wide IoT network, in: *2015 13th International Symposium on*

Modeling and Optimization in Mobile, Ad Hoc, and Wireless Networks (WiOpt), IEEE, pp. 84–89, 2015.

36. Reiter, G., Wireless connectivity for the Internet of Things. 433, Europe, 868MHz, 2014.
37. Sharma, R., Top 15 Sensor Types Being Used Most By IoT Application Development Companies, 2019, source: https://www.finoit.com/blog/top-15-sensor-types-used-iot/.
38. Sethi, P. and Sarangi, S.R., Internet of things: architectures, protocols, and applications. *J. Electr. Comput. Eng.*, 2017, 1–25, 2017.
39. Shang, W., Yu, Y., Droms, R., Zhang, L., Challenges in IoT networking *via* TCP/IP architecture. Technical Report NDN-0038. NDN Project, 2016.
40. Shinde, S.A., Nimkar, P.A., Singh, S.P., Salpe, V.D., Jadhav, Y.R., MQTT-message queuing telemetry transport protocol. *Int. J. Res.*, 3, 3, 240–244, 2016.
41. Singh, A., Payal, A., Bharti, S., A walkthrough of the emerging IoT paradigm: Visualizing inside functionalities, key features, and open issues. *J. Netw. Comput. Appl.*, 143, 111–151, 2019.
42. Singh, B. and Verma, M., Working, Operation and Types Of Arduino Microcontroller. *Int. J. Eng. Sci. Res. Technol.*, 6, 155–158, 2017, https://www.academia.edu/33401314/WORKING_OPERATION_AND_TYPES_OF_ARDUINO_MICROCONTROLLER.
43. Singh, M., Rajan, M.A., Shivraj, V.L., Balamuralidhar, P., Secure mqtt for internet of things (iot), in: *2015 Fifth International Conference on Communication Systems and Network Technologies*, IEEE, pp. 746–751, 2015.
44. Choudhury, S., Types of Network Topology, access on 2019, 2019, source: https://www.geeksforgeeks.org/types-of-network-topology/).
45. Suresh, P., Daniel, J.V., Parthasarathy, V., Aswathy, R.H., A state of the art review on the Internet of Things (IoT) history, technology and fields of deployment, in: *2014 International conference on science engineering and management research (ICSEMR)*, IEEE, pp. 1–8, 2014.
46. Muddana, V., What is the Future of IoT or Internet of Things in next 5 years?, Jan 18, 2019, source: https://www.softscripts.net/blog/2019/01/future-of-iot/.
47. Vermesan, O., Friess, P., Guillemin, P., Gusmeroli, S., Sundmaeker, H., Bassi, A., Jubert, I.S., Mazura, M., Harrison, M., Eisenhauer, M., Doody, P., Internet of things strategic research roadmap, in: *Internet of things-global technological and societal trends*, vol. 1, pp. 9–52, 2011.
48. Yaqoob, I., Ahmed, E., Hashem, I.A.T., Ahmed, A.I.A., Gani, A., Imran, M., Guizani, M., Internet of things architecture: Recent advances, taxonomy, requirements, and open challenges. *IEEE Wireless Commun.*, 24, 3, 10–16, 2017.
49. Yiğit, O., Bilişik, H.E., Demir, E., Sokullu, R., Yeğin, K., GPS Signal Channel Modeling and Verification. *Procedia Comput. Sci.*, 113, 621–626, 2017.
50. Zamfir, S., Balan, T., Iliescu, I., Sandu, F., A security analysis on standard IoT protocols, in: *2016 International Conference on Applied and Theoretical Electricity (ICATE)*, IEEE, pp. 1–6, 2016.

51. Zhang, D.G., Zhu, Y.N., Zhao, C.P., Dai, W.B., A new constructing approach for a weighted topology of wireless sensor networks based on local-world theory for the Internet of Things (IOT). *Comput. Math. Appl.*, 64, 5, 1044–1055, 2012.
52. Zhao, W., Wang, C., Nakahira, Y., Medical application on internet of things, 2011.
53. Zhu, Q., Wang, R., Chen, Q., Liu, Y., Qin, W., Iot gateway: Bridgingwireless sensor networks into internet of things, in: *2010 IEEE/IFIP International Conference on Embedded and Ubiquitous Computing*, IEEE, pp. 347–352, 2010.

7

Architectures and Protocols for Next-Generation Cognitive Networking

R. Ganesh Babu[1]*, V. Amudha[2] and P. Karthika[3]

[1]*Department of Electronics and Communication Engineering, SRM TRP Engineering College, Tamil Nadu, India*
[2]*Department of Electronics and Communication Engineering, Saveetha School of Engineering, Tamil Nadu, India*
[3]*Kalasalingam Academy of Research and Education, Tamil Nadu, India*

Abstract

Cognitive Radio (CR) supports more software flexibility and affordability features than other radio classes. CR is a radio with intelligence for spectrum sensing, spectrum sharing, and spectrum management with self-aware capability. It can learn and sense the environment to detect the operating conditions and reconfigure its own characteristics to provide the best suitable conditions for secondary communication. The quality of transmission is based on their type of modulation, frequency, and power. If there is any interference occurring in the cognitive radio network, it can automatically adjust to provide the best suitable conditions for data rate, power, and frequency. The key advantage of the cognitive radio network is self-awareness. The process of dynamically accessing the unused spectral bands (spectrum holes/white spaces) is known as Dynamic Spectrum Access (DSA). Better spectrum communication of the xG network is maintained without spectrum space, by allowing CR to operate any one of the best available spectrum band. If primary communication occurs in channel sensing state, the occupied CR user should vacate the current position with informing the remaining CR users. The Occurrence of primary signal decision about time delay is less.

Keywords: Cognitive radio, Dynamic Spectrum Access (DSA), NeXt Generation (xG) network, spectrum sensing, spectrum sharing, spectrum management, self awareness

---

*Corresponding author: ganeshbabu.r@trp.srmtrichy.edu.in

Krishna Kant Singh, Akansha Singh, Korhan Cengiz and Dac-Nhuong Le (eds.) Machine Learning and Cognitive Computing for Mobile Communications and Wireless Networks, (155–178) © 2020 Scrivener Publishing LLC

7.1   Introduction

The Dynamic Spectrum Access of NeXt Generation (xG) network architecture [1] can be classified into two main components, namely, the (1) primary network and (2) CR network (Figure 7.1).

7.1.1   Primary Network (Licensed Network)

The main network module comprises the primary user (licensed user) and primary base station (licensed base station). The main network is functioning on the primary user and primary base station to access a particular spectrum band. The primary network components consist of the primary user (licensed user) and primary base station (licensed base station).

Primary user (licensed/noncognitive user): Primary users are users licensed to access a spectrum from the government, such as Jio, Vodafone, MTNL, Tata Docomo, and Airtel. An assured range of the spectrum band is permitted for

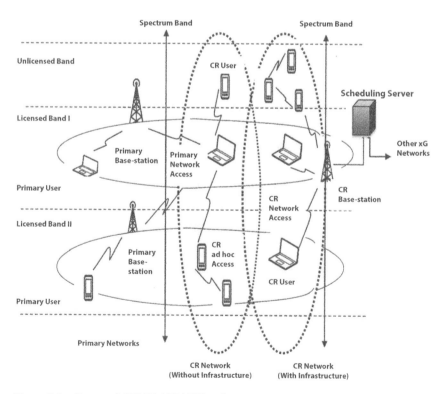

Figure 7.1 xG network/DSANs/CRAHN architecture.

access by primary users. Whole licensed users accessing facility is controlled by the primary base station. It cannot be affected by the actions from unlicensed users. Licensed users do not change with alteration for living with CR users and CR base stations over the spectrum band.

Primary base station (licensed base station): The main network base station does not involve next-generation spectrum capability with secondary users. It may have additional functionality to ensure both CR protocols and legacy for licensed access of multiple secondary users.

7.1.2 CR Network (Unlicensed Network)

It is not licensed to access particular band frequencies in the spectrum. The secondary users, unlicensed base station (CR base station), and scheduling server are the main components of a secondary network.

Secondary user (unlicensed/cognitive Radio/xG user): A cognitive radio user does not specify spectrum communication. The secondary networks do not have license to access the spectrum bands. Hence, additional functionality to access the spectrum band.

Secondary base station (unlicensed base station): The secondary base station makes available single-hop access communication over a set of unlicensed spectrum bands in a CR user. From this linking, a secondary user is able to communicate over other networks.

Scheduling server (spectrum broker): It is an essential set-up object that has a major role in accessing the spectrum resource assets between different next-generation networks.

Unlicensed Network Access Types

The dynamic accessing unlicensed network depends on CR network access, CR ad hoc access, and primary network access.

1. CR network access: Cognitive users able to access both primary and secondary spectral bands with the help of a secondary base station.
2. CR ad hoc access: The ad hoc association on multiple CR users is performed at both primary and secondary spectral bands. Dynamically requests and accesses the available spectrum of PU. By accessing licensed spectrum band, additional functionalities are required.
3. Primary network access: CR users able to access the licensed spectrum band through a primary base station.

CR Network Functions

The next-generation network is suitable for accessing licensed bands and unlicensed bands in a CR network.

1. CR network on a licensed band: The specific spectrum bands can be accessed on the same location along with the CR network on the primary network (Figure 7.2). If primary users exist to access a certain spectrum band employed by secondary users, secondary users should shift unoccupied vacant spectrum positions immediately. The operation is called a spectrum handoff.
2. CR network on an unlicensed band: All network activities have the same privileges to operate particular spectrum bands when there are no license owners (Figure 7.3). Multiple operators coexist with the same area in the spectrum portions.

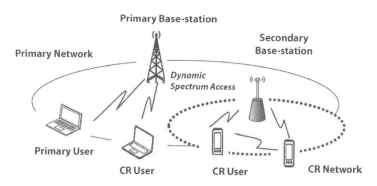

Figure 7.2 CR network on a licensed band.

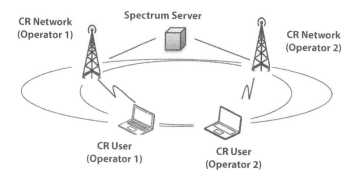

Figure 7.3 CR network on an unlicensed band.

7.2   Cognitive Radio Network Technologies and Applications

A software-defined radio (SDR) united with a clever system that has the ability of identifying locations, enhancing radio resources. and acquiring system enactment is called a cognitive radio (CR). Dillinger *et al.* [9] illustrate that SDR technology is feasible and controls congestion management and spectrum management. CR supports more software flexibility and affordability features than other radio classes. Software flexibility has to be adaptive and compassionate to a current scheme if new software is executed and software affordability is economical to support the present system. Wyglinski *et al.* [22] state that CR is a radio with intelligence for spectrum sensing, spectrum sharing, and spectrum management with self-aware capability. Celebi and Arslan [6] say that it can learn and sense the environment to detect the operating conditions and reconfigure its own characteristics to provide the best suitable conditions for secondary communication.

Hassim and Ghazali, [17] discussed that the quality of transmission is based on the type of modulation, frequency, and power. If there is any interference occurring in the cognitive radio network, it can automatically adjust to provide the best suitable conditions for data rate, power, and frequency. The key advantage of a cognitive radio network is self-awareness. The unemployed spectral bands accessing dynamically (spectrum holes/white spaces) are known as dynamic spectrum access (DSA). Kokar and Lechowicz [19] discussed that better spectrum communication of the CR network is maintained without spectrum space, by permitting CR to work any one of the finest unfilled spectrum band. In conventional radio, there is no ability to change the parameters dynamically and the spectrum band in response to environmental interferences.

7.2.1   Classes of CR

Arslan [4] presents a CR which is the advanced evolution of SDR technology. CR is programmed and configured dynamically. It can make link optimization decisions. Fette [11] describes that CR is equipped with more reconfigurable features than other radio classes. Table 7.1 shows the performance of different classes of radio property.

Haykin [18] illustrates that CR is implemented using ultra-wide-band (UWB) antennas (3.1 to 10.6 GHz) and spread over a wide frequency

Table 7.1 Advanced classes of radio properties.

Radio property	Software capable radio	Software programmable radio	Software defined radio	Aware radio	Adaptive radio	Cognitive radio
Frequency hopping	X	X	X	X	X	X
Automatic link establishment (i.e., channel selection)	X	X	X	X	X	X
Programmable crypto	X	X	X	X	X	X
Networking capabilities		X	X	X	X	X
Multiple waveform interoperability		X	X	X	X	X
In-the-field upgradable		X	X	X	X	X
Full software control of all signal processing, crypto, and networking functionality			X	*	*	*

(Continued)

Table 7.1 Advanced classes of radio properties. (*Continued*)

Radio property	Software capable radio	Software programmable radio	Software defined radio	Aware radio	Adaptive radio	Cognitive radio
QoS measuring/ channel state information gathering				X	X	X
Modification of radio parameters as function of sensor inputs					X	X
Learning about environment						X
Experimenting with different settings						X

* The industry standards organizations are in the process of determining the details of what properties should be expected of aware, adaptive and CRs.

band for spectrum detecting and tunable/smart antennas and is used for communication. Mitola [20] describes that the cognitive radio system frequency bands are as follows:

1. UHF bands: 470-806 MHz used by broadcast television
2. Cellular bands: 800/900 MHz, 1.8/1.9 GHz, 2.1 GHz, 2.3 GHz, and 2.5 GHz
3. Immovable wireless bands: two-way broadband facility and are targeted near 2.5 and 3.5 GHz
4. Ideal SDR device ability to reasonably contact three-octave bands from 0.4 to 0.96 GHz, from 1.3 to 2.5 GHz, and from 2.5 to 5.9 GHz

7.2.2   Next Generation (xG) of CR Applications

A CR network is best suitable for the ensuing applications to improving the detecting performance cooperatively with cognitive and non-cognitive users.

1. Cooperative leased network: The main network is responsible for a leased network by authorizing adaptable access to its registered spectrum range with a third-party treaty without sacrificing the facility of the licensed user. Ex: Mobile Virtual Network Operator (MVNO).
2. Cognitive mesh network: A wireless mesh network is offered with a high-speed Internet connection. However, with the increased network density, the network needs more capability to meet applications. The sensible CR technology gets into larger radio frequencies. Hence, CR networks with mesh networks situated in dense urban areas.
3. Safety emergency network: In situations of natural disasters, it may lead to the destruction of the existing infrastructure. The emergency network deals with important information, where reliable communication is guaranteed with minimal delays. The CR network can access the existing spectrum by keeping priority communication and response time without requiring the infrastructure.
4. Military network: It provide safeguard transfer information to the hostile environment with strong protection. Hence, it performs secured spectral band themselves.

5. Cooperative dynamic spectrum access for IoT service: IoT-capable objects will be interconnected through wired and wireless communication technologies in the CR networks.

7.3   Cognitive Computing: Architecture, Technologies, and Intelligent Applications

7.3.1   CR Physical Architecture

Figure 7.4(a) shows the CR transceiver section components of RF front-end and baseband processing. The control bus is used every module to establish the time-varying RF environment by a reconfiguration process. Rondeau and Bostain [21] present that the received radio-frequency (RF) signal is amplified from the antenna; mixing and conversion of A/D by RF front-end and amplified signal is then down-converted/up-converted to baseband for demodulation/modulation by baseband processing.

Figure 7.4(b) shows the RF front-end structure of a wideband antenna, a low-noise amplifier (LNA), a mixer, a voltage-controlled oscillator

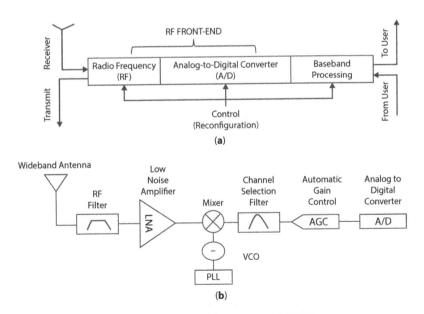

Figure 7.4 CR physical architecture: (a) CR transceiver and (b) RF front-end structure.

(VCO), a phase-locked loop (PLL), a channel selection filter, intermediate frequency (IF)/automatic gain control (AGC), and an analog-to-digital converter (ADC), Chaudhari, [7]. The received radio-frequency signal selects band-pass filter (BPF), followed by LNA. LNA is the amplified noise reduction of the desired signal. A mixer is used to mix with the received signal, and a local oscillating signal converts them to the IF range of the signal. VCO performs the specified voltage to mix the entering signal at the particular frequency. The selection of the channel is filtered to reject adjacent network channels and selects the desired response of the channel. AGC controls the constant amplifier output power level of the wide-band signal.

7.4   Functionalities of CR in NeXt Generation (xG) Networks

Biglieri *et al.* [5] present the enhancement of spectral efficiency in CR networks, cooperative features incorporated with spectrum sensing and spectrum sharing with each other. Figure 7.5 shows dynamic access of

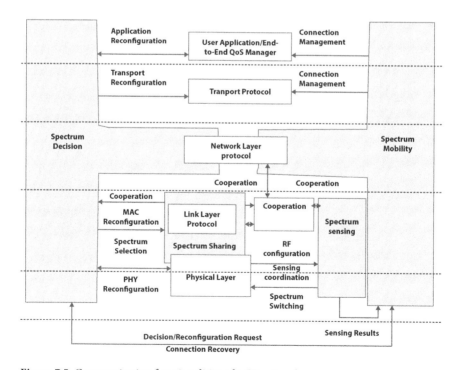

Figure 7.5 Communication functionalities of a CR network.

cooperative spectral functionalities, which are spectrum management, spectrum decision, spectrum mobility, user applications, transport, network, data link, and physical layer.

7.5 Spectrum Sensing

The unemployed spectral bands accessing dynamically (spectrum holes/ white spaces) and sharing spectral bands without harmful interference to other users are shown in Figure 7.6.

7.5.1 Spectrum Decision

The spectrum decision decides the characteristics of the spectrum, user requirement selection, and CR reconfiguration functions. The CR network adopts the finest suitable spectral band to improve the necessities of the overall spectrum quality of service (QoS) and capture the best obtainable spectral bands.

7.5.2 Spectrum Mobility

A transition of the better spectrum of the CR network is maintained by the seamless communication requirements.

Spectrum Sharing

Spectrum sharing is a facility to allow spectrum functionality resources with various secondary users (unauthorized users). The spectrum sharing access techniques in a CR network consists of underlay and overlay. In Figure 7.7(a), underlay process the simultaneous transmissions are allowed

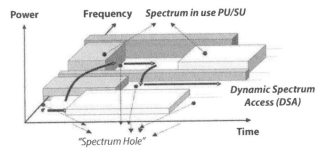

Figure 7.6 Spectrum hole concept.

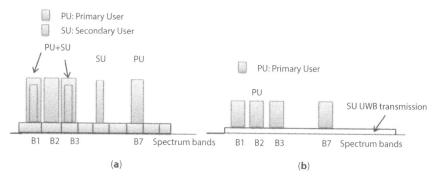

Figure 7.7 Spectrum sharing access techniques: (a) underlay and (b) overlay.

by authorized and unauthorized users as long as the noisiness at the PU is at a tolerable level.

But in Figure 7.7(b), overlay process the cognitive devices overhear the knowledge of channel conditions, activity, signal codebooks, and messages of the non-cognitive radio users (primary users) and enhance the primary communication or avoid the interferences by the primary users.

7.5.3 CR Network Functions

Chen and Prasad [8] present a CR network function that varies according to licensed and unlicensed spectrum bands.

CR Network on an Authorized Band

Figure 7.8 shows that a CR network can communicate with the primary network for accessing the particular spectral band on the same

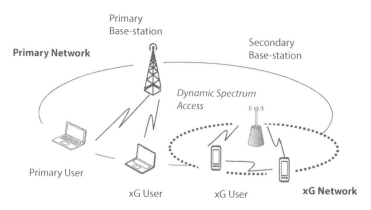

Figure 7.8 CR network accessing an authorized band.

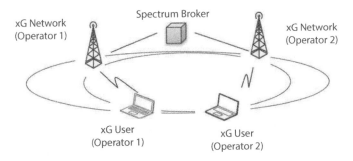

Figure 7.9 CR network accessing an unauthorized band.

location. Ekram and Bhargava [10] stated that PUs request for spectrum, xG users shift to the newly available spectrum band and vacate from the current spectrum band immediately; this is called a spectrum handoff.

CR Network on an Unauthorized Band

All network activities have the same privileges to operate particular spectrum bands when there are no license owners (Figure 7.9). Multiple operators coexist with the same area in the spectrum portions.

7.6 Cognitive Computing for Smart Communications

7.6.1 CR Technologies

The CR technology involves the Voice over Internet calls, video streaming, and data downloading (music, audio) for smart communications. Communications in a cognitive radio network are shown in Figure 7.10. These communications are defined based on their modulation, frequency, and power [12–16]. Power is the important parameter in the mobile phones. Minimum power for transmission is achieved with a patch antenna with sectoring in an array fashion. The patch antenna covers 360 degrees of signal radiation, and it can transmit and receive. In this example, the network consists of two different Voice over Internet calls and they are differentiated by their modulation and frequency. Voice over Internet call 1 has low-bit-rate modulation, frequency of 5 GHz, and low power. Voice over Internet call 2 has medium-bit-rate modulation, frequency of

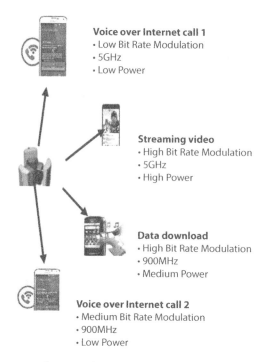

Voice over Internet call 1
• Low Bit Rate Modulation
• 5GHz
• Low Power

Streaming video
• High Bit Rate Modulation
• 5GHz
• High Power

Data download
• High Bit Rate Modulation
• 900MHz
• Medium Power

Voice over Internet call 2
• Medium Bit Rate Modulation
• 900MHz
• Low Power

Figure 7.10 Cognitive radio network.

900 MHz, and low power. This is how the communication happens with the antenna.

Figure 7.11 shows that interference occurs in a cognitive radio environment. For example, let us consider interferers occurring in Voice over Internet call 2, video streaming, and data downloading. The video streaming, data downloading, and Voice over Internet call 2 operations are disturbed and interfered by any device or mobile phone. So it can affect the type of modulation, frequency range, and power level.

Figure 7.12 shows the self-adjusting of the dynamic cognizance radio network. The key advantages of a cognitive radio network are self-awareness and self-adjusting. Whenever interference is detected in a cognitive radio network, it can be rectified automatically. But in the conventional radio, there is no ability to change the dynamic parameter and spectrum band response to having an unacceptable level of interference for communicating. Similarly, the data download power is adjusted from medium to high power, and Voiceover Internet call bit rate modulation is adjusted from medium to low.

Voice over Internet call 1
• Low Bit Rate Modulation
• 5GHz
• Low Power

Streaming video
• High Bit Rate Modulation
• 5GHz
• High Power

Data download
• High Bit Rate Modulation
• 900MHz
• Medium Power

Voice over Internet call 2
• Medium Bit Rate Modulation
• 900MHz
• Low Power

Figure 7.11 Interferers are detected in a CR network.

7.7   Spectrum Allocation in Cognitive Radio

There are wireless devices growing day by day utilizing the radio spectrum. The spectrum bands are fixed, but the accessing devices are growing rapidly. Hence, improving dynamic spectrum resources opportunistically through cognitive radio (CR). Cognitive radio is a radio with intelligence to assign a spectrum between primary and secondary users. Paid users with a license to use the spectrum are called primary users; the other type without a license is known as secondary users. Allocation of channels in a fixed spectrum band is done by many methods such as cooperative and noncooperative ones. Artificial intelligence techniques play a major role in spectrum allocation, such as neural networks, fuzzy logic, ant colonies, particle swarm algorithms, genetic algorithm, and deep learning. In this section, the idea of dynamic spectrum allocation (DSA) method using genetic algorithm is discussed [3]. This spectrum management selection is allotted in an overlay manner; i.e., secondary users are allotted band access

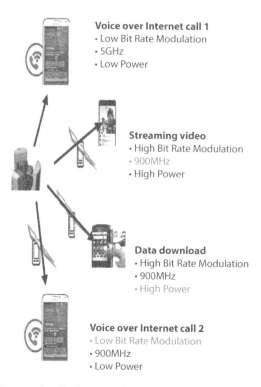

Voice over Internet call 1
• Low Bit Rate Modulation
• 5GHz
• Low Power

Streaming video
• High Bit Rate Modulation
• 900MHz
• High Power

Data download
• High Bit Rate Modulation
• 900MHz
• High Power

Voice over Internet call 2
• Low Bit Rate Modulation
• 900MHz
• Low Power

Figure 7.12 A CR network self-adjusts its characteristics.

in the nonappearance of primary users on the condition that the secondary users switch to a free band whenever a primary user enters the band. To proceed with this method, the RF parameters of primary and secondary users must be known. In genetic algorithm, the RF parameters of the channels are represented in the form of chromosomes.

Genetic algorithm is a biological evolutionary algorithm based on chromosomes and genes. The best genes in each chromosome can be selected, and these will be overlapped by crossover and mutation processes. The main advantage of GA is its flexibility and random nature. Unlike HMM, it does not need to allot a spectrum by any channel prediction state. So the trained set of chromosomes is available by the given input algorithm. A genetic-algorithm-based chromosome consists of genes; here the genes are the parameters of the CR network, i.e., modulation, power, frequency, and BER. The decision-making process is considered by each gene. The genes and their ranges for the operation of cognitive radio are assigned as frequency range from 40 MHz to 910 MHz, the power is -90 to -40 dBm, and the bit error rate is 10^{-9} to 10^{-1} (Table 7.2). The modulation techniques used are BPSK, QPSK, 8QAM, and 16QAM. Each gene value is important to decide its primary characteristics or secondary characteristics.

For the frequency gene, the total bandwidth is 800 MHz and each channel bandwidth B (channel) = 8 MHz is used to transmit and receive for a particular CR network. The frequency band considered for this research would range from 40 to 840 MHz with a step size = 8 MHz; each band is assigned to a decimal number. For example, 40-48 is assigned a decimal value of "1," 49-56 is assigned to "2," and so on up to 832-840, which is assigned to "100," as shown in Table 7.3.

Compared to all genes in the chromosome, the important parameter is the power gene. The range of power values specified in IEEE 802.22 varies from -90 dBm to -40 dBm. The power gene is considered the standard values from 90 dBm to -40 dBm with a step size of 1 dBm is characterized in Table 7.4. Power is an important parameter for the detection of the presence of the primary node. Because if the power is less, it indicates the absence of the primary node and the secondary node can start transmission.

Another parameter is the bit error rate (BER), defined as ratio of erroneous bits to the total transmitted bits. BER may vary depending

Table 7.2 Selected genes and their ranges.

Gene parameter	Values
Frequency (MHz)	40 to 910
Power (dBm)	-90 to -40
BER	10^{-1} to 10^{-9}
Modulation	BPSK, QPSK, 8-QAM, 16-QAM

Table 7.3 Frequency gene representation.

Decimal value	1	2	...	100
Frequency band MHz	40-48	48-56		832-840

Table 7.4 Power gene representation.

Decimal value	1	2	....	50
Power dBm	-90	-89	...	-40

upon certain service applications. The bit error rates can be reduced by either coding schemes or the use of certain modulation at the receiver and transmitter. One more way to reduce the bit error rates is to increase the transmission power of the device that is limited by FCC. Here the bit error rates ranges between 10^{-1} and 10^{-9} with a step size of 10^{-1}. Each value is assigned to a decimal number. For example, 10^{-1} is assigned to "1" and similarly 10^{-9} is assigned to "9" in Table 7.5.

The last gene considered is the type of modulation used for transmission and reception. Here four modulation schemes are considered. These are binary phase shift keying (BPSK), quadrature phase shift keying (QPSK), quadrature amplitude modulation (8QAM), and 16QAM. Each modulation scheme is assigned to a decimal number from "1" to "4" as shown in Table 7.6.

The four genes, as discussed above, all together define the structure of the CR channel chromosome. The arrangement of all genes in the chromosome structure is shown in Table 7.7.

The primary chromosomes is considered the value of 20 with high-power and low-BER conditions. Low-power and high-BER conditions are assumed to characterize the presence of secondary chromosomes; with this characterization, a set of 20 secondary chromosomes is considered. The assumed conditions are represented in Table 7.8.

Table 7.5 BER gene representation.

Decimal value	1	2	...	9
BER	10^{-1}	10^{-2}	...	10^{-9}

Table 7.6 Modulation gene representation.

Decimal value	1	2	3	4
Mod.	BPSK	QPSK	8QAM	16QAM

Table 7.7 Chromosome structure.

Order	1	2	3	4
Gene	Frequency	Power	BER	Mod

Table 7.8 Assumed conditions.

Parameters	Primary	Secondary
Power dBm	-60 to -40	-90 to -70
BER	10^{-9} to 10^{-6}	10^{-4} to 10^{-1}
Mod. & freq.	Fixed	Fixed

The set of chromosomes will be selected, and the fitness value will be calculated. Depending upon the fitness value, a conclusion will be made to decide to continue or to do crossover and mutation. Finally, the iteration is stopped after a number and the chromosome values are checked to occupy the whole spectrum or to vacate by the secondary node. It is observed that best fitness higher values will result in correct classification.

7.8   Cooperative and Cognitive Network

Cooperative cognitive network is capable of mitigating the uncertainty of noise power and the effect of fading and shadowing by providing spatial diversity [2]. The detection in a cognitive radio spectrum, the spectrum sensing time required to successfully detect a PU, is inversely proportional to the PU's signal strength. When the PU operates in a low-SNR region, the effective transmission time of a CR system with a fixed transmission window can be extremely short for the CR system to fully utilize the spectrum. The performance of various cooperative spectrum-sensing comparison techniques is discussed in Table 7.9.

The techniques are (see Figure 7.13)

1) Cooperative centralized coordinated
2) Cooperative decentralized (distributed) coordinated
3) Cooperative decentralized (distributed) uncoordinated

7.8.1   Cooperative Centralized Coordinated

In a cluster based cognitive radio network, the wideband spectra could share some common spectral components; such a data fusion center based cooperative wideband sensing technique will lead to a heavy data transmission burden in the common control channels (see Figure 7.14(a)).

Table 7.9 Comparison of cooperative wideband spectrum-sensing algorithms.

Cooperative sensing algorithms	Advantages	Disadvantages
Centralized coordinated	• Decision center fusion and data fusion based cooperative wideband sensing techniques	• Individualistically to detect the channel by CR users • Controller unit of secondary base station is essential • Occurrence of primary signal decision about time delay is more • Small accessible, robustness is slow and computational cost is very high
Decentralized (distributed) coordinated	• Coordinates to detect the channel by CR users • Controller unit of secondary base station is not essential • Occurrence of primary signal decision about time delay is less • Large accessible, robustness is fast and computational cost is low • Resistant to security attacks and network failures (e.g., jamming)	• Does not differentiate users by poor performance of low SNR
Decentralized (distributed) uncoordinated	• Controller unit of secondary base station is not essential • Occurrence of primary signal decision about time delay is less • Large accessible, robustness is fast and computational cost is low • Resistant to security attacks and network failures (e.g. jamming)	• Individualistically to detect the channel by CR users

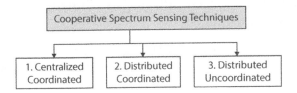

Figure 7.13 A CR network self-adjusts its characteristics.

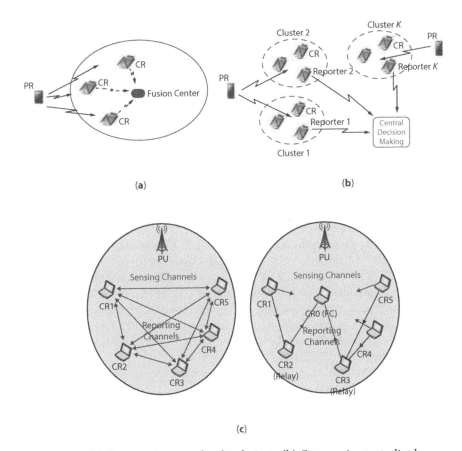

Figure 7.14 (a) Cooperative centralized technique. (b) Cooperative centralized decision fusion technique. (c) Cooperative decentralized (distributed) coordinated and uncoordinated.

An alternative is to develop a decision fusion central based cooperative wideband sensing technique if each cognitive radio is able to detect wideband spectrum independently (see Figure 7.14(b)).

7.8.2 Cooperative Decentralized (Distributed) Coordinated and Uncoordinated

A cognitive radio network accessing spectrum resources without required controller unit. Each cognitive user collect information and coordinate with each other which means individualistically to detect the channel by CR users. If primary communication occurs in channel sensing state, the occupied CR user should vacate the current position without informing the remaining CR users (Figure 7.14(c)).

References

1. Akyildiz, I.F., Lee, W.-Y., Vuran, M.C., Mohanty, S., NeXt generation/dynamic spectrum access/cognitive radio wireless networks: A survey. *Comp. Netw. Elsevier*, 50, 2127–2159, 2006.
2. Akyildiz, I.F., Lo, B.F., Balakrishnan, R., Cooperative spectrum sensing in cognitive radio networks: A survey. *Phys. Commun.*, 4, 40–62, 2011.
3. Amudha, V., Ramesh, G.P., Dynamic spectrum allocation for cognitive radio using genetic algorithm. *Int. J. Tech. Eng. Sci.*, 1, 1092–1097, 2013.
4. Arslan, H., *Cognitive Radio, Software Defined Radio, and Adaptive Wireless Systems,* Springer, Netherlands, 2007.
5. Biglieri, E., Goldsmith, A.J., Greenstein, L.J., Mandayam, N.B., Poor, H.V., *Principles of Cognitive Radio*, Cambridge University Press, USA, 2013.
6. Celebi, H. and Arslan, H., Enabling Location and Environment Awareness in Cognitive Radios. *Comp. Commun. Elsevier*, 31, 1114–1125, 2008.
7. Chaudhari, S., *Spectrum sensing for cognitive radios: Algorithms, performance, and limitations, Schools of Electrical Engineering*, Helsinki, Finland, 2012.
8. Chen, K.-C. and Prasad, R., *Cognitive Radio Networks*, John Wiley & Sons, Ltd, Chichester, UK, 2009.
9. Dillinger, M., Madani, K., Alonistioti, N., *Software Defined Radio: Architectures, Systems and Functions*, John Wiley, USA, 2003.
10. Ekram, H. and Bhargava, V.K., *Cognitive Wireless Communications Networks*, Springer Science & Business Media, Springer USA, 2007.
11. Fette, B.A., *Cognitive Radio Technology*, Elsevier, UK, 2009.
12. Ganesh Babu, R. and Amudha, V., Allow an Useful Interference of Authenticated Secondary User in Cognitive Radio Networks. *Int. J. Pur. Appl. Math.*, 119, 3341–3354, 2018.
13. Ganesh Babu, R. and Amudha, V., Cluster Technique Based Channel Sensing in Cognitive Radio Networks. *Int. J. Con. Theor. Appl.*, 9, 207–213, 2016.
14. Ganesh Babu, R. and Amudha, V., Comparative Analysis of Distributive Firefly Optimized Spectrum Sensing Clustering Techniques in Cognitive Radio Networks. *J. Adv. Res. Dyn. Cont. Syst.*, 10, 1364–1373, 2018.

15. Ganesh Babu, R. and Amudha, V., Comparative Analysis of Distributive Optimized Clustering Techniques in Cognitive Radio Networks, *proce. 1st Int. Conf. Emerg. Techno. Dat. Mini. Inform. Secu.*, (IEMIS) in association with Springer Advances in Intelligent Systems and Computing Series, February 23-25, 2018.

16. Ganesh Babu, R. and Amudha, V., Dynamic Spectrum Access Techniques in Cognitive Radio Networks, *proce. 4th Int. Conf. Rec. Tren. Comp. Sci. Engg.*, (ICRTCSE) in association with Elsevier-Procedia Computer Science, April 29-30, 2016.

17. Hassim, Y.M.M. and Ghazali, R., *Improving Functional Link Neural Network Learning Scheme for Mammographic Classification*, Springer, Cham, 2016.

18. Haykin, S., Cognitive Radio: Brain-Empowered Wireless Communications. *IEEE J. Sel. Area. Commun.*, 23, 201–220, 2005.

19. Kokar, M.M. and Lechowicz, L., *Cognitive Radio Interoperability through Waveform Reconfiguration*, Artech House, Norwood, 2016.

20. Mitola, J., *Software Radio Architecture: Object-Oriented Approaches to Wireless System Engineering*, John Wiley & Sons Ltd, USA, 2000.

21. Rondeau, T.W. and Bostain, C.W., *Artificial Intelligence in Wireless Communication*, Artech House, USA, 2009.

22. Wyglinski, A.M., Nekovee, M., Hou, Y.T., *Cognitive Radio Communication and Networks*, Elsevier, USA, 2010.

8

Analysis of Peak-to-Average Power Ratio in OFDM Systems Using Cognitive Radio Technology

Udayakumar Easwaran[1*], Poongodi Palaniswamy[1] and Vetrivelan Ponnusamy[2]

[1]Dept. of ECE, KIT-Kalaignarkarunanidhi Institute of Technology, Coimbatore, Tamilnadu, India
[2]Dept. of ECE, PSG Institute of Technology and Applied Research, Coimbatore, Tamilnadu, India

Abstract

Cognitive radio is a wireless intelligent system that has an altering parameter of radio activity through sensing. It is able to learn and adjust the wireless transmission as indicated by the encompassing radio environment through a physical layer (PHY). This radio framework has a bit of leeway of utilizing a frequency band in an authorized way. OFDM is a multicarrier regulation procedure utilized in many propelled telecommunication, remote, and broadcasting norms. OFDM is viewed as muddled as different flag, yet additionally it has high information rate transmissions with generally wide transfer speeds. CR is utilized to diminish the ISI through spectrum detecting. For the most part, OFDM-based cognitive radio spectrum gives a higher peak-to-average power ratio, slow information transmission, and huge side flaps. The significant disservice incorporated into OFDM sign is peak-to-average power ratio (PAPR), which is of higher level and has complex to carrier balance. Subsequently the decrease systems of high PAPR is numerous to resolve and it is future challenge benchmarks. The principal purpose behind lessening PAPR is to maintain a planned distance from non-linearity at the less than desirable end in rapid remote correspondence.

Keywords: OFDM, PAPR, computational complexity, partial transmit sequence, cognitive radio, neural networks, mobile communications, bit error rate

---

*Corresponding author: udayakumar.sujith@gmail.com

Krishna Kant Singh, Akansha Singh, Korhan Cengiz and Dac-Nhuong Le (eds.) Machine Learning and Cognitive Computing for Mobile Communications and Wireless Networks, (179–202) © 2020 Scrivener Publishing LLC

8.1   Introduction

Voice and information can be transmitted by utilizing electromagnetic waves in open space. Remote correspondence is the exchanging of data at any rate between two that are not related by an electrical channel. The term is ordinarily utilized in the conveyed trades industry to recommend media correspondence structures, for example, radio transmitters and recipients and remote controls, that utilize some sort of vitality, for example, radio waves and acoustic hugeness, to move data without the utilization of wires. Data are moved along these lines over both short and long parcels. Remote activities grant associations, for example, long time back run exchanges that are generally inconvenient [1].

The most exceptional remote movements utilize electromagnetic remote media correspondences, for example, radio signals. With infrared waves, separations are short, for example, a couple of meters for a TV remote control, while radio waves can land at like thousands or even an enormous number of kilometers for huge space radio correspondence. It unites different kinds of fixed, versatile, and negligible applications, including two-way radios, cell phones, personal digital assistants (PDAs), and remote structure association. Different events of livelihoods of radio remote headway combine GPS units, parking spot passage openers, remote PC mice, consoles and headsets, earphones, radio recipients, satellite TV, pass on TV, and cordless phones. Less customary strategies for accomplishing remote exchanges meld the use of light, enduring, engaging, or electric fields. A remote framework is a PC orchestrate that uses a remote framework relationship, for instance, Wi-Fi. It licenses homes, media correspondence frameworks, and associations to avoid the costly strategy of bringing joins into a structure or between equipment zones. Remote media interchange frameworks are regularly completed and controlled using radio correspondence. This utilization occurs at the physical level layer of the OSI model framework structure [3].

Since radio can be utilized straightforwardly with low frequencies, for example, those in a human voice, it is important to superimpose the data content onto a higher recurrence transporter signal at the transmitter, utilizing a procedure called adjustment. The utilization of tweak additionally permits multi data signal to utilize the radio channel by essentially utilizing an alternate transporter recurrence for each. The backward procedure, demodulation, is performed at the recipient to recover the noisy data. The data signal likewise once in a while is called the insight, the adjusting signal, or the baseband signal. A perfect correspondence framework would recreate the data signal precisely at the collector, with the exception of the unavoidable time delay as it goes among the transmitter and beneficiary and aside from potentially for an adjustment [7]. Some other changes establish twisting. In media interchanges, a point-to-point affiliation insinuates a correspondence relationship between two center points or endpoints. A model is a telephone call, in which one telephone is related to another, and what is said by one visitor must be heard by the other. Point-to-multipoint correspondence is correspondence which is cultivated by means of a particular kind of one-to-numerous association, giving various ways from a solitary area to different areas. Point-to-multipoint broadcast communication is most normally utilized in remote Internet and IP communication by means of gigahertz radio frequencies.

Broadcasting is the dissemination of sound and video substance to a dissipated group by methods for any stable or visual mass exchange medium, anyway by and large one using electromagnetic radiation. The getting social affairs may join the general populace or a reasonably tremendous subset thereof. Broadcasting has been used for inspirations driving private stimulation, non-business exchange of messages, experimentation, self-getting ready, and emergency correspondence, for instance, beginner radio and amateur television despite business purposes like understood radio or TV stations with ads. Employment of wireless communication is an essential fragment of compact enlisting. The diverse available progressions change in close by availability, consideration range, and execution, and in specific conditions, customers should likely use various affiliation types and switch between them. Wi-Fi is a remote neighborhood that enables minimized enrolling devices to interface successfully to the Internet. Standards such as IEEE 802.11, Wi-Fi procedures paces of specific sorts of wired Ethernet. Wi-Fi has transformed into a genuine standard for access in private homes, inside work environments, and at open hotspots. A couple of associations charge customers a month-to-month cost for organization, while others have begun offering it to no end with the ultimate objective to construct the ideas of their product [8].

8.2 OFDM Systems

Orthogonal frequency division multiple access is a multicarrier modulation method used to transmit the frequencies very quickly. OFDM has formed into an exceptional course of action for modernized wideband correspondence, paying little personality to whether remote or over copper wires, utilized in applications, for example, moved TV and sound telecom, DSL Internet get to, remote systems, control line structures, and 4G versatile exchanges. OFDM is a frequency-division multiplexing (FDM) plot utilized as a robotized multi-transport balance method. Countless ardently parceled adjusted sub-transporter signs are utilized to pass on information on two or three parallel information streams or channels. Each sub-transport is changed with a standard rule plan, for example, quadrature amplitude modulation or phase-shift keying at a low picture rate, keeping up full-scale information rates like normal single-transporter adjustment plots in a near data move limit [10].

The essential bit of space of OFDM over single-transport plans is its capacity to conform to real channel conditions, for instance, incapacitating of high frequencies in a long copper wire, narrowband deterrent and rehash express clouding due to multipath without complex equality channels. Channel night out is improved considering the manner in which that OFDM might be seen as utilizing different logically balanced narrowband pennant instead of one promptly adjusted wideband sign. The low picture rate utilizes a gatekeeper break between pictures moderate, making it conceivable refrain from cover symbol interference (ISI) and use echoes and time spreading on essential TV these are recognizable as ghosting and blurring, independently to accomplish an OK variety gain, for example a sign to-disturbance degree improvement. This portion in like way invigorates the course of action of single-frequency networks (SFNs), where a couple flanking transmitters send an equivalent sign at the same time at a near rehash, as the sign from different far-off transmitters might be joined accommodatingly, rather than meddling as would routinely happen in a standard single-bearer structure. OFDM has a dash of slack as immunity to explicit darkening, adaptable to obstacle, ISI, thin band impacts, and more straightforward channel night out. As such, OFDM has inadequacy as PAPR and is sensitive to transporter parity and float. The key pieces of OFDM frameworks are depicted underneath [12].

Orthogonality: In OFDM structures, the two rare signs are in any event, when the basic of their thing over a period is equivalent to zero.

Sub-carriers in OFDM systems: Each subcarrier in an OFDM structure is a sinusoid with a repeat that is an entire number different of key repeat. Each subcarrier can be imparted as a Fourier course of action fragment of the composite sign, for instance, an OFDM picture.

Inter symbol interference: Inter symbol interference (ISI) is a kind of turning of a sign wherein one picture encroaches with coming about pictures. This is an irksome marvel as the past pictures have for all intents and purposes indistinguishable impact as turmoil, thusly making the correspondence less solid. ISI is ordinarily accomplished by multipath causing or the normal non-straight recurrent reaction of a channel making dynamic pictures "cloud" together. The closeness of ISI in the framework presents mess up in choice contraption at the beneficiary yield. Thusly, in the structure of transmitting and getting channels, the goal is to limit the impacts of ISI and; as such, give the modernized information to its goal with the most minute spoil rate conceivable.

Inter-carrier interference: The presence of Doppler advancements and rehash and stage adjusts an OFDM structure causes parity of the subcarriers. Thusly, impediment is seen between subcarriers. This miracle is known as between transporter obstruction (ICI).

Cyclic prefix: The cyclic prefix (CP) or guard interval is an unpredictable increment of the last piece of an OFDM picture that is added to the front of picture in a transmitter and is expelled at the beneficiary before demodulation. The cyclic prefix goes about as a guard interim. It disposes of the between-picture hindrance from the past picture. It goes about as an accentuation of the bit of the arrangement, all things considered permitting the straight convolution of a recurrent express multipath channel to be appeared as circuitous convolution which in this way might be changed to the recurrent space utilizing a discrete Fourier change. This system thinks about basic recurrent space managing, for example, channel estimation and adjustment [12].

8.3   Peak-to-Average Power Ratio

The PAPR is the relationship between the peak & average power. PAPR happens when a non-linearity takes place. it is the major drawback in OFDM, because of power amplifiers. the power be increased due to amplifiers, takes more PAPR in OFDM during the transmission. PAPR is portrayed as

$$\text{PAPR} = \frac{P_{\text{PEAK}}}{P_{\text{AVERAGE}}} = \frac{\max\left[|x_n|^2\right]}{E[|x_n|^2]}$$

where P_{PEAK} = peak power of the OFDM system.
P_{AVERAGE} = average power of the OFDM system.

OFDM frameworks are the supposed PAPR issue. The information image stream of the inverse finite Fourier transform (IFFT) ought to have a uniform power range; however, the yield of the IFFT may effect in a non-uniform or spiky power range. The greater part of transmission vitality would be apportioned for a couple rather than the lion's share subcarriers. This issue can be evaluated as the PAPR measure. It causes numerous issues in the OFDM framework at the transmitting end [8].

The effect of PAPR is RF control intensifiers ought to be worked in a huge direct locale. The sign pinnacles get into non-direct district of the power enhancer causing signal contortion and signal mutilation presents between adjustment among the subcarriers and out of band radiation. Huge pinnacles cause immersion in power intensifiers, prompting bury tweak items among the subcarriers and dispersing out of band vitality. S-PTS plan is to partition the covered OFDM signals into various fragments, and afterward some disjoint sub-squares are separated and duplicated with various stage revolution factors in each portion [15].

8.4   Cognitive Radio (CR)

CR is a clever radio that utilizes the range authorized to different clients when they are not utilizing it. It is a product structured radio [7] with psychological programming. Software-defined Radio is a latest wireless method, smart servicing technique using hardware & software to send and receive data signals. the radio spectrum available at primary users are able to used by secondary users by this techniques. It is used in 4G technology, etc. The cognitive radio cycle appears in Figure 8.1.

Spectrum sensing is utilized to distinguish the under-used part of a range. Range detecting is a key item that makes conceivable to artful range access in CR systems [11]. Be that as it may, range detecting can give blunder bring about the type of false caution and misdetection [13]. The allocated/used spectrum band and un-allotted bands/spectrum holes appear in Figure 8.1.

Cutting is a nonlinear process which causes two impacts: (i) out-of-band radiation [4], and (ii) in-band distortion of the ideal signal, which expands the bit error rate. Clipping is the low demanding system for decreasing the power by setting the transmitted signal as high. The filtering is the out-of-band transmitted can and frequently is smothered by separating, which leads top regrowth [14]. The clipping procedure alone in OFDM sign have a few impediments of about the exhibition of BER could be influenced adversely due to the in-band twisting brought about by the section.

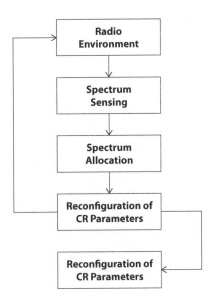

Figure 8.1 Cognitive radio cycle.

Additionally out-of-band radiation generally shows up with section system that could bother the adjoining channels. Be that as it may, we can utilize sifting activity to diminish the presence of the out-of-band radiation, yet the sign may surpass the most extreme degree of the section activity.

An artificial neural network (ANN) is a logical model that endeavors to reproduce the structure and functionalities of normal neural frameworks. Major structure square of each fake neural framework is a phony neuron, that is, a fundamental logical model (work). Such a model has three clear game plans of standards: expansion, summation, and inception. At the entry of the phony neuron, the data sources are weighted what suggests that every data worth is copied with individual weight. In the middle region of fake neuron is all out limit that wholes each and every weighted data and tendency. Bury associated gathering of hubs is named as systems. These hubs can be considered as computational units. These hubs get information sources and procedure them to acquire a yield [11]. On the off chance that the system considers to be as fake neurons, they are named as fake neural systems (ANN). ANNs join fake neurons so as to process data. The NNs considered here depend on the multilayer feed forward system, that is, with two layers and two neurons for every each layer with triangular actuation work. Triangular premise move capacity is a neural exchange work that computes a layer yield from its net sources of info. Here, NNs are utilized at both the collector and transmitter. Since neural systems are versatile, there is no requirement for from the earlier numerical model for info yield change. Consequently, neural systems are not modified but rather prepared.

The basic goal of the endeavor is to decrease the PAPR and lessening the computational multifaceted plan of the offset quadrature amplitude modulation based orthogonal frequency-division multiplexing (OQAM-OFDM) structure. The significant work is to build up an ideal ability since it can accomplish the required PAPR decay with least in-band reshaping and far less emphasis. For lessening the peak-to-average power ratio, consider the section hullabaloo instead of cutting sign close by the confining strategy and artificial neural network for diminishing the oddity in the PAPR decay [7]. The need of OQAM-OFDM structure is utilized to improve the phantom proficiency and information transmission rate. Regardless, an imperative disadvantage of OQAM-OFDM sign is their high PAPR. Since the transmitter's power amplifiers (PAs) are top power constrained, the colossal PAPR prompts in-band contorting and out-of-band radiation. Huge peak-to-average power (PAP) degree which ruins the sign if the transmitter contains nonlinear parts, for example, PAs.

8.5 Related Works

OFDM is generally utilized in present-day remote correspondence frameworks in light of its high range productivity and low powerlessness to multiway impacts Luo. Z. Q and Wang. Y. C (2011) [18]. The iterative clipping and filtering (ICF) technique is perhaps the most straightforward to approach for PAPR decrease in the extremely effective OFDM sign, and this reason out of band ghostly development and in band bending causing bit error rate (BER) corruption. The curved optimization is worldwide ideal answer for PAPR decrease and can be registered proficiently. The exemplary ICF is altered by incorporating rectangular window channel with curved streamlining which diminishes the emphasis check to accomplish decreased PAPR level which is of a sharp drop in complementary cumulative distribution Function (CCDF) produce a littler image of twisting and lower out of band radiation. Be that as it may, the present optimized iterative clipping with filtering (OICF) uses error vector magnitude (EVM). At the point when compared with exemplary ICF the proposed EVM strategy presents the inside point technique for second-order cone program (SOCP) which will diminish the computational intricacy which happens at high rate in the greater part of the applications. OICF has less contortion, high

PAPR reduction, and better out of band radiation with usage in OFDM signal [5].

Neural networks (NN) have been one of the extraordinary frameworks in lessening the PAPR as a result of their incredible hypothesis properties with versatile showing and learning limits. Another method that uses NNs arranged on the dynamic star gathering development (ACE) sign to diminish the PAPR of OFDM signals Insoo Sohn (2014) [19]. One of the major drawbacks of orthogonal frequency division multiplexing (OFDM) is the gigantic instabilities of its ability envelope. In this paper, a novel and successful arrangement subject to multi-layer perceptron (MLP) neural networks (NN) is proposed. The NN joins the active constellation expansion (ACE) framework which can reduce envelope fluctuations Younes Jabrane, Victor P. Gil Jimenez et al. (2010) [20]. This is practiced with a lot of lower capriciousness, snappier intermixing, and better execution [7].

OQAM-OFDM is utilized in current remote computerized correspondence applications to improve ghostly productivity with the goal that a cyclic prefix (CP) is not required and expands information transmission rate Chen Ye, Chunxing Ni et al. (2014) [21]. The OQAM-OFDM framework has its own lower side projections which are absent in an OFDM framework. The quadrature amplitude modulation based orthogonal frequency division multiplexing (QAM-OFDM) framework can remunerate the channel mutilations and adapt to lingering timing balances with appropriate equalizer. In the segmental partial transmit sequence (S-PTS) conspire, the stage revolution activity is utilized for the covered flag in a few back-to-back information squares, be that as it may, the stage pivot activity is utilized for each transmit signal autonomously in the complementary partial transmit sequence.

A C-PTS plan isolates the covered OQAM-OFDM signals into various portions. In each fragment, some disjoint subsquares are apportioned; at that point, they are increased with various stage turn factors. S-PTS includes the motivation reaction channel and the square root raise cosine (SRSC) and furthermore the OQAM-OFDM sign made out of various information obstructs, rather than the PAP of every datum square freely. S-PTS furnishes high PAPR reduction with lower unpredictability, and the information rate can be diminished further [6].

MCM have pulled in a great deal of consideration running from wire line to remote interchanges because of its ability to proficiently adapt to recurrence particular channels Bingham. J (1990) [5]. Much of the consideration in the present writing stresses on the utilization of regular OFDM. In an improved partial transmit sequence (PTS) plot is utilized by utilizing multi-block joint optimization (MBJO) for the

PAPR decrease of filter bank multicarrier based (FBMC-OQAM) signals Lacaille. N, Siclet. C and *et al.* (2002) [22] called as MBJO-PTS conspire. In PTS conspire, one information square is separated into a few subsquares and each subsquare is duplicated by a stage turn factor for the subsquare Jiang T *et al.* (2014) [23]. The PTS plan looks over all blends of permitted stage variables to bring down the PAPR. Not at all like existing PAPR decrease plans of freely advancing the information hinders, the MBJO-based plan misuses the covering structure of the FBMC-OQAM sign and together streamlines numerous information squares. Additionally, create two calculations for the advancement issue in the MBJO-PTS conspire, including a dynamic programming (DP) calculation to ensure the ideal arrangement and keep away from comprehensive hunt. Hypothetical examination and reproductions demonstrate that the proposed MBJO-PTS plan could give a noteworthy PAPR decrease in the FBMC-OQAM framework Arndt. D. M *et al.* (2011) [24], by abusing the covering structure of the FBMC-OQAM signal. Improved PTS has inconvenience of less improvement in BER and high multifaceted nature with less clamor and PAPR decrease [9].

High PAPR of the transmitted sign is a noteworthy disadvantage of OFDM Han. S. H. *et al.* (2004) [11]. Albeit numerous PAPR decrease methods for OFDM have been proposed, strategies for lessening the PAPR of an OFDM signal with channel coding are yet to be created. This procedure, an adjusted selected mapping (SLM) technique, is utilized for the PAPR decrease of coded OFDM signal. The real preferred position of the changed SLM procedure is that there is no information rate misfortune from the transmission of the side data. Here, a stage grouping plan strategy is utilized for coded OFDM signal, a technique to insert the stage arrangement on the check images of the coded OFDM information square, and a strategy to dependably recuperate the stage succession at the recipient. It is demonstrated that it can accomplish both PAPR decreases from the SLM strategy just as blunder execution improvement from the channel coding with no misfortune in information rate from the transmission of side data. Additionally in this work, inexact articulation for the PAPR measurement of an OFDM signal in the wake of applying changed SLM system is inferred. It is demonstrated that the inexact articulation coordinates very well with the recreation results. SLM system has an advantage of high transmission rate and less clamor with an issue [6].

SLM is one of the most encouraging among every one of these strategies since it is easy to execute, i.e., at any rate from a reasonable perspective, presents no bending in the transmitted sign, and can accomplish huge PAPR decrease Goff S. Y. L *et al.* (2008) [8]. The essential thought in SLM comprises of creating a lot of sign, every one of them speaking to similar information square, and after that transmitting the one with the most minimal PAPR. The execution of SLM prompts an abatement in information rate on the grounds that the chose sign list, called side data, should likewise be transmitted to consider the recuperation of the first information hinder at the beneficiary side. The inevitable loss of the side data during transmission fundamentally [2] debases the blunder execution of the framework since the entire information square is lost for this situation. This is the reason it is, practically speaking, essential to ensure the side data utilizing a ground-breaking channel code, which makes the framework progressively unpredictable, builds the transmission deferral, and further decreases the information rate. This procedure delivers to the issue by depicting a novel SLM strategy is utilized without side data and examining its presentation regarding PAPR decrease, likelihood of mistaken side data discovery, just as bit error rate (BER) at the recipient yield. In the SLM technique, each side data record is related with a specific arrangement of areas inside the information hinder at which the regulation images have been broadened. In the beneficiary, a side data identification square endeavors to decide the areas of the all-encompassing images. Novel SLM strategy has an advantage of improved BER and less transmission delay with less execution issue [15].

OFDM has been thoroughly perceived as the most captivating structure for high information rate remote correspondences because of its essential execution, wellbeing against rehash explicit darkening channels, and relative ease of utilizing particular receiving wire transmission frameworks Au. E. K. S, Gao et al. (2011) [2]. Beginning late, single-carrier frequency division multiple access (SC-FDMA) has been comfortable all together with beat such a weakness by getting key highlights of the single-transporter transmission in an OFDM framework, and the discrete Fourier transform (DFT)-spread OFDM (DFTS-OFDM) confirmation of such a structure has been proposed for uplink correspondence applications Tsai. Y et al. (2008) [25]. Gone for SC-FDMA applications, a CP variety of the OQAM-OFDM is first proposed in this work. By then apply CP-OQAMOFDM to SC-FDMA transmission in rehash express clouding channels. Sign model and joint least minimum mean square error (LMMSE) evening out utilizing earlier data with low whim are made. Separated and the current DFTS-OFDM based SC-FDMA, the proposed SC-FDMA can on an extremely fundamental level decline envelope fluctuation (EF) of the transmitted sign while keeping up the data move limit capacity. The inalienable structure of

CP-OQAM-OFDM empowers low-multifaceted nature joint evening out in the recurrent domain to battle both the different section square and the ISI. The joint WLMMSE night out utilizing earlier data ensures flawless minimum mean square error (MMSE) execution and supports turbo recipient for improved BER execution. CP-OQAM-OFDM has an issue of high multifaceted nature and progressively expensive with a preferred position of BER improvement and decline in PAPR [15].

OFDM has been as of late observed rising notoriety in remote applications. Huge PAPR could cause poor power proficiency or genuine execution corruption to transmit control intensifier Gu. J, Huang. X *et al.* (2004) [10]. So as to lessen PAPR of OFDM signals, two gatherings of strategies have been proposed. One gathering expects to decrease the event of enormous flag before multicarrier tweak. The truth of the matter is that if the freedom among sign on various subchannels is obliterated by coding or particular mapping, or the quantity of autonomous subchannels is diminished by incomplete transmitting, PAPR would be decreased. In these strategies, be that as it may, either excess or computational multifaceted nature is generally high, which may bring about enormous deferral or overhead in reasonable frameworks. In this system, a general companding change strategy Ai. B, Gee *et al.* (2012) [1] is proposed to viably diminish PAPR of OFDM signals. By packing huge sign while improving little flag alongside considering their measurable qualities, this strategy can accomplish critical decrease in PAPR with low execution multifaceted nature. In particular, present the plan criteria of the change, which empower powerful tradeoff between decrease in PAPR and BER execution of the OFDM framework. Companding change technique gives interference is high and less information rate with an advantage of improve the exhibition and less execution unpredictability [13].

OFDM is an exceptionally encouraging procedure for fast information transmission in remote correspondence frameworks Jiang T *et al.* (2008) [15]. Nonetheless, as the consequence of superposition of numerous individual subcarriers, OFDM sign have a PAPR. At the point when enormous pinnacles come to the transmit speaker immersion district, signal twisting happens, prompting the BER execution debasement at the recipient. This procedure has five novel plans dependent on avaricious calculation are proposed to lessen the PAPR in OFDM frameworks. For each proposed plan, a basic change is performed on the halfway transmit groupings in an iterative design to bring down the PAPR. PC reenactments results demonstrate that all the proposed plans can accomplish PAPR decreases, yet the exhibitions of the PAPR decrease are extraordinary [5].

OFDM has gotten insistence for applications in multipath darkening channels and is a promising framework for wideband correspondence structures Beaulieu N. C *et al.* (2009) [3]. The non-relentless envelope property of OFDM sign is a striking suppression that prompts non-linear bowing in reasonable executions. Different methods have been proposed to lessen the PAPR of OFDM signals. A specific time-zone separating system for PAPR decrease is proposed. This course of action shows a period zone channel bank Lacaille. N *et al.* (2002) [22] to get distinctive mixed applicant signals with various PAPRs and picks the one with the base PAPR for transmission. By utilizing scrambling in the time an area rather than in the recurrent space, this game plan does not require extra IFFTs. Moreover, the power sees the impacts of the time-space channels as a touch of the multipath clouding channel reaction and can recuperate the information utilizing just standard channel estimation and demodulation methodologies for multipath darkening channels. It is noteworthy that by ideals of OFDM frameworks with pilot pictures embedded in the recurrent space, the recipient structure can be kept unaltered. Express time-area separating structure causes less information rate [6].

The PAPR frameworks have been proposed in the composition to diminish the PAPR. These methodologies can generally be arranged into hail scrambling frameworks and sign mutilation strategies. Sign scrambling techniques are by and large minor departure from how to scramble the codes to reduce the PAPR Lacaille. N *et al.* (2002) [22]. Coding methodologies can be utilized for sign scrambling. Golay reciprocal groupings, Shapiro-Rudin movements, M game-plans, and Barker codes can be utilized feasibly to decrease the PAPR. Regardless with the improvement in the measure of bearers the overhead connected with concentrated pursue of the best code would increment exponentially. Logically commonsense blueprints of the sign scrambling methods are square coding, Selective level mapping (SLM) and partial transmit sequences (PTS). Sign scrambling systems with side information reduces the amazing throughput since they present reiteration. The sign bending strategies present both in-band and out-of-band impedance and eccentrics to the structure. The sign bending methods lessen high zeniths honestly by curving the sign before increase. Cutting the OFDM signal before increase is a direct procedure to oblige PAPR. At any rate removing may cause immense out-of-band (OOB) and in-band impedance, which brings about the structure execution corruption. Continuously practical courses of action are peak windowing, top clearing out, peak control camouflage, weighted multicarrier transmission, companding, etc. Basic need of rational PAPR decline frameworks fuse the likeness with the gathering of existing equalization plans, high apparition capability, and low multifaceted nature. No specific PAPR decline procedure is the best response for all multicarrier transmission. Or on the other hand possibly the PAPR decline technique should be purposely picked by various system necessities [6].

Evening out quadrature amplitude modulation based orthogonal frequency-division multiplexing (OQAM-OFDM) framework is made to improve the crazy ampleness and enlargement information transmission rate. Like OFDM frameworks, one of the significant disadvantages in OQAM-OFDM structures is the high peak-to-average power ratio (PAPR). Several plans have been proposed unequivocally for the PAPR decrease in OQAM-OFDM structures. An overlapped SLM (O-SLM) conspire has been proposed to diminish the PAPR of OQAM-OFDM signals. For the O-SLM framework, the present information square and the past information squares are as one considered to pick the ideal stage turn game-plan. Additionally, a sliding window tone reservation (SW-TR) system has been proposed. For the SW-TR plot, the peak lessening tones of a couple back-to-back information squares are utilized to drop the summit power of the OQAM-OFDM signal inside a window.

In this manner, in the present strategy, a novel segmental PTS plot, named as S-PTS plan, is used for straightforwardness, to diminish the PAPR in OQAM-OFDM structures. For the S-PTS plot, the stage upset action is used for the shrouded banner in a couple consecutive data squares. The block diagram of TX NN and RX NN using ACE schemes is shown in Figure 8.2.

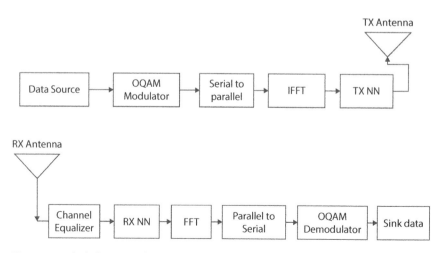

Figure 8.2 Block diagram of TX NN and RX NN using ACE schemes.

8.6   Neural Network System Model

Top-to-average power proportion (PAPR) decrease is one of the key parts in symmetrical recurrence division multiplexing (OFDM) frameworks. Among different PAPR decrease procedures, fake neural system (NN) has been one of the ground-breaking methods in lessening the PAPR because of its great speculation properties with adaptable demonstrating and learning abilities. Where the customary ACE plan and time-frequency neural network (TFNN) plan and after that contrasts their presentation and proposed procedure [2].

In ACE plan, both time space and recurrence area sign handling is required. The primary thought behind dynamic group of stars augmentation is to move the external heavenly body focuses towards outside of unique star grouping producing an elective portrayal of a similar image. Subsequently, PAPR can be diminished with low BER. Here, time space sign cut-out and recurrence area group of stars point expansion are considered. Sign section is accomplished for decreasing sign tops with extents higher than the objective pinnacle level. Henceforth the fundamental disadvantage of ACE plan is the huge number of IDFT and DFT activities. Dynamic heavenly body augmentation in QPSK and 16QAM another plan that exists for PAPR decrease is the time recurrence neural system. TFNN utilizes complex recurrence space neural system modules for PAPR decrease. Consequently contrasting and ACE plan, TFNN conspire additionally accomplishes a proportionate power decrease. While considering higher request adjustment blurring channels, TFNN procedure demonstrates a poor bit-error rate (BER) execution. The plan additionally requires countless mind boggling and genuine computational tasks. Consequently, we need to propose another technique that can decrease top to-average-control proportion and accomplishes a superior BER simultaneously with lower unpredictability. In this framework propose another strategy that utilizations NNs prepared on the active constellation extension (ACE) sign to decrease the PAPR of OFDM signals. The proposed arrangement has a lot of lower multifaceted nature and better BER execution diverged from other ACE-based systems with little PAPR decline execution adversity [13].

In the ACE game plan, the PAPR is lessened through L number of iterative dealing with between the time and rehash an area. The sign pinnacles are diminished by section the sign with sizes beating a specific objective peak level in time space and BER corruption is kept up an essential decent ways from in rehash an area by persuading the progression of the magnificent body exhibits due cut out to just exemplary advancement headings

[17]. In the TFNN plot, the PAPR is lessened by the utilization of two phase neural system structuring dependent on time domain neural network (TNN) for time space preparing and frequency domain neural network (FNN) for rehash locale dealing with. Both TNN and FNN depend upon the multilayer feed forward system with two layers and two neurons for each layer with triangular incitation work. The TFNN is prepared utilizing the ACE sign as the ideal sign with the Levenberg-Marquardt calculation as the learning estimation.

8.7   Complexity Examination

The computational bizarreness of the ACE, the TFNN, and the proposed plans is considered in Table 8.1. The table displays the measure of complex duplications and expands by virtue of the utilization of (I) FFT modules, confirmed extensions and increments because of the utilization of NN modules, and the attainable region check assignments. It is ordinary that the measure of complex duplications and augmentations expected of the N point (I) FFT modules are (N/2) log2(N) and N log2(N), freely. Also, the NN modules subject to the multilayer feed-forward system with two layers and two neurons for each layer require 8N genuine developments and 6N genuine enlargements. In the ACE game plan, L iterative preparing of N point IFFT estimation is required for time space cutting and extra L iterative treatment of N point FFT calculation is required for rehash locale social event of stars increment. Likewise, LN possible area check tasks are required to complete worthy expansion constrainment. In the TFNN plot, one N point IFFT figuring is required for TNN managing and one N point FFT tally is

Table 8.1 Comparison table for BER and PAPR of original and proposed methods.

BER		PAPR	
Original	Proposed	Original	Proposed
0.4887	0.2887	6.7318	4.2038
0.4830	0.2830	6.8318	4.3038
0.4687	0.2687	6.9318	4.4038
0.4216	0.2216	–	–
0.3749	0.1749	–	–

required for FNN preparing. In like manner, 2 NN tallies are required for the authentic and eccentric TNN dealing with and 8 NN figurings are required for the veritable and nonexistent FNN arranging. Additionally, N reachable area check practices are required to realize praiseworthy advancement fundamental. With respect to the proposed game plan, just a lone N point IFFT calculation is required for TXNN preparing. What is more, 2 NN estimations are required for the genuine and offbeat TXNN preparing and extra 2 NN tallies are required for the valid and nonexistent RXNN dealing with. In any case, no possible zone check development is required in the proposed course of action. From Table 8.1, it may be seen that the proposed course of action lessens the computational multifaceted nature stood apart from different structures like the measure of complex growths and expands, genuine duplications and increases, and the check practices [7].

8.8   PAPR and BER Examination

The CCDF of the PAPR was utilized to assess the PAPR decrease execution of the proposed game plan veered from different plans. It was seen that the ACE course of action, TFNN plot, and the proposed NN plan can essentially lessen the PAPR veered from the first OFDM signal for both QPSK and 16-QAM social occasions of stars. For a 10−3 CCDF, ACE plan accomplishes 3.75 dB PAPR decrease for 16-QAM [16]. Concerning the TFNN and the proposed NN plans, with much lower fancy separated from the ACE scheme, 3dB PAPR decreasing is searched for a 10−3 CCDF. The TFNN plan offers better PAPR decrease execution stood apart from the proposed NN create for low catch level PAPR0 values. This is considering the way that the TFNN utilizes extra eccentric recurrent zone NNs to improve PAPR decrease and BER execution. By the by, the proposed NN plan shows little execution difficulty, under 0.25 dB, with much lower number of NN modules showed up distinctively in connection to the TFNN plot. The BER introductions of the first OFDM framework, the ACE game plan, the TFNN plot, and the proposed NN conspire in the Rayleigh clouding channel with QPSK and 16-QAM, independently. The station is accepted to be semistatic recurrent express and perfect station estimation is considered. It may be seen from that the ACE and NN based frameworks accomplish BER improvement over the first OFDM signal considering the star gathering advancement, acknowledging broadened edge and lower botch rates. What is more, the TFNN and the proposed NN plans show better BER execution veered from the ACE course of action, showing mind boggling rehash an area arranging [7].

In the proposed plan, the FNN unit is expelled and an extra basic NN unit is utilized at the recipient side. Reduction of multifaceted nature is perceived by utilizing a solitary time an area NN unit for PAPR decrease and BER execution improvement is developed through the time space NN unit at the position. The proposed transmitter NN (TXNN) and the gatherer NN (RXNN) depend upon the multilayer feed-forward structure with two layers and two neurons for each layer with triangular incitation work.

8.9   Performance Evaluation

In this piece, the showcase of the current and the proposed structure is thought about. In the present structure, a novel S-PTS plan is proposed for the PAPR decrease. In the proposed framework, optimized iterative clipping with filtering (OICF) and Neural Networks (NNs) technique is utilized for the PAPR-decrease in the OQAM-OFDM Signals. This undertaking entertainment and execution evaluation are endeavored and avowed by utilizing the MATLAB software.

8.10   Results and Discussions

OFDM is a phenomenal example of multicarrier transmission, where a lone data stream is transmitted over different lower rate subcarriers. It justifies referencing here that OFDM can be seen as either a guideline framework or a multiplexing strategy. One of the essential inspirations to use OFDM is to grow the quality against repeat explicit obscuring or narrowband block. In a lone transporter system, a singular haze or interferer can make the entire association miss the mark, yet in a multicarrier structure, only somewhat level of the subcarriers will be affected. Misstep amendment coding would then have the option to be used to address the couple of erroneous subcarriers [5].

OFDM is a multicarrier transmission structure. It is seen as modification or multiplexing frameworks. OFDM sign has various amounts of solidly scattered sub-bearers. By non-linearity, it causes impedance between the bearers as a sort of between modification contorting and conveys balance of the transmission. It will cause unwanted sign insinuate as impedance. This mutilation causes progressively raised measure of data goofs. The information signal OFDM appears in Figure 8.3.

FFT is only founded on deterioration and breaking the changes and joining them for getting the general change. Where it lessens calculation

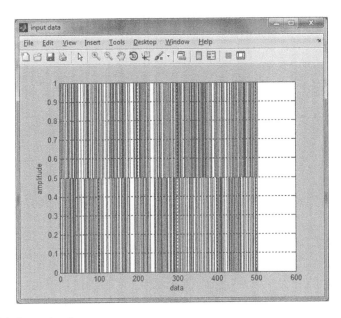

Figure 8.3 Input signal.

time requires to finishing the DFT and improves the presentation factor by at least 100 than it. It for the most part utilized in computerized unearthly examination and autocorrelation capacities. The PAPR reduction over different sampling rates is shown in Figure 8.4.

Since it can accomplish the required PAPR decay with least in-band twisting and far less emphases. Rehash space segregating is point by point as a movement issue and the streamlining parameters are the channel coefficients. By utilizing the ideal coefficients to quantify the cut sign, one can compel the sign reshaping under the targets of PAPR decrease and out-of-band radiation. The connection table for BER and PAPR of original and proposed method is shown as Table 8.1. The ANN contains different non-straight computational parts working in parallel and sifted through in models taking after those of trademark neurons. The neurons are interconnected into systems by techniques for weighted affiliations, which are normally adjusted through a learning approach to get a specific execution. Neurons are collected into lays relying on their level of association with the outside world. The neurons are usually depicted by an inner limit and by the sort of their presentation work. The neurons in the information layer are upheld with information. Every neuron totals the entirety of the wellsprings of information and moves the data, as shown by an authorization work, to all of the parts in the accompanying layer.

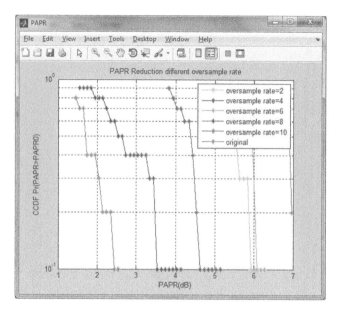

Figure 8.4 PAPR reduction over different sampling rates.

The average probability of picture botch is known as bit error rate (BER) where the ordinary probability of picture goof is the probability that the changed picture at the recipient yield contrasts from the transmitted twofold picture. BER comparison of OICF and ANN techniques appears in Figure 8.5 and Figure 8.6. The procedure of consistently inspecting a sign in the time area brings about an intermittent range in the recurrence space with period equivalent to examining rate. Where the BER diminishes the impedance will be diminished. In like manner the BER diminishes the peak-to-average power ratio (PAPR) additionally diminishes.

PAPR is just subjectively sinusoidal leads causes during transmission of the OFDM signal. Where the extent between most outrageous force of pass-band sign and mean power of pass-band signal. PAPR is a truly prominent extent of the envelope changes of a sign. Proximity of huge number of self-rulingly adjusted sub-bearers in an OFDM structure the apex estimation of the system can be high when stood out from the typical of the whole system. This extent of the peak to average power worth is named as peak-to-average power ratio. Clear development of N indication of same stage conveys a zenith which is N times the typical sign. The genuine weights of a high PAPR are extended multifaceted design in the easy to mechanized and progressed to basic converter and reduction is adequacy of RF speakers.

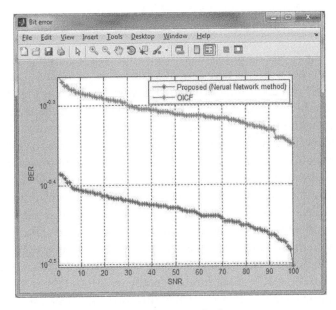

Figure 8.5 BER comparison of OICF and ANN methods.

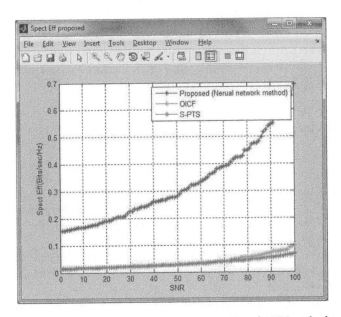

Figure 8.6 Spectral efficiency comparison for S-PTS, OICF, and ANN methods.

8.11 Conclusion

The first OICF calculation is an elite cut-out and separating strategy. Be that as it may, it needs to take care of a curved improvement issue related with channel, which prompts high intricacy which prompts high multifaceted design. In this work, the streamlining issue has been changed similarly to an issue with the PAPR decline vector as the headway parameter, which can be generally clarified by using some clear undertakings. Considering this examination, an improved OICF count with a lot of lower unpredictability has been proposed. The entertainment results show that the first and improved computations have almost a comparative introduction with respect to PAPR lessening, BER and out-of-band radiation. At that point, the reenactment results similarly show the transcendence of the estimation when differentiated and the other cut-out and isolating methodology. It ought to be noticed that the PAPR worth is diminished from 6.7000 dB in S-PTS to 6 dB in OICF, albeit fundamentally researched the instance of the oversampling factor L = 2, 4, 6 and 8 in this work. The decrease of the computational multifaceted nature of the proposed strategy can be anticipated and prepared utilizing neural networks (NN) for higher PAPR decrease can be executed. Fake neural network (NN) has been an incredible method where diminishing the PAPR because of its great speculation properties with adaptable displaying and learning abilities. Another technique that utilizations NNs prepared on the active constellation extension (ACE) sign to diminish the PAPR of OFDM signals. At long last, it ought to be noticed that the PAPR worth is diminished from 6 dB in OICF to 4.2038 dB in NN, albeit the instance of the testing rate 2, 4, 6, 8 and 10 was primarily examined in this work.

References

1. Ai, B., Gee, J.H., Wang, Y., Wang, L.H., An efficient nonlinear companding transform for reducing PAPR of OFDM signals. *IEEE T. Broadcast.*, 58, 677–684, 2012.
2. Au, E.K.S., Gao, X., Wang, W., Xia, X.G., You, X., Cyclic prefixed OQAM-OFDM and its application to single-carrier FDMA, *IEEE T. Comm.*, 59, 5, 1467–1480, 2011.
3. Beaulieu, N.C., Du., Z., Zhu., J., Selective time-domain filtering for reduced-complexity PAPR reduction in OFDM. *IEEE T Wirel Commun*, 58, 1170–1176, 2009.
4. Udayakumar, E. and Vetrivelan, P., PAPR Reduction for OQAM/OFDM Signals using Optimized Iterative Clipping and Filtering Technique.

Proceedings of IEEE International Conference on Soft-Computing and Network Security (ICSNS '15), SNS College of Technology, Coimbatore, 2015.

5. Bingham, J., Multicarrier modulation for data transmission: an idea whose time has come. *IEEE Commun. Mag.*, 28, 5–14, 1990. May.

6. Santhi, S, SoS Emergency Ad-Hoc Wireless Network, in: *Computational Intelligence and Sustainable Systems (CISS)*, EAI/Springer Innovations in Communications and Computing, pp. 227–234, 2019.

7. Farhang Boroujeny, B. and Kempter, R., Multicarrier communication techniques for spectrum sensing and communication in cognitive radios. *IEEE Commun.*, 46, 80–85, 2008.

8. Goff, S.Y.L., Khoo, B.K., Sharif, B.S., Tsimenidis, C., A novel selected mapping technique for PAPR reduction in OFDM systems. *IEEE T Commun*, 56, 1775–1779, 2008.

9. Udayakumar, E. and Vetrivelan, P., PAPR Reduction for OQAM/OFDM Signals by using Neural Networks. *Int. J. Appl. Eng. Res. Research India Publications*, 30292–30297, 2015.

10. Gu, J., Huang, X., Letaief, K.B., Lu, J., Companding transform for reduction in Peak-To-Average Power Ratio of OFDM signals. *IEEE T Wirel Commun.*, 3, 2030–2039, 2004.

11. Han, S.H. and Lee, J.H., Modified selected mapping technique for PAPR reduction of coded OFDM signal. *IEEE T Broadcast*, 50, 335–341, 2004.

12. Ghassemi, A. and Gulliver, T.A., PAPR reduction in OFDM based cognitive radio with blockwise-subcarrier activation, in: *2012 IEEE International Conference on Communications (ICC)*, Ottawa, ON, pp. 5598–5602, 2012.

13. Udayakumar, E. and Krishnaveni, V., A Review on Interference Management in Millimeter-Wave MIMO Systems for future 5G Networks. *Innovations in Electrical and Electronics Engineering, Lecture Notes in Electrical Engineering (LNEE) series*, Springer Nature, vol. 626, Issue 1, pp. 715-721, 2020 March.

14. Udayakumar, E. and Krishnaveni, V., Analysis of various Interference in Millimeter-Wave Communication Systems: A Survey. *2019 10th International Conference on Computing, Communication and Networking Technologies (ICCCNT)*, Kanpur, India, pp. 1–5, 2019.

15. Jiang, T. and Wu, Y., An overview: Peak-To-Average Power Ratio reduction techniques for OFDM signals. *IEEE T Broadcast*, 54, 2, 257–268, 2008.

16. Udayakumar, E., Balamurugan, S., Vetrivelan, P., A Neural Network-Based Automatic Crop Monitoring Robot for Agriculture. in: *The IoT and the Next Revolutions Automating the World*, IGI Global Publisher, pp. 203–212, 2019.

17. Sivaganesan, S. *et al.*, An Event based Neural Network Architecture with Content Addressable Memory. *Int. J. Embed Real-Time Commun. Syst. IGI Global*, 11, 1, 23–40, 2020.

18. Luo, Z.Q. and Wang, Y.C., Optimized Iterative Clipping with Filtering for PAPR Reduction of OFDM Signals, *IEEE T. Comm.*, 59, 1, pp. 33–37, 2011.

19. Insoo, S., A Low Complexity PAPR Reduction Scheme for OFDM Systems via Neural Networks, *IEEE Commun. Lett.*, vol. 18, 2, 225–228, 2014.

20. Gil Jimenez, V.P., Armada, A.G., Ait Es Said, B., Ait Ouahman, A., Reduction of Power Envelope Fluctuations in OFDM Signals by using Neural Networks. *IEEE Comm. Lett.*, 14, 7, 2010.

21. Ye, C., Ni, C., Qi, Q., Jiang, T., Li, Z., PAPR Reduction of OQAM-OFDM Signals Using Segmental PTS Scheme With Low Complexity. *IEEE T Broadcast.*, 60, 1, pp. 141–147, 2014.

22. Lacaille, N., Siclet, C., Siohan, P., Analysis and design of OFDM - OQAM systems based on filterbank theory. *IEEE Trans. Signal Processing*, 50, 5, pp. 1170–1183, 2002.

23. Jiang, T., et.al., PAPR Reduction of OQAM-OFDM Signals Using Segmental PTS Scheme With Low Complexity. *IEEE T Broadcast.*, 60, 1, pp. 141–147, 2014.

24. Arndt, D.M. and Da Rocha, C.A.F., Performance comparison between OFDM and FBMC systems in digital TV transmission. *IEEE Latin-American Conference on Communication*, pp 1– 6, 2011.

25. Tsai, Y., Wang, X., Zhang, G., Polyphase codes for uplink OFDM-CDMA systems. *IEEE T. Comm.*, 56, 6, pp. 435–444, 2008.

9

A Threshold-Based Optimization Energy-Efficient Routing Technique in Heterogeneous Wireless Sensor Networks

Samayveer Singh

Department of Computer Science & Engineering, National Institute of Technology Jalandhar, Punjab, India

Abstract

In wireless sensor networks (WSNs), clustering plays the greatest role for persisting the lifespan of the networks and helps in stabilizing the vitality/energy consumption among the existing sensor nodes of the networks. In this paper, a threshold-based optimization energy-efficient direction-finding technique in heterogeneous WSNs is proposed. It considers weighted election probabilities of sensor nodes for electing the master node/cluster heads (CHs). This method also deliberates an approach for transmission of data among the nodes and clusters and data collection in intra- and inter-cluster communication. The performance of the proposed technique is estimated against that of existing protocols using given performance matrices as network lifetime, network stability period, number of CHs, total energy depletion, throughput, etc. The investigational outcomes demonstrate the lifespan of the network, and the throughputs of the suggested method are increased by 25.03%, 31.76%, and 48.91% and 25.38%, 46.02%, and 67.03% in respect of those of hetDEEC-4, EDDEEC-4, and DDEEC-4, respectively, for 100 J network energy in the case of level-4 heterogeneity, correspondingly.

Keywords: Energy efficiency, wireless sensor network, WSNs, clustering, network lifetime, cluster heads

Email: samayveersingh@gmail.com

Krishna Kant Singh, Akansha Singh, Korhan Cengiz and Dac-Nhuong Le (eds.) Machine Learning and Cognitive Computing for Mobile Communications and Wireless Networks, (203–224) © 2020 Scrivener Publishing LLC

9.1 Introduction

In earlier limited periods, significant development has been done in the arena of wireless sensor networks (WSNs) because of the improvement in the latest technology of sensors. WSNs having or consisting of different abilities link automatic sensing, computing, and communication, and these nodes are easily added into existing networks because of their self-organizing nature [1]. The characteristics of WSNs are self-organizing capability from various failures, constraints of node energies, ease of use, usage of homogeneity and heterogeneity nodes in a defined network, and absorption of various harsh environmental conditions. The sensors are positioned in the observing field for gathering data/information. These sensors collect information from the deployed field and forward the gathered information to other sensor nodes, and then the next node forwards that information to another nearer node. Then, at last, the collected information is communicated to the base station (BS). The BS is unswervingly or indirectly associated with the server with the help of the Internet [2].

Nowadays, WSNs are being deployed in numerous solicitation applications, for example, various fields in health care, water quality monitoring, landslide recognition, industrial and consumer applications, armed reconnaissance, natural disaster deterrence, building/bridge structural health, various types of data centers, forestry fire detection, and data classification. Generally, there are two possible methods to organize/deploy sensors in monitoring fields, namely, deterministic and non-deterministic. The sensors are deployed manually in the case of deterministic deployment, whereas in non-deterministic deployment, sensors are thrown using aircraft or deployed randomly [2].

Sensor networks/systems can be characterized into two comprehensive categories, namely, homogeneous and heterogeneous, depending upon the node's energy levels and nodes capabilities. Homogeneous networks consist of similar types of sensor nodes, meaning they have the same amount of preliminary vitality/energy, whereas energy is not the same in the situation of heterogeneous networks. The heterogeneous nodes are positioned in all the possible groups in the observing area. These groups are called levels or tiers. The above discussion is founded on the vitality of the sensors; thus, it is called energy heterogeneity. The energy heterogeneity is only possible when the nodes are heterogeneous in the nature. There are two more types of heterogeneity in heterogeneous WSNs, i.e., link and computational heterogeneity [3]. In link heterogeneity, sensors have different-different transmission bandwidth, whereas sensors have different-different computational resources such as the microprocessor in computational heterogeneity as an associate to the normal nodes.

Sensor nodes are restricted due to the limited dimensions, vitality, storing, and cost. Therefore, there is a dire need to design an energy-efficient network to overcome the limitations of sensor networks up to some extent. Clustering shows a vital role for efficient utilization of the limited size, power, storage, and cost of sensor devices. It also helps in efficiently gathering data from the monitoring field using the size of the cluster, the election of CHs, intra and inter-cluster announcement, and data aggregation. Thus, this work is an attempt to determine the problems and provides the solution of energy efficiency by proposing a threshold-based optimization energy-efficient routing technique in heterogeneous WSNs.

The leading influences of the projected work may be itemized as follows: In this work, an innovative methodology for electing the cluster head (CH) by weighted election probabilities of the deployed sensors in heterogeneous WSNs is proposed. This method is capable of selecting the highest energy node with the minimum distance from the base station in the suggested clustering process. It also uses a chain process for gathering information from the nodes inside the clusters and from the cluster heads outside of the cluster and forwards the gathered data to the BS. The proposed heterogeneous model can define four levels of heterogeneity. The various performance matrices are considered for evaluating the performance, which are given as network lifetime and network stability (first node dead), throughput, number of CHs, total energy consumption, etc.

The roadmap of the chapter is given as follows. Section 9.2 discusses the literature review. In Section 9.3, energy and radio models are discussed. In Section 9.4, the proposed model is discussed. Section 9.5 discusses the simulation result and their deliberations. Finally, Section 9.6 concludes the chapter.

9.2   Literature Review

In the last decade and so, there has been a proportion of research on clustering techniques which are established on the load dissemination among nodes to address the energy constraint issue of both homogeneous and heterogeneous networks. The first distributed clustering protocol, which is popularly known as "low-energy adaptive clustering hierarchy" (LEACH), works in two phases, specifically setup and steady-state phases [4]. In the setup phase, the sensor nodes are first grouped into bunches or clusters and then their master node/cluster heads (CHs) are identified. In the steady-state phase, the collected information is conveyed. The LEACH elects CHs arbitrarily using a probability function. To extend the work of LEACH, "power-efficient gathering in sensor information systems" (PEGASIS) forms chains using nodes in WSNs [5]. In the chains, the farthest node gathers data and guides the collected data to its nearer node. The nearer node then forwards the information to a nearer one, and the process continues until the base station receives the information. The PEGASIS protocol is not appropriate for huge-sized systems or networks.

To increase the longevity of the wireless sensor network, a "heterogeneous stable election protocol" (hetSEP) was introduced for 2-level heterogeneity and 3-level heterogeneity [3]. The hetSEP uses functions, namely, weighted election probability and the threshold for CH election and cluster member selection. However, hetSEP may increase overhead in the case of long-distance transmission. For two-level and multilevel energy heterogeneities, the distributed energy-efficient clustering (DEEC) protocol was proposed [6]. The cluster heads are elected using the ratio residual energy of each node and the average energy of the network. Nevertheless, the additional vitality of superior sensor nodes is not professionally consumed, as the vitality is randomly allocated, which leads to infeasibility issues. In [7], the CHs are assigned based on the remaining essentialness of sensors to heightening the lifespan of the WSN if there should be an occurrence of three-level heterogeneity. However, this system requires extra essentialness to remake the groups in each cycle. The convention may endure information misfortune issues in the event of correspondence issues of group heads with one another. To diminish the entomb bunch vitality, Maheswari et al. presented vitality productive two-level grouping convention dependent on the node's degree [8]. The convention utilizes multi-bounce correspondence, which thusly experiences a surprising burden at the sink. Istwal et al. presented the double group head directing convention for lessening the vitality utilization in WSNs [9]. In any case, convention expends a huge measure of vitality in the inter/bury bunch correspondence. In [10, 11], the energy/vitality, clustering of the sensor nodes is depend on the remaining energy of every sensor node, normal energy, node density, and distance between the sensor nodes and sink. These systems acquire high overhead because of the complex nature of the WSN for bury and intragroup correspondences. Su et al. presented a fluffy-rationale-based vitality effective bunching procedure [12]. The procedure utilizes uneven conveyance of the sensors and the vulnerability of the radio channel utilizing a fluffy rationale for bunch development. The strategy experiences the issue of uneven vitality utilization. Sodairi *et al.* presented a multi-bounce LEACH for drawing out the vitality lifetime of a WSN [13]. An arbitrary challenge-based vitality compelling group head political decision system was proposed by Narendran *et al.* which fundamentally uses improved obtrusive weed streamlining (EIWO) metaheuristic for the appointment of bunch heads [14]. Be that as it may, the irregular appointment of CHs builds the correspondence cost. To limit vitality exhaustion between sensors, Ke *et al.* presented a progressive bunch-based directing convention [15]. The convention utilizes arched capacity with a nonlinear programming issue to locate the ideal arrangement. A circulated vitality productive grouping plan for heterogeneous remote sensor systems is created by Elbhiri *et al.* [16]. The vitality of this system proficiently chooses CHs utilizing remaining vitality. Javaid *et al.* examined an improved DEEC conspire for heterogeneous WSNs [17]. This plan proficiently discovers group heads utilizing lingering vitality and political decision likelihood. In the following sections, the heterogeneous energy consumption models will be discussed.

9.3   System Model

In this segment, first deliberate the assumptions made for the projected network and then discuss network and radio energy dissipation models. The basic assumptions are given as follows:

- All the sensors are stationary and have unique ID, and deployed randomly in the monitoring area.
- Nodes can be homogeneous or heterogeneous, and their initial energies rely upon the level of heterogeneity.
- Sensors have symmetric connections, comparative capacities, and constrained computational supremacy, memory, and vitality.
- Base station (BS) is placed in the central of the monitoring filed and sensors and BS distance can be calculated using received signal strength.
- Sensors have self-organising capabilities.

There are three reference models considered in the proposed work, which are as follows: heterogeneous system, radio, and vitality models. The nitty-gritty depiction of the heterogeneous system, radio, and vitality models is given beneath.

9.3.1   Four-Level Heterogeneous Network Model

In this section, a 4-level heterogeneity model that can designate four levels of heterogeneity is discussed. First of all, an N number of sensors are arbitrarily deployed in the characterized observing zone. Fundamentally, sensors are heterogeneous in nature. The heterogeneous sensors have a diverse measure of energy/vitality levels. The heterogeneous nodes might be called level-1, level-2, ..., level-4 nodes. The energies of level-1, level-2, ..., level-4 nodes/hubs are indicated as E_0, E_1, ..., E_3, individually, which must fulfill the imbalance $E_0 < E_1 < \cdots < E_3$, and their numbers are meant as N_1, N_2, ..., N_4, separately, which must fulfill the disparity $N_1 > N_2 > \cdots > N_4$. The entire network energy can be calculated as follows:

$$E_T = \rho * N * E_0 + \rho^2 * N * E_1 + \rho^3 * N * E_2 + \cdots + \rho^4 * N * E_3 \quad (1)$$

where ρ is a system constraint.

The nodes' vitalities are associated as $E_i = E_0 + \theta_i$, $i = 1, 2, 3$. Where θ_1, θ_2, θ_3 are the parameters.

Putting $E_i = E_0 + \theta_i$ in (1), we get

$$E_T = N * (E_0 * (\rho + \rho^2 + \rho^3 + \rho^4) + (\rho^2 * \theta_1 + \rho^3 * \theta_2 + \rho^4 * \theta_3)) \quad (2)$$

Level-1 Heterogeneity

For $\theta_i = 0$, $i = 1,2,3$, the separated framework has just level-1 nodes/hubs; for example, all have similar vitality, and for this situation, the complete system vitality is given by

$$\mathrm{E}_{\text{level-1}} = E_0 * (\rho + \rho^2 + \rho^3 + \cdots + \rho^n)$$

The number of nodes/hubs in level-1 heterogeneity is given as

$$N_1 = N * (\rho + \rho^2 + \cdots + \rho^n) \text{ with condition } \rho + \rho^2 + \cdots + \rho^n = 1.$$

The level-1 heterogeneity consists of only single type of nodes means entire nodes consist ofidenticalquantity of energy. So, this network is also called the *homogeneous networks*.

Level-2 Heterogeneity

For $\theta_i = 0$, i=2,3, the system has level-1 and level-2 nodes, and for this situation, the complete system vitality is given by

$$E_{level-2} = E_0 * (\rho + \rho^2 + \rho^3 + \cdots + \rho^n) + \rho^2 * \theta_1$$

The quantities of level-1 and level-2 nodes, denoted by N_1 and N_2, correspondingly, are as follows:

$$\left. \begin{array}{l} N_1 = N*(\rho+\rho^2+\rho^3+\cdots+\rho^n) \\ N_2 = N*\rho^2*\theta_1 \end{array} \right\} \tag{3}$$

with conditions $(\rho + \rho^2 + \rho^3 + \cdots + \rho^n) * N = N_1$, $\rho^2 * \theta_1 = N - N_1$.

Level-3 Heterogeneity

For $\theta_i = 0$, i=3,4, the system has level-1, level-2, and level-3 nodes, and for this situation, the complete system vitality is given by

$$E_{tier-3} = E_0 * (\rho + \rho^2 + \rho^3 + \cdots + \rho^n) + \rho^2 * \theta_1 + \rho^3 * \theta_2$$

The quantities of level-1, level-2, and level-3 nodes, denoted by N_1, N_2 and N_3, correspondingly, are as follows:

$$\left. \begin{array}{l} N_1 = N*(\rho+\rho^2+\rho^3+\cdots+\rho^n) \\ N_2 = N*\rho^2*\theta_1 \\ N_3 = N*\rho^3*\theta_2, \end{array} \right\} \tag{4}$$

with conditions $(\rho + \rho^2 + \rho^3 + \cdots + \rho^n) * N = N_1$, $(\rho^2 * \theta_1 + \rho^3 * \theta_2) * N = N - N_1$.

Level-4 Heterogeneity

For $\theta_i = 0$, i=4, the system has level-1, level-2, level-3, and level-4 nodes, and for this situation, the complete system vitality is given by

$$E_{tier-3} = E_0 * (\rho + \rho^2 + \rho^3 + \cdots + \rho^n) + \rho^2 * \theta_1 + \rho^3 * \theta_2 + \rho^4 * \theta_3$$

The quantities of level-1, level-2, level-3, and level-4 nodes, denoted by N_1, N_2, N_3 and N_4, correspondingly, are as follows:

$$
\left.
\begin{aligned}
N_1 &= N * (\rho + \rho^2 + \rho^3 + \cdots + \rho^n) \\
N_2 &= N * \rho^2 * \theta_1 \\
N_3 &= N * \rho^3 * \theta_2 \\
N_4 &= N * \rho^4 * \theta_3
\end{aligned}
\right\}
\tag{5}
$$

with conditions $(\rho + \rho^2 + \rho^3 + \cdots + \rho^n) * N = N_1$, $(\rho^2 * \theta_1 + \rho^3 * \theta_2 + \rho^4 * \theta_3) * N = N - N_1$.

9.3.2   Energy Dissipation Radio Model

In this section, a radio dispersal vitality model is talked about. The vitality consumption for communicating L-bit data over the short (E_{TXS}) and long (E_{TXL}) separation d is assumed as follows [4]:

$$
E_{TXS} = L * \in_{elec} + L * \in_{fs} * d^2 \quad \text{if } d \le d_0
\tag{6}
$$

$$
E_{TXL} = L * \in_{elec} + L * \in_{mp} * d^4 \quad \text{if } d > d_0
\tag{7}
$$

where $\in_{elec}$, $\in_{fs}$, and $\in_{mp}$ are the vitality scattered and d_0 is the separation limit between a sensor and the BS as given below:

$$
d_0 = \sqrt{\frac{\in_{fs}}{\in_{mp}}}
\tag{8}
$$

The absolute vitality devoured by the transmitter in advanced coding and adjustment is characterized in the principal term of (7) and (8). The energies spent in getting (E_{Rx}) and in detecting (E_{Sx}) are yielded (10) and (11) as follows:

$$
E_{Rx} = L * \in_{elec}
\tag{9}
$$

$$
E_{Sx} = L * \in_{elec}
\tag{10}
$$

9.4 Proposed Work

In this section, a description of optimum cluster head election, chain-based information congregation and communication procedure for intra and inter-cluster announcement, and employed procedure of the proposed method is discussed.

9.4.1 Optimum Cluster Head Election of the Proposed Protocol

In this section, the selection of the cluster heads for the proposed method is discussed as follows. The heterogeneous distributed energy-efficient clustering (hetDEEC) protocol is considered for evaluating the performance of the suggested four-level network model, which is one of the important protocols [7]. Let us consider that the average number of CHs is $N * p_{opt}$ and a node becomes a CH after $r_j = 1/p_{opt}$ rounds, where p_{opt} and r_j are the optimal probability to become a CH of a node and the number of rounds, respectively. The network average vitality $\bar{E}(r)$ for round r is as follows:

$$\bar{E}(r) = \frac{1}{N} \sum_{j=1}^{N} E_j(r) \tag{11}$$

The average probability of a node to be CH is given as follows:

$$p_j = P_{opt} \left[1 - \frac{\bar{E}(r) - E_j(r)}{\bar{E}(r)} \right] = P_{opt} * \frac{E_j(r)}{\bar{E}(r)} \tag{12}$$

where $E_i(r)$ is residual energy and the total CHs are given as follows:

$$\sum_{j=1}^{N} p_i = \sum_{j=1}^{N} P_{opt} * \frac{E_j(r)}{\bar{E}(r)} = P_{opt} \sum_{j=1}^{N} \frac{E_j(r)}{\bar{E}(r)} = N * p_{opt} \tag{13}$$

$$r_j = \frac{1}{p_j} = \frac{\bar{E}(r)}{P_{opt} * E_j(r)} = r_{opt} * \frac{\bar{E}(r)}{E_j(r)} \tag{14}$$

In this scenario, a sensor node has more chance to become a CH if it has the highest residual energy among the sensors. Equation 2 defines the total vitality of the heterogeneous system as $N * ((\rho + \rho^2 + \rho^3 + \cdots + \rho^n) + \rho^2 * \theta_1 + \rho^3 * \theta_2 + \rho^4 * \theta_3)$. It chooses $N * p_{opt}$ nodes as the average number of CHs which help in minimizing the energy dissipation among the nodes. In this networks, every sensor becomes a cluster head after $1/p_{opt} * ((\rho + \rho^2 + \rho^3 + \cdots + \rho^n) + \rho^2 * \theta_1 + \rho^3 * \theta_2 + \rho^4 * \theta_3)$ rounds. It is also equal to $((\rho + \rho^2 + \rho^3 + \cdots + \rho^n) + \rho^2 * \theta_1 + \rho^3 * \theta_2 + \rho^4 * \theta_3) * N * p_{level-1}$, where $p_{level-1}$ is the probability of the level-1 sensor nodes. For differentiating the threshold value, incorporate the level of heterogeneity (as level-1, -2, -3, -4) in the threshold formula to become a CH after $N * p_{opt}$ rounds. In the case of level-1 heterogeneity, every sensor node becomes a CH once in every $((\rho + \rho^2 + \rho^3 + \cdots + \rho^n) + \rho^2 * \theta_1 + \rho^3 * \theta_2 + \rho^4 * \theta_3)/p_{opt}$ rounds. Similarly, each level-2 node becomes a CH $(1 + \alpha)$ times more than the level-1 node in every $((\rho + \rho^2 + \rho^3 + \cdots + \rho^n) + \rho^2 * \theta_1 + \rho^3 * \theta_2 + \rho^4 * \theta_3)/p_{opt}$ round, and each level-3 and level-4 node becomes a CH $(1 + \beta)$ and $(1 + \gamma)$ times more than the level-1 nodes in every $((\rho + \rho^2 + \rho^3 + \cdots + \rho^n) + \rho^2 * \theta_1 + \rho^3 * \theta_2 + \rho^4 * \theta_3)/p_{opt}$ and $((\rho + \rho^2 + \rho^3 + \cdots + \rho^n) + \rho^2 * \theta_1 + \rho^3 * \theta_2 + \rho^4 * \theta_3)/p_{opt}$ round, respectively.

The proposed approach gives weights for each type of heterogeneity to obtain optimal probability. By using (15), weighted probabilities are calculated. The weighted probabilities of the level-1, -2, -3, and -4 nodes for the proposed method, denoted by $p_{level-1}$, $p_{level-2}$, $p_{level-3}$, and $p_{level-3}$, respectively, are given by

$$p_{level-1} = \frac{P_{opt} * E_j(r)}{\left((\rho + \rho^2 + \rho^3 + \cdots + \rho^n) + \rho^2 * \theta_1 + \rho^3 * \theta_2 + \rho^4 \theta_3\right) * \overline{E}(r)}$$

$$(15)$$

$$p_{level-2} = \frac{P_{opt}(1 + \alpha) * E_j(r)}{\left((\rho + \rho^2 + \rho^3 + \cdots + \rho^n) + \rho^2 * \theta_1 + \rho^3 * \theta_2 + \rho^4 * \theta_3\right) * \overline{E}(r)}$$

$$(16)$$

$$p_{level-3} = \frac{P_{opt}(1 + \beta) * E_j(r)}{\left((\rho + \rho^2 + \rho^3 + \cdots + \rho^n) + \rho^2 * \theta_1 + \rho^3 * \theta_2 + \rho^4 * \theta_3\right) * \overline{E}(r)}$$

$$(17)$$

$$P_{level-4} = \frac{P_{opt}(1+\gamma)*E_j(r)}{\left((\rho+\rho^2+\rho^3+\cdots+\rho^n)+\rho^2*\theta_1+\rho^3*\theta_2+\rho^4*\theta_3\right)*\overline{E}(r)} \tag{18}$$

The choice of CH is based on the likelihood formula, which is specified as follows:

$$T(s) = \begin{cases} \dfrac{P_{opt}}{1-P_{opt}\cdot\left(r \bmod \dfrac{1}{P_{opt}}\right)} & \text{if } s \in G \\ \\ 0 & \text{Otherwise} \end{cases} \tag{19}$$

Where p_{opt} and G are the predetermined % of CHs and set of nodes that have not been CHs in the last $1/p_{opt}$ rounds.

Election of CH in each round can be calculated by putting the value of the $p_{level-1}$, $p_{level-2}$, $p_{level-3}$, and $p_{level-4}$ in (19). Thus, the thresholds $T(s_j)$ for level-1, level-2, level-3, and level-4 are given by

$$T(s_i) = \begin{cases} \dfrac{P_{nrm}}{1-P_{level-1}*\left(r \bmod \dfrac{1}{P_{level-1}}\right)} & \text{if } P_{level-1} \in G' \\ \\ \dfrac{P_{adv}}{1-P_{level-2}*\left(r \bmod \dfrac{1}{P_{level-2}}\right)} & \text{if } P_{level-2} \in G'' \\ \\ \dfrac{P_{sup}}{1-P_{level-3}*\left(r \bmod \dfrac{1}{P_{level-3}}\right)} & \text{if } P_{level-3} \in G''' \\ \\ \dfrac{P_{usup}}{1-P_{level-3}*\left(r \bmod \dfrac{1}{P_{level-3}}\right)} & \text{if } P_{level-4} \in G'''' \\ \\ 0 & \text{Otherwise} \end{cases} \tag{20}$$

where G′, G″, G‴, and G⁗ are conventional of level-1, -2, -3, and -4 nodes that have not become CHs within the last $1/p_{nrm}$, $1/p_{adv}$, $1/p_{sup}$ and $1/p_{usup}$ rounds, respectively.

9.4.2   Information Congregation and Communication Process Based on Chaining System for Intra and Inter-Cluster Communication

Stage 1. Compute the distance of each sensor from the CHs and distance among the other sensors in the cluster or distance amongst each CHs and the BS in the specified network.

Stage 2. Select the furthest sensor node from the cluster head (CH)/BS which will be the first sensor/ cluster head node of the intra/inter communication chaining process in the clusters/networks.

Stage 3. The farthest sensor/CH begins to pick the following sensor/ CH to develop the chain by considering the eager approach. This methodology considers the base far-off sensor/group head node as the following node from the farthest node. Correspondingly, the subsequent least far-off sensor/group head node is picked. This procedure proceeds until the following least far-off node/bunch head is the group head/systems.

Stage 4. After forming the first chain in the cluster/networks, if any sensor/ CH node is not connected with the respective cluster head/base station then construction of a new chain will start by consider the same process as defined in Step 3 in the cluster/networks distinctly.

Stage 5. When the energy of a sensor/cluster head become zero means the sensor/cluster headexpires in the chain and the chain is again reassembled to avoid the dead node/cluster head.

Stage 6. Repeat Step 1 to Step 5 for all the possible clusters.

9.4.3   The Complete Working Process of the Proposed Method

In this section, the total portrayal working procedure of an upgrade vitality effective steering method in heterogeneous WSNs is talked about, which aids in prolonging the network/system lifespan. The proposed method is worked into two stages: setup/arrangement and steady/unfaltering state stages.

Setup Phase

In the arrangement stage, at first, a remote system is framed, and afterward, the method for appointment of CH node is prepared. The bit-by-bit arrangement is examined as follows.

Stage 1. First of all, an N number of sensors are arbitrarily deployed in the characterized observing zone. Fundamentally, sensors are heterogeneous in nature. The heterogeneous nodes have the diverse measure of energy/vitality levels. The heterogeneous nodes might be called as level-1, level-2, ..., level-4 nodes. The energies of level-1, level-2, ..., level-4 nodes/hubs are indicated as $E_0, E_1, ..., E_3$ individually, which must fulfill the imbalance $E_0 < E_1 < \cdots < E_3$, and their numbers are meant as $N_1, N_2, ..., N_4$ separately, which must fulfill the disparity $N_1 > N_2 > \cdots > N_4$. A solitary BS is conveyed in the observing zone which gathers the information from each group head.

Stage 2. After network formation, procedure for election of CHs discussed in section 9.4.1

Steady-State Phase

After CH determination, the genuine information accumulation and communications to the CHs and the BS happen in the steady/consistent state stage. This procedure is talked about in the accompanying advances.

Stage 1. Subsequently in the CHs election, each CH starts the process of chain construction in the respective cluster for intra-cluster communications. The chain construction is constructed on the distance among the nodes and the CH which is calculated by the RSSI.

Stage 2. After forming the chain within the cluster intra-cluster communication starts. In the intra cluster announcement farthest node join itself as the first node in the chain and starts to collect the information and forwards it to the nearest node.

Stage 3. The selection of the nearest node from the farthest sensor node is grounded on the minimum distant node in the chain and once a node is already in the chain will not be consider again. The CHsreceived the data from the respective sensors in each cluster after chain construction process.

Stage 4. After intra cluster communication data gathering process from each cluster, the inter-cluster communication takes place. In this process, all cluster heads adopted both single hop and multi-hop communication and direct their information to the BS using the same chaining approach similar as intracommunication by considering the sink as cluster head.

Stage 5. In this proposed method, each sensor and cluster node perform the data aggregation in both inter- and intra-cluster communication in order to removal of the duplicate data.

Stage 6. Moreover, on the off chance that the leftover vitality of any node has become zero, at that point the node/hub is said to be a dead hub and it is erased from the networks/systems. Notwithstanding, when every sensor is dead, the system stops working.

9.5 Simulation Results and Discussions

In this section, the re-enactment consequences of the proposed methods and the current DEEC convention variations are contrasted. The deterministic energy-efficient clustering (DEEC) chooses CHs by utilizing the proportion of lingering energy/vitality of every sensor and normal vitality of the network. It does not utilize the additional vitality of more elevated level nodes effectively, as the vitality of the nodes is haphazardly assigned from a given vitality interim. In this manner, it cannot be achievable to structure such a network. The proposed convention is the changed execution of DEEC using limit remaining vitality for cluster head determination. It chooses higher remaining vitality sensors for cluster/bunch head in an effective way. The projected strategy is executed utilizing transmission and accumulation of information, and a chain-based information social occasion and communication procedure for intra- and between-cluster/bunch correspondence. All the planned executions are functional on four-level heterogeneous systems for assessing the exhibition. The trial arrangement for all the projected and existing conventions is given beneath.

The networks are reproduced in MATLAB adaptation R2014. The proposed network system comprises 100 heterogeneous nodes which are in an irregular arrangement in a square field of measurement 100 m × 100 m in every one of the reproductions. The BS is situated in the checking region at measurement 50 m × 50 m, and the underlying energy/vitality of the typical or level-1 nodes is 0.50 J. The outcomes introduced are the found middle value of the 20-recreation run by thinking about similar parameters. We deliberate distinctive execution grids for assessing the exhibition of the proposed technique against the other existing conventions given as follows: network lifetime, network sustainability, complete energy/vitality utilization, throughput, and the number of bunch heads.

For a similar investigation of the reproduction results, a heterogeneous system is considered. The proposed heterogeneous system comprises four types of nodes, in particular level-1, -2, -3, and -4 networks. This network contains level-4 heterogeneity where the quantity of level-1 (N_1) nodes, level-2 (N_2) nodes, level-3 (N_3) nodes, and level-4 (N_4) nodes are 46, 27, 16, and 11, with their energies as 0.50 J (E_0), 1.25 J (E_1), 1.75 J (E_2), and 2 J (E_3), correspondingly. Consider energy disbursed by amplifier to transmit data at shorter ($\in_{fs}$) and longer distance ($\in_{mp}$) and the energy consumption to transmit or receive signal ($\in_{elec}$) are 10nJ/bit/m^2, 0.0013pJ/bit/m^4, and 50nJ/bit, respectively. Additionally, think that the vitality for information conglomeration ($\in_{DA}$), threshold separation (d0), message size (L), and vitality steady (δ) are 5nJ/bit/signal, 70 m, 4000 bits, and 1.5, separately.

In this section, the exhibition assessment of the DDEEC [16], EDDEEC [17], hetDEEC-4 [7], and proposed strategy conventions are talked about for heterogeneous networks. We have considered four degrees of heterogeneity for breaking down the presentation of the networks. The outcomes for various frameworks such as network lifespan, vitality utilization, throughput, and the quantity of group heads are assumed as follows.

9.5.1 Network Lifetime and Stability Period

Figure 9.1 shows the number of alive nodes in regard to the number of rounds for DDEEC-4 [16], EDDEEC-4 [17], hetDEEC-4 [7], and proposed strategy in level-4 networks. It is seen that the proposed technique covers 7002 rounds though hetDEEC-4, EDDEEC-4, and DDEEC-4, spread 5600, 5314, and 4702 rounds, individually, before exhausting the total energy/vitality of the considerable number of nodes. In this way, the proposed technique increments 25.03%, 31.76%, and 48.91% in the lifespan of the network in regard to hetDEEC-4, EDDEEC-4, and DDEEC-4, separately. The proposed limit leftover energy/vitality helps to increase the lifespan

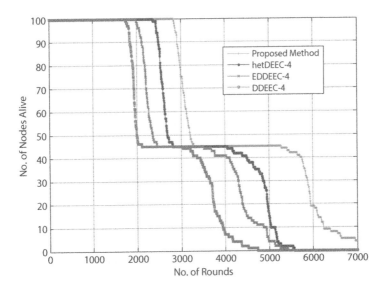

Figure 9.1 Alive nodes vs number of rounds.

of the network since the node distance decreases the correspondence cost between the sensors and BS. Moreover, the nodes in the proposed method die leisurelier than the hetDEEC-4, EDDEEC-4, and DDEEC-4 because it chooses the head nodes proficiently which helps in extending the network lifespan. It is also evident from the Figure 9.1; any increases in tire of heterogeneity show a significant increment in the network lifespan. Figure 9.2 demonstrates the number of dead nodes in regard of the number of rounds for DDEEC-4 [16], EDDEEC-4 [17], hetDEEC-4 [7], and proposed strategy in level-4 networks. It is showing similar behaviour as presented in Figure 9.2.

The economical time of the proposed technique is 2831, 3208, and 7002, individually, for first node dead as demonstrated in Figure 9.3 in level-4 systems. It is evident from the Figure 9.3 the sustainable period of the proposed method for first node dead significantly exceeds by 19.04%, 41.26%, and 59.85% as comparison with the hetDDEEC-4, EDDEEC-4, and DDEEC-4, respectively because the proposed methods considered the threshold residual energy. The weighted election decision probabilities guarantee the base vitality consumption in the intra- and inter/bury cluster/bunch transmission among the sensors and the base station. It is manifest the sustainable period of the proposed significantly exceeds by 18.37%, 36.56%, & 59.92% and 25.03%, 31.76%, &48.91%as comparison with the hetDDEEC-4, EDDEEC-4,& DDEEC-4, respectively, for half and

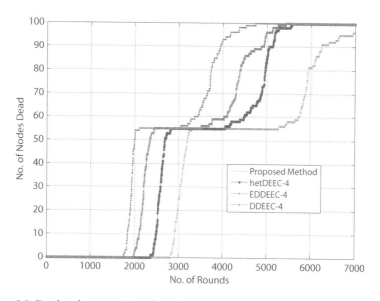

Figure 9.2 Dead nodes vs number of rounds.

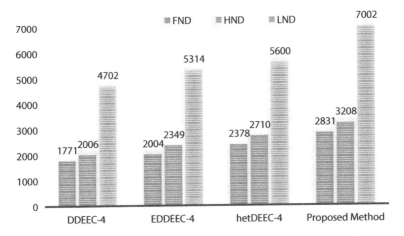

Figure 9.3 First node dead (FND), half node dead (HND), and last node dead (LND) vs number of rounds.

last node dead, separately. Along these lines, this vitality protection helps in the supportability of the systems. Figure 9.3 shows as the tire of heterogeneity increase the network lifespan of the increases.

9.5.2 Network Outstanding Energy

The normal energy/vitality dissemination of the DDEEC-4, EDDEEC-4, hetDDEEC-4, and proposed strategies in regard of the quantity of rounds is demonstrated in Figure 9.4 in the level-4 systems. The beginning vitality of the system is considered as 107 J. The proposed method outperforms as compare to the DDEEC-4, EDDEEC-4, and hetDDEEC-4 because it covers more number of rounds. The results show the higher energy consumption in DDEEC-4, EDDEEC-4,and hetDDEEC-4 because they do not consider any chaining approach for data transmission among the nearby nodes and BS. Moreover, the proposed method considers both intra and inter cluster communication by chaining approach which preserves energy of the sensors in the effective manner. Along these lines, it decreases the computational vitality cost of the CHs in the systems. It is likewise clear that as the tier of heterogeneity expands, the vitality consumption diminishes as demonstrated in Figure 9.4.

9.5.3 Throughput

The quantity of packets acknowledged by the BS in respect of the quantity of rounds till the networks alive using the DDEEC-4, EDDEEC-4,

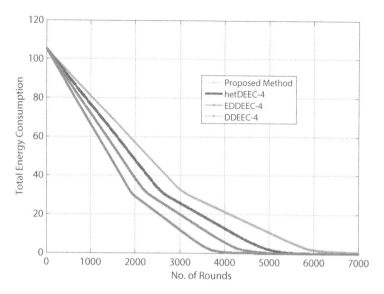

Figure 9.4 Energy consumption vs number of rounds.

hetDDEEC-4, and proposed strategies is indicated in Figure 9.5. The proposed strategy sent 25.38%, 46.02 %, and 67.03% progressively the number of packets to the BS regarding hetDEEC-4, EDDEEC-4, and DDEEC, separately. It is likewise seen that the proposed technique sent information

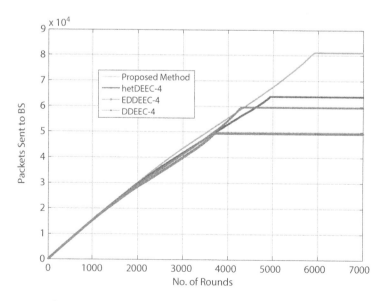

Figure 9.5 Packets sent to BS vs number of rounds.

Table 9.1 Illustrations of the total energy of the network, FND, HND, LND, throughput, increment % in lifetime, and throughput for the proposed method, hetDEEC-4, EDDEEC-4, and DDEEC-4 for four levels of heterogeneity.

Results for tier-4 network protocols

Approaches	Total energy	FND	HND	LND	Throughput	% increment in lifetime	% increment in throughput
Proposed method	107	2831	3208	7002	62185	–	–
hetDEEC-4	107	2378	2710	5600	49597	25.03	25.38
EDDEEC-4	107	2004	2349	5314	42584	31.76	46.02
DDEEC-4	107	1771	2006	4702	37228	48.91	67.03

packets at a higher rate to the BS as related to DDEEC-4, EDDEEC-4, and hetDDEEC-4. The proposed technique produces the most elevated number of packets because the nodes in the proposed strategy stay alive more as far as the number of rounds.

9.5.4   Comparative Analysis of the Level-4 Network Protocols

Table 9.1 demonstrates the relative examination of the absolute network power, first node dead (FND), half node dead (HND), last node dead (LND), throughput, rate increase in lifetime, and throughput for the proposed strategy and the current strategies, for example, hetDEEC-4 [7], EDDEEC-4 [17], and DDEEC-4 [16], separately by considering level-4 heterogeneity. If there should arise an occurrence of level-4 heterogeneity, the network lifetime and throughput of proposed strategy are expanded by 25.03%, 31.76%, and 48.91% and 25.38%, 46.02 %, and 67.03 % in regard of hetDEEC-4, EDDEEC-4, and DDEEC-4, separately, using network energy of 107 J, individually. It is shown from Table 9.1 that the supportable time of the proposed technique fundamentally increases by 19.04%, 41.26%, and 59.85%; 18.37%, 36.56%, and 59.92%; and 25.03%, 31.76%, and 48.91% as examination with hetDEEC-4, EDDEEC-4, and DDEEC-4, separately, for first, half, and last node dead, individually, for level-4 heterogeneity. The proposed strategy performs best among hetDEEC-4, EDDEEC-4, and DDEEC-4, separately, on the grounds that it accomplishes burden adjusting by considering weighted political election probabilities-based grouping and fastening approach. Thus, it is evident from the results weighted election probabilities based clustering and chaining approach enhance the reliability and also improve the sustainable period of the networks in the cases of four level of heterogeneity.

9.6   Conclusion

In this paper, a threshold-based optimization energy-efficient directing method for prolonging the lifespan of the network in a heterogeneous environment is proposed. The proposed protocol used weighted election probabilities for CH election and a chaining approach for proficient information/data gathering. The proposed method delivers a sustainable region for heterogeneous networks since it elects the highest energy nodes for CH efficiently. The network lifetime and throughput of the proposed method are presented as increased by 25.03%, 31.76%, and 48.91% and 25.38%, 46.02%, and 67.03% in respect of hetDEEC-4, EDDEEC-4, a DDEEC-4, using 107 J network energy in the case of level-4 heterogeneity, respectively. The proposed method performs best among hetDEEC-4, EDDEEC-4, and DDEEC-4. The simulation results of the proposed method also show that as the level of heterogeneity increased, the lifespan of the networks increased, accordingly. This work can be extended using multiple sinks instead of single and mobile sinks, and sensors can be added for monitoring the different applications.

References

1. Chand, S., Singh, S., Kumar, B., Heterogeneous HEED Protocol for Wireless Sensor Networks. *Wireless Pers. Commun.*, 77, 3, 2117–2139, 2014.

2. Singh, S., Chand, S., Kumar, R., Malik, A., Kumar, B., NEECP: Novel energy-efficient clustering protocol for prolonging lifetime of WSNs. *IET Wireless Sens. Syst.*, 6, 5, 151–157, 2016.

3. Singh, S. and Malik, A., hetSEP: Heterogeneous SEP protocol for increasing lifetime in WSNs. *J. Inf. Optim. Sci.*, 38, 5, 721–743, 2017.

4. Heinzelman, W.R., Chandrakasan, A.P., Balakrishnan, H., An application-specific protocol architecture for wireless microsensor networks. *IEEE Trans. Wireless Commun.*, 1, 4, 660–670, 2002.

5. Lindsey, S., Raghavendra, C.S., Sivalingam, K.M., Data gathering algorithms in sensor networks using energy metrics. *IEEE Trans. Parallel Distrib. Syst.*, 13, 9, 924–935, 2002.

6. Qing, L., Zhu, Q., Wang, M., Design of a distributed energy-efficient clustering algorithm for heterogeneous wireless sensor networks. *Comput. Commun.*, 29, 12, 2230–2237, 2006.

7. Singh, S., Malik, A., Kumar, R., Energy efficient heterogeneous DEEC protocol for enhancing lifetime in WSNs. *Eng. Sci. Technol.*, an International Journal, 20, 1, 345–353, 2017.

8. Maheswari, D.U. and Sudha, S., Node Degree Based Energy Efficient Two-Level Clustering for Wireless Sensor Networks. *Wireless Pers. Commun.*, 104, 3, 1209–1225, 2018.

9. Istwal, Y. and Verma, S.K., Dual Cluster Head Routing Protocol with Super Node in WSN. *Wireless Pers. Commun.*, 104, 2, 561–575, 2019.

10. Singh, S., Chand, S., Kumar, B., Multilevel heterogeneous network model for wireless sensor networks. *Telecommun. Syst.*, 64, 2, 259–277, 2017.

11. Singh, S., Chand, S., Kumar, B., Energy-efficient protocols using fuzzy logic for heterogeneous WSNs. *Wireless Pers. Commun.*, 86, 2, 451–475, 2017.

12. Su, S. and Zhao, S., An optimal clustering mechanism based on Fuzzy-C means for wireless sensor networks. *Sustain. Comput.: Informat. Syst.*, 18, 127–134, 2018.

13. Sodairi, S.A. and Ouni, R., Reliable and energy-efficient multi-hop LEACH-based clustering protocol for wireless sensor networks. *Sustain. Comput.: Informat. Syst.*, 20, 1–13, 2018.

14. Narendran, M. and Prakasam, P., An energy aware competition based clustering for cluster head selection in wireless sensor network with mobility. *Cluster Comput.*, 22, 11019–11028, 2019.

15. Ke, W., Yangrui, O., Hong, J., Heli, Z., Xi, L., Energy aware hierarchical cluster-based routing protocol for WSNs. *J. China Univ. Posts Telecommun.*, 23, 4, 46–52, 2016.

16. Elbhiri, B., Saadane, R., El Fkihi, S., Aboutajdine, D., Developed Distributed Energy-Efficient Clustering (DDEEC) for heterogeneous wireless sensor networks. *5th International Symposium on I/V Communications and Mobile Network (ISVC)*, 2010.

17. Javaid, N., Qureshi, T.N., Khan, A.H., Iqbal, A., Akhtar, E., Ishfaq, M., EDDEEC: Enhanced Developed Distributed Energy-Efficient Clustering for Heterogeneous Wireless Sensor Networks. *International Workshop on Body Area Sensor Networks (BASNet-2013)*.

10

Efficacy of Big Data Application in Smart Cities

Sudipta Sahana*, Dharmpal Singh and Pranati Rakshit

Department of CSE, JIS College of Engineering, Kalyani, Nadia, W.B., India

Abstract

Smart cities play a vital role in the lifestyle of humans, and these are just like smart phones, which provide information to persons based on their different needs. Several governments/private organizations are planning to make many cities as smart cities with the help of big data. As for the smart phone, many technologies are required to make it smart; many technologies are also required to make a city smart. Big data analytics is one of the modern technologies that have a huge potential to enhance the services in a smart city. Therefore, the concept of big data application can be used in health monitoring, efficiency in transportation, energy, smart education, and water management system multiple technologies to move the lifestyle of the people to a higher level. This involves cost optimization and resource utilization properly in addition to more efficiently and vigorously engaging with their citizens. Currently, one of the integral outcomes of daily life is digitization, which produces a large volume of data, and analysis of those data can be used in various beneficial application domains. The prime factor for achievement in several commerce and technology domains, including the domain of smart cities, is effectual analysis and utilization of big data. The main concept of this book chapter is to focus on different applications of big data to make cities smarter with various opportunities, challenges, and benefits. Furthermore, the solution of the challenger is also discussed in this chapter.

Keywords: Big data, smart city, structured data, unstructured data, big data analytics

Corresponding author: ss.jisce@gmail.com

Krishna Kant Singh, Akansha Singh, Korhan Cengiz and Dac-Nhuong Le (eds.) Machine Learning and Cognitive Computing for Mobile Communications and Wireless Networks, (225–250) © 2020 Scrivener Publishing LLC

10.1 Introduction

Big data [3] is now a trendy ground that treats ways to investigate, analytically take out data from, or else manage informational indexes that are colossal or composite to be managed by conventional information-handling application programming. When conventional data mining and handling systems could not expose the insights and meaning of the underlying data, the big data technique was introduced.

Big data employment is nearly as differed as they work with huge datasets. Unmistakable models you are presumably effectively used to include online internetworking systems examining their personages' data to become familiar with them and partner them with substance and commercial enterprise Brobdingnagian to their inclinations, or Internet crawlers trying association among request and results to supply higher reactions to customers' request.

In any case, the potential uses go much further! There are two utmost origins of facts in tremendous sums those are based on esteem information. This includes stock expenses along with banking details to particular sellers' purchase narratives and sensor information, a ton of it beginning dependent on what is customarily implied as the Internet of Things (IoT). This sensor statistics fall under the category ranging from approximations taken from robots on an automaker's amassing line, to zone information on a cellphone arrange, to provoke power-driven use information in homes and associations, to explorer boarding information taken on a movement system.

By analyzing this information, affiliations can learn slants about the information they are evaluating, similarly as the people creating this information. The desire for this huge information examination is to give progressively changed help and extended efficiencies in whatever industry the information accumulated from.

Getting programs on different machines to collaborate in a capable way so each program realizes which parts of the information to process and a short time later having the alternative to put the results from all of the machines together to comprehend a tremendous pool of information takes unprecedented programming methods. Since it is commonly much faster for undertakings to get to information set away locally instead of over a framework, the allotment of information over a bundle and how those machines are masterminded together are also huge thoughts when contemplating enormous information issues.

The occupations of huge information are almost as changed as they are tremendous. Observable models you're probably viably familiar with include web based systems administration frameworks analyzing their people's information to think about them and interface them with substance and elevating relevant to their inclinations, or web search instruments looking association among request and results to offer better reactions to customers' request.

10.1.1 Characteristics of Big Data

The data size which can be viewed as big data [2] is a continually shifting component, and progressively, current devices are constantly being created to deal with this huge information. It is changing our world absolutely and gives no indications of being a passing predominant style that will obscure away at whatever point soon. In order to look good out of this staggering proportion of information, it is consistently isolated utilizing five V's: velocity, volume, value, variety, and veracity.

10.1.1.1 *Velocity*

Velocity suggests the swiftness at which tremendous proportions of facts are being made, assembled along with dismembered. Reliably the amount of messages, Twitter data, pictures, audiovisual cuts, etc., upsurges at lighting speeds far and wide. Each second of reliable information is extending. In addition to the fact that it should be broken down, in any case the speed of transmission and access to the information should in a like way stay smart to think about relentless access to site, Mastercard check, and informing. Gigantic information improvement engages us right presently to isolate the information while it is being made, while never placing it into databases.

10.1.1.2 *Volume*

Volume refers to the unfathomable extent of information conveyed each second from online life, mobile phones, vehicles, visas, snapshots, audiovisual, and so on. The monster extent of information has wound up being so expansive in affirmation that we can never again store and examine information utilizing standard database headways. We straightforwardly use orbited frameworks, where parts of the information is dealt with in various zones and joined by programming. With Facebook alone, there are 10 billion messages, 4.5 on different events that the "like" get is squeezed, and more than 350 million new pictures are moved each day. Gathering and isolating this information is clearly a structure challenge of enormously colossal degrees.

10.1.1.3 Value

When we call attention to worth, we are bearing on the value of the fact being unglued. Facts having unlimited measures are a matter of concern, anyway except if it will be wound up justified, despite all the troubles futile. While there is a straightforward connection among information and bits of knowledge, this does not constantly mean there is value in monstrous learning. The preeminent essential a piece of setting out on a gigantic information activity expresses to know the expenses and focal points of bringing together and breaking down the information to certify that at last the data that are procured will stand adapted.

10.1.1.4 Variety

The term *variety* deals with the differing sorts of facts we would presently have the option to use. Data today seem, by all accounts, to be very novel than data from a prior time. Generally, information is stored from sources like spreadsheets and databases. Presently information comes as messages, photographs, recordings, checking gadgets, PDFs, sound, and so on. This assortment of unstructured information leads to issues in capacity, mining, and breaking down of information. Jeff Veis, VP of Solutions at HP Autonomy, displayed how HP is helping associations manage huge difficulties, including information assortment. New and creative colossal data advancement is right now empowering sorted out and unstructured data to be gathered, taken care of, and used simultaneously.

10.1.1.5 Veracity

Enormous data veracity alludes to the inclinations, clamor, and anomaly in information. Is the information that is being put away and mined significant to the issue being broken down? Inderpal feel veracity in information investigation is the greatest test when looking at things like volume and speed. In investigating your enormous information procedure, you have to have your group and accomplices work to help keep your information clean and procedures to keep "messy information" from collecting in your frameworks.

10.1.2 Definition of Smart Cities

The first question is, what is meant by a smart city [4]. The appropriate response is, no fixed meaning of smart city is present as of now. Various stuffs to various personages have been implied by it. In this way, the smart city thinking shifts across the city and nation to nation, contingent upon the degree of progression, eagerness to alteration, assets, and yearnings of the city inhabitants. There is an alternate undertone regarding the smart city concept in India than, state, Europe. Indeed, even in India, there is no method for characterizing a keen city.

The urban region, specifically the smart city, utilizes various sorts of electronic Internet of things (IoT) sensors to gather data and afterward utilize these data to manage resources and assets effectively. This integrates data grouped from gadgets, natives, and assets that are handled and broken down to screen and superintend traffic and transportation contexts, control plants, water supply systems, squander the executives, wrongdoing recognition, data frameworks, schools, libraries, medical clinics, and other network administrations.

10.2   Types of Data in Big Data

Mostly big data incorporate data sets with different sizes past the capacity of normally applied programming instruments to hook, clergyman, oversee, and process data inside an endurable slipped by time. Big data theory incorporates unstructured, semi-structured, and structured data; anyway, the primary spotlight is on unstructured data. Big data "size" is an always moving objective, starting at 2012 extending from a couple of dozen terabytes to numerous zettabytes of data. Big data involve a lot of systems and develop with new types of reconciliation to uncover experiences from datasets that are various, complex, and of a gigantic scale. Generally, big data are commonly gathered into three guideline types, which are as follows.

10.2.1   Structured Data

Structured data are accustomed to insinuate the facts which are starting at now taken care of in databases, in an organized way. It speaks to approximately 20% of the full-scale prevailing data and is used the most in programming- and PC-associated accomplishments.

Two wellsprings are there of structured data technologies and individuals. All of the facts got from sensing instruments, web logs, and budgetary structures are portrayed underneath machine-delivered data. These fuse therapeutic contraptions, GPS data, and usage data estimations gotten by servers and applications and the enormous proportion of data that by and large travel through transaction stages, to give a few models.

Structured data made by persons generally join all every fact a human commitment to a PC, for instance, his personal details and other individual nuances. Exactly when an individual snaps a connotation on the web, or even makes a move in a preoccupation, data are created and can be used by associations to comprehend their customer lead and choose the appropriate decisions and modifications.

10.2.2 Unstructured Data

While structured data live in the regular line fragment databases, unstructured data are the opposite they have no undeniable course of action away. The rest of the data made, about 80% of the hard and fast record for unstructured gigantic data. The huge amount of data that an individual encounters has a spot with this characterization, and starting quite recently, there was almost nothing to do with it besides taking care of it or looking at it physically.

Unstructured data are furthermore gathered reliant on its basis, into machine-delivered or human-made. Machine-made data speak to entire satellite pictures, the intelligent information from numerous tests, and radar data gotten by various highlights of advancement.

Unstructured data made by human beings are found abundantly on the web, still the same fuses online life data, compact facts, and webpage content. These include the photographs we upload to Facebook or Instagram handles, the accounts we lookout on YouTube, and even the texts we send all add to the colossal stack, i.e., unstructured data.

10.2.3 Semi-Structured Data

The difference stuck between unstructured data and semi-structured data has consistently stood misty, since the vast majority of the semi-structured data look as if to be unstructured at a look. Data, not inside the antiquated data group as structured data, anyway contain some structure properties that assemble it simpler to technique, zone unit encased in semi-structured data. For instance, NoSQL reports zone unit thought of being semi-structured, since they contain watchwords which will be wont to technique the record basically.

Big data examination has been originated to claim a specific business worth, as its investigation and procedure will encourage a company convey the merchandise value decreases and sensational development. In this way, it is basic that you basically do not stand by too long to even consider taking favorable position of the capability of this wonderful business shot.

10.3   Big Data Technologies

Big data are a collection of data sets which are so large and very complex to process using traditional applications/tools. These exceed terabytes in data size. As these data are coming from various sources and because of their volume and complexity, big data always face a number of challenges. A recent survey says that the maximum part of datasets (almost 80%) produced in the world is unstructured. One challenge is to find the method of structuring these unstructured data and try to know and incarcerate the valuable and important data subsequently. Another challenge is how we can store these. Here are some top technologies or mechanisms used to store and analyze big data.

10.3.1   Apache Hadoop

Apache Hadoop is a Java-based programming system that can proficiently store enormous compute of information in a bunch. This arrangement keeps running in comparable on a bunch and has an ability to allow us to process information over all hubs.

Apache Hadoop is an open-source platform which gives remarkable dependable, flexible, circulated handling of huge informational collections utilizing straightforward programming models. Hadoop is based on groups of ware PCs, giving a financially savvy answer for putting away and preparing enormous measures of organized, semi-structured, and unstructured information with no configuration prerequisites. This makes Hadoop perfect for structure information lakes to help huge information investigation activities.

Hadoop does not depend on apparatus to give fault tolerance and high availability, but the Hadoop library itself has been projected to recognize and handle failures at the application layer.

Hadoop keeps on working without interference of servers that can be included or expelled from the group progressively. Hadoop is open source, and it is perfect on every one of the stages since it is Java based.

10.3.2   HDFS

The Hadoop distributed file system (HDFS) is a dispersed, adaptable, and versatile file-based system printed in Java for the Hadoop structure. Every center in a Hadoop incidence typically has a solitary namenode, and a group of data nodes structure the HDFS bunch. The circumstance is run in fact that every hub does not require a datanode to be available.

Each datanode presents squares of information in excess of the system utilizing a square convention explicit to HDFS.

HDFS stores enormous files (gigabytes/terabytes) over a variety of machines. It accomplishes firm quality by repeating the information over different hosts and henceforth does not require RAID stockpiling on hosts.

HDFS included the high-availability abilities for free 2.x, permitting the main metadata server (the NameNode) to be failed over bodily to reinforcement in case of failure, programmed fail-over.

10.3.3 Spark

Apache Spark is an unlocked source of huge information-handling structure worked in the region of speed, convenience, and refined test. It was publicly released in 2010.

Spark gives us a far-reaching, brought collectively system to oversee huge information preparing necessities with a hotchpotch of informational collections that are in variety of nature just as the source of information.

Spark support applications in Hadoop bunches to enhance the running capability of memory on same plate.

Spark helps us to compose applications in Java, Scale, or Python. It also helps in implicit arrangement of above 80 significant level administrators. Furthermore, you can use it for inside information of the shell.

10.3.4 Microsoft HDInsight

Microsoft HDInsight is big data arrangement Apache Hadoop of Microsoft. This one is accessible as an assistance in the cloud and also utilizes the HDInsight utilizes Windows Azure Blob stockpiling as the default document framework. This likewise gives far above the ground accessibility in minimal effort. Microsoft Azure PaaS uses Azure HDInsight as an assistance that sends and arrangements Apache Hadoop groups in the cloud. Furthermore, Microsoft Azure PaaS gives a product structure planned to oversee, investigate, and report on big data.

It has been observed that our information generates exponential data once a day, and it ends up hard to process utilizing these produced data. Therefore, Azure HDInsight comes into picture and provides the close by database the board apparatuses or conventional information-handling applications.

We can dissect formless information from Azure HDInsight in Microsoft Excel and use Microsoft Excel's innovative cutting-edge tools such as Power Pivot, Power Query, and Power View to perform active examination on the joined informational index. We can outline information effectively with Power Map—an amazing 3D mapping instrument in Excel.

It comes into picture since Windows Azure HDInsight brings undertaking prepared. All clients can pick up bits of knowledge through Excel, while designers are bolstered in .NET and Java, and that is just the beginning.

.NET designers can utilize the intensity of language-coordinated question with LINQ to Hive.

SQL abilities can be utilized by database designers to inquiry and change information through Hive.

10.3.5   NoSQL

NoSQL is a way to deal with database structure that can suit a wide variety of information and is an option in difference to conventional relational databases. NoSQL databases are particularly obliging for operational with enormous arrangements of dispersed information.

The NoSQL look can be applied to certain databases that originated before the relational database management system (RDBMS), worked in the mid-2000s data with the end objective of enormous level database bunching in cloud and web applications.

In NoSQL, consistency is possibly ensured after some timeframe when composes stop. This implies it is conceivable that questions will not see the most recent information. This is generally executed by putting away information in memory and after that lethargically sending it to different machines.

10.3.6   Hive

Apache Hive is a data division hub framework for data shabby and investigation and for inquiring of huge data frameworks in the open-source Hadoop stage. It changes over SQL-like questions into MapReduce occupations for easy implementation and handling of very enormous volumes of data.

In today's world, Hadoop has the advantage of being one of the most enhanced tools across the board with regard to crunching gigantic actions of big data. Hadoop resembles as a huge immense range of apparatuses and advancements to connect with each other to perform the task. The innovation which satisfies aforesaid needs is known as Apache Hive. Apache Hive is a Hadoop section that is characteristically sent by data evaluators. Apache Pig can also used for a similar reason, but Hive is utilized more by scientists and developers all over the world. It is an open-source data warehousing framework used for inquiry and investigation of enormous datasets which were put away in Hadoop.

The three major functionalities for which Hive is sent are data outline, data examination, and data inquiry. The question language, only upheld by Hive, is named as HiveQL. This HiveQL makes an interpretation of SQL-like inquiries into MapReduce occupations for sending them on Hadoop. HiveQL as well use MapReduce contents that can be linked to the questions. Hive is used to form constructive plans for adaptability, data serialization, and deserialization.

Hive is used as most appropriate for group occupations who opposed to work with web log data and attach data. Hive does not give continuous questioning to push level updates, and hence, it cannot work for online transaction-processing frameworks.

10.3.7 Sqoop

Apache Sqoop is a technique intended for proficiently moving mass data between outside datastores and Apache Hadoop. Data can also be stored in social databases, venture data stockrooms, etc.

Sqoop is utilized to bring in data from external datastores place into the Hadoop Distributed File System or related Hadoop eco-systems such as Hive and HBase. Correspondingly, Sqoop can also be utilized to take out data from Hadoop or from its eco-systems and send these into outside datastores, viz., social databases, undertaking data distribution centers. The Sqoop mechanism is suitable for social databases, for example, Teradata, Netezza, Oracle, and MySQL, Postgres.

Sqoop mechanizes a large portion of the procedure and relies upon the file to depict the composition of the facts to be imported. Sqoop utilizes the MapReduce system to bring in and fare the data, which gives a similar component just as adaptation to non-critical failure. Sqoop makes designers' life simpler by giving an order line interface. Designers simply need to give fundamental data such as source, goal, and database verification subtleties in the Sqoop order. Sqoop deals with the outstanding part.

The robust nature of Sqoop makes it an extraordinary network-backing and commitment software. Sqoop is broadly utilized in the greater part of big data organizations to move facts between social databases and Hadoop.

As day-to-day information is managed by big data, Hadoop stores and procedures the big data utilizing diverse preparing systems such as MapReduce, Hive, HBase, Cassandra, and Pig and capacity structures such as HDFS to achieve the advantage of dispersed processing and distributed stockpiling. Data should be moved between database systems and the Hadoop Distributed File System (HDFS) to store and examine the big data. Therefore, Sqoop is used to provide the solution and used as a moderate layer among Hadoop and social database systems. You can bring in the data and charge data between social database systems and Hadoop. Furthermore, its eco-systems uncomplicatedly utilize Sqoop.

10.3.8   R

R, a programming language which is an open-source venture, is intended for working with measurements. It is overseen by the R Foundation and is easy to get to under the GPL 2 permit. It is especially favored by information researchers. It is sustained by numerous mainstream incorporated advancement situations (IDEs), including Eclipse and Visual Studio.

R has turned out to be one of the most well-known dialects on the planet. A few associations such as IEEE, Tiobe, and RedMonk rank the prominence of R. IEEE indicate that R is the fifth most famous programming language. For a language that is utilized solely for enormous information activities, to be so close to the top exhibits the criticalness of huge information and the significance of this language in its field.

10.3.9   Data Lakes

These are immense data files that meet data from a broad range of sources and store these in their characteristic state. Numerous undertakings are setting up data lakes to get to their huge stores of data effectively. This is not the same as a data distribution centre that collects data from different sources and yet to form in structures for better use. On the off chance that data resemble water, a data lake is frequent and unfiltered like a waterway, while a data distribution center is increasingly similar to a gathering of water containers put away on racks.

Markets and Markets predicts that data lake income will increase from $2.53 billion in 2016 to $8.81 billion by 2021.

10.4   Data Source for Big Data

Data analytics is one of the major jobs of organizations. For this purpose, big data are usually used. Knowledge of different big data sources is very much important to get insights on big data and extract valuable information from that. Here, the data are huge and exist in diverse forms. In the concept of big data, these should be classified properly or sourced well;

otherwise, it will be a wastage of valuable time and resources. To reach success through big data, companies need to know how they can sift from one source to another and classify the usability with proper relevance.

10.4.1 Media

As we know, media generally means social media and also some interactive platforms such as Google, Twitter, Facebook, Instagram, and YouTube in addition to some generic media such as images, audios, and videos that afford quantitative as well as qualitative insights of user interaction. So this is the main reason that media is the most accepted foundation of big data.

10.4.2 Cloud

Nowadays, organizations or companies usually move their traditional data sources to the cloud [4]. Structured as well as unstructured data are accommodated in cloud storage and give some real-time information and insights on demand. Flexibility and scalability are the main characteristics of cloud computing. As big data can be sourced and stored on private or public clouds, by means of networks along with servers, the cloud makes for a proficient and low-priced data source.

10.4.3 The Web

The web is constituted with big data which is extensive and very easily accessible. Web data are generally available to persons and companies as well. Furthermore, different web services such as Wikipedia make available free and quick informational insights to everyone. The vastness of the Internet or web ensures their various usability, and it becomes especially advantageous to start-ups and small-scale enterprises. The reason is that they do not have to wait to build up their own big data repositories and infrastructure before they can leverage big data.

10.4.4 IOT

Machine-generated content or data created from IoT [6] comprise a valuable resource of the big data. These sensor-generated data are usually referred here. The sensors are attached to electronic devices. The sensors offer real-time correct information, and this sourcing capability depends on the sensor's ability. IoT is now getting hold of thrust and also includes big data which are generated not only from smartphones and computers but also perhaps from each device which can produce data. Now data can be gathered from different sources such as medical devices, video games, cameras, vehicular processes, household appliances, and meters with the help of IoT.

10.4.5   Databases as a Big Data Source

A combination of modern and traditional databases is preferred to be acquired by different businesses which are acted as big data. The hybrid data model is used for this integration, and it incurs a low investment cost. IT-infrastructure-related cost is not so high. These databases, furthermore, are deployed for several business intelligence purposes also. These databases, perhaps, can then be afforded for the taking out of insights which are used to achieve business profits. Popular databases such as MS Access, Oracle, DB2, and SQL are included as a range of data sources.

The method of extraction and analyzing data among extensive big data sources is a compound process and can be time-consuming and annoying. These type of complications may be resolved if organizations include all the required considerations of big data and take into consideration pertinent data sources as well as organize them in a proper manner so that these will be well tuned to their organizational goals.

Big data are basically around us everywhere even including places wherever we normally do not think about. Some sources of big data are obvious. Software log files, databases that house customer records, and the like are designed for the specific purpose of collecting and storing data.

As a consequence, when we seek data sources, these places are looked for doing analytics.

10.4.6   Hidden Big Data Sources

It is actually big data, what we normally do not think as big data as it is yet beyond the noticeable thinking.

Considering the subsequent big data sources which can put forward valuable imminent for marketing, business operations, and beyond.

10.4.6.1   Email

Usually, an office employee normally sends 35 official emails/day and receives almost 100. Really, it is a lot of statistics—in particular if we count the attachments which are attached to many mails.

Drawing out data from one's organization's electronic mail accounts can give insights into the whole thing from the efficiency of employees. The strength of one's production pipeline depending on the times of the day when our clients are mainly expected to take action to emails and, perhaps, other forms of commitment, are as well added to the mined data.

10.4.6.2   Social Media

Facebook posts, Tweets, Instagram images, and data streams of all the other social media offer possessions of information which one can evaluate to get knowledge of social media, for example, what people are chatting or talking about, how persons are talking, about themselves, and about their business.

10.4.6.3   Open Data

There are lots of data in gigabytes which are called "open" data, are free, one can take. Some government agencies provide open data sets, for example, the US federal government, the city of New York, which are published that can be shared by anyone. We do not know about the types of data that are collected as well as reported, of course. There is a good chance of getting the relevant information which we can find from these data sets for our business. As an additional benefit, numerous open data sets are moderately well maintained as well as all set to be analyzed out-of-the-box.

10.4.6.4   Sensor Data

One of the important hidden big data comes from sensor data. Conventionally, network switches and servers produce log files which are the sources for machine data. Gradually, though, IoT devices are added by the organizations to their infrastructures. IoT devices create data as well, which may perhaps be recorded in conventional logs. They produce vast data if sensors or else other devices (smart) are used.

In brief, Big Data sources are all over the place. We just require to see the surface to find wealthy data sources which we might or else be missing.

10.4.7   Application-Oriented Big Data Source for a Smart City

10.4.7.1   Healthcare

Healthcare systems are a huge source of big data. In 2011 alone, the U.S. healthcare system reached 150 exabytes (one billion gigabytes) of data.

Predicting the rate of growth, the U.S. healthcare will soon reach the zetta-byte (10^{21} gigabytes) scale and, thereafter, the yottabyte (10^{24} gigabytes) scale.

"Big data in healthcare" is basically referring to the plentiful cumulative health data from a variety of sources together with medical imaging, electronic health records (EHRs), pharmaceutical research, wearables, genomic sequencing, medical devices, etc. Three characteristics—high volume, high velocity, and highly variable structure and nature—discriminate these from conventional electronic and medical or human health data needed for decision-making.

Big data in healthcare usually may be disordered and distributed, while it is also much less expensive to have and operate than it is done in relational databases.

The extraction and analyzing process amongst widespread big data sources is an intricate process and can be annoying and time-taking.

Outcomes

- Health care providers can develop new strategies of big Data application [1] to care for patients before it is too late, which minimizes the number of needless hospitalizations.
- Improvement in the health of patients while diminishing the costs of care.
- It will be sometimes better to combine several predictive models of big data.

10.4.7.2   Transportation

Transportation is as always an important factor of a smart city. By reducing traffic problems, an intelligent transport system (ITS) tries to accomplish traffic efficiency. Citizens with an ITS can save transportation time, and the city becomes even smarter. Users are enriched with earlier information about local conveyance, traffic situation, seat availability, real-time information, etc. This facility reduces travel time as well as improves the security and comfort of commuters.

The progress of Internet and information and communications technology (ICT) makes ITS available with a significant quantity of real-time data. To enhance knowledge in the region of the transport system, the data which are the called as "big data" can be gathered and analyzed in a suitable way. The utilization of these technologies has really improved the user-friendliness and competence of ITS.

The appliance and relevance of ITS is extensively used and accepted in different countries nowadays. It is mainly used in traffic overcrowding management and information, but it is also used for road safety and proficient infrastructure usage.

Glasgow is one such example of the smart city which effectively uses ITS. In the city, ITS provides usual information to the daily traveler about public bus timings, availability of seats, the time needed to reach a specific destination, the current position/location of that vehicle (bus), the next stoppage of the, bus and the crowd of passengers within the bus.

Sensors are the main or important things which are used in the bus of a smart city. With the help of these sensors, the bus, which is going faster and is early for the next stoppage, can temporarily slow down and can stop a little longer at the red light to be sure that the bus is on scheduled time. The total systematic approach has been achieved so smartly and efficiently that passengers are unaware of the delay or fastness.

10.4.7.3   Education

Education is the most vital area of smart city which can significantly change one's life. Furthermore, as big data can bear the traditional educational system by helping the teachers scrutinize and analyze the knowledge of the students and the techniques which are mostly effective for them. In this method, teachers are capable of learning new techniques and methods about their edifying work.

Hence, different technologies like data mining and data analytics [7] are used to provide a fast feedback about the academic performance of teachers and students. Extraction of valuable knowledge and thorough analysis of different education patterns can be provided by these technologies. In this way, collective and big scale [5] data are used to predict students who need more assistance from the edification system, evading the hazard of failure or dropout.

Digital learning is basically the outcome of digital transformation of the teaching-learning process. Actually, a group of data and associated analytics contribute to the process of teaching and learning. Many online teaching-learning methods and mobile learning methods are made available, and in this way, several students are participating in those learning methodologies and from where new data continuously are being created. These types of new data, in association with social networks, are serving the students by helping them understand core subjects/courses of the different background and to find correlation between them.

10.5   Components of a Smart City

Different components are there to make a city smart. Some of those are listed below.

10.5.1   Smart Infrastructure

The worldwide market for savvy urban foundation in keen urban areas incorporates progressed associated roads, shrewd stopping, brilliant lighting, and other transportation developments. Here is the manner by which they work.

10.5.1.1   Intelligent Lighting

With savvy lighting, city experts can keep continuous following of lighting to guarantee improved enlightenment and convey request-based lighting in various zones. Savvy lighting likewise helps in sunlight collecting and spare vitality by darkening out segments without any inhabitances such as parking areas can be diminished amid work timing and when a vehicle is entering, it can be distinguished and suitable parts can be enlightened, while others can be set aside at subtle setting.

10.5.1.2   Modern Parking Systems

Smart leaving the board framework can be utilized to locate the empty area for a vehicle at various open spots. Keen parking' in-ground vehicle detection sensors are center advanced, having the main impact in intelligent parking arrangement that is directing about searching the parking spot by the drivers in the shopping centers and downtown areas. Remote sensors are inserted into parking spots, transmitting information on the planning and term of the space utilized by means of nearby flag processors into a focal stopping the executives application. Savvy parking diminishes clogging, diminishes vehicle emanations, brings down requirement expenses, and cuts down driver stress. For viable arrangement of savvy stopping advances, every gadget needs a solid availability with the cloud servers.

10.5.1.3   Associated Charging Points

Smart framework additionally incorporates executing charging stations in leaving frameworks, city armadas, shopping centers and structures, air terminals, and transport stations over the city. Electronic vehicle (EV) charging stages can be incorporated with IoT to streamline the activities of EV charging and addresses the effect of the power framework.

10.5.2   Smart Buildings and Belongings

Smart buildings [8] use distinctive frameworks to guarantee the wellbeing and security of structures, upkeep of benefits, and by and large soundness of the encompassing.

10.5.2.1   Safety and Security Systems

These incorporate actualizing remote observing, biometrics, IP reconnaissance cameras, and remote alerts to lessen unapproved access to structures and odds of burglaries. To stop admittance to limited territories of the property and recognize individuals in non-approved regions, perimeter access control may be incorporated.

10.5.2.2   Smart Sprinkler Systems for Gardens

To water the plants with the confirmation that plants get the appropriate measure of water, smart sprinkler frameworks can be synchronized with associated advances and the cloud can be utilized. Savvy garden gadgets can likewise perform assignments, for example, estimating soil dampness and dimensions of compost, assisting the city experts with saving on water charge (shrewd sprinkler gadgets utilize climate projections and consequently modify their calendar to remain off when it rains), and shielding the grass from congesting in the helpful manner (robot lawnmowers).

10.5.2.3   Smart Heating and Ventilation

Smart warming and ventilation frameworks screen different parameters, for example, temperature, weight, vibration, dampness of the buildings, and properties, for example, cinemas, and authentic landmarks. Remote sensor arranges sending is the way to guaranteeing suitable warming and ventilation. These sensors likewise gather data to upgrade the HVAC frameworks, improving their effectiveness and execution in the structures.

10.5.3   Smart Industrial Environment

The distinctive opportunities are gift from the smart industrial environments for embryonic applications interrelated to the IoT and connected technologies which may be utilized within the following areas.

Timberland fire exposure: The observation of burning gases and preemptive flame conditions to characterize ready zones can be identified by it.

Air/noise contamination: Helps in controlling of CO_2 emanations of industrial facilities, contamination transmitted via vehicles, and poisonous gases produced on ranches.

Snow level monitoring: It introduces to recognize the ongoing state of ski tracks, giving permission to security organizations for torrential slide aversion.

Avalanche avoidance: To check the soil dampness, earth thickness, just as vibrations to distinguish risky examples in land conditions.

Earthquake early discovery: Helps in distinguishing the odds of tremors by using conveyed controls at explicit spots of tremors.

Fluid existence: To identify the nearness of fluid in server farms, building grounds, and distribution centers to anticipate breakdowns and consumption it plays a vital role.

Emission levels: Helps in disseminated estimation of the levels of radiation in atomic power stations surroundings to produce spillage cautions.

Dangerous and hazardous gases: Helps in recognizing gas levels and spillages in compound manufacture lines, mechanical situations, and within mines.

10.5.4   Smart City Services

IoT answer for smart city [4] incorporate administrations for open security and crises. The following are the key regions where IoT and associated advances can help.

10.5.4.1   Smart Stalls

Smart kiosks assume a critical job in giving diverse city administrations to the open, for example, wireless networking administrations, observation of

IP cameras in 24 × 7 basis and examination, digital signage for promotion, and open declarations. Now and again, free video calling and free portable charging station, just as ecological sensor reconciliation can likewise be actualized. Savvy booths additionally give data about eateries, retail locations, and occasions in the prompt territory. These can likewise give mapping to guests and can match up with cell phones to give extra information as required.

10.5.4.2   Monitoring of Risky Areas

Sensors (cameras, road lights) and actuators for constant observing can be actualized in dangerous territories or regions inclined to mishaps. After identifying any wrongdoing, or setback, these sensors can alarm the natives to stay away from such territories briefly.

10.5.4.3   Public Safety

IoT sensors can be introduced at open associations and houses to ensure residents and give ongoing data to flame and police officers when it distinguishes a robbery.

10.5.4.4   Fire/Explosion Management

Smart flame sensors can recognize and consequently take activities dependent on the dimension of seriousness, for example, distinguishing false cautions, illuminating firemen and emergency vehicles, closing off close-by roads/structures on the prerequisite, helping individuals to clear, and planning salvage automatons and robots.

10.5.4.5   Automatic Health-Care Delivery

Smart human services gadgets can be executed at open spots to give day-in and day-out social insurance for patients like apportioning prescriptions and medications to patients. These gadgets can likewise be utilized to call a rescue vehicle to get the patients in instances of urgent situation.

10.5.5   Smart Energy Management

Here's the manner by which IoT answers for shrewd urban communities can be executed for brilliant vitality the executives.

10.5.5.1   Smart Grid

Smart lattices are carefully observed, self-recuperating vitality frameworks that convey power or gas from age sources. Shrewd network arrangements can be crosswise over modern, private just as in transmission and dispersion ventures. Different IoT arrangements like portals can be utilized to accomplish vitality preservation at both the transmission level and buyer level. For example, doors can give a more extensive perspective on vitality dispersion examples to service organizations with high availability and ongoing examination. Likewise, it builds up a demand-response system for the utility suppliers to improve vitality circulation dependent on the utilization designs.

10.5.5.2   Intelligent Meters

These meters can be utilized in private and modern metering divisions for power and gas meters where there is a need to distinguish the constant data on vitality use. Shoppers and utilities with shrewd meters can screen their vitality utilization. Besides, vitality investigation, reports, and open dashboards can be additionally gotten to over the web utilizing portable applications coordinated with these keen meters.

10.5.6   Smart Water Management

Smart water management is empowered by IoT and associated gadgets in the accompanying ways.

Water outflows: Detects of fluid leakage outside tanks and monitor the pressure in the pipes.

Observation of potable water: Monitors the nature of faucet water in the urban communities.

Swimming pool remote measurement: Controls the pool conditions remotely.

Chemical leakage: Identifies leakage and waste of processing plants in rivers.

Levels of the pollution of the ocean: Identify and controls the contamination in the ocean.

10.5.7   Smart Waste Management

Smart way out for tracking wastes help municipalities and waste service managers the facility to optimize wastes, cut operational expenses, and suitable field the environmental issues connected with an incompetent waste collection.

Realization of a smart city moves toward enormous prospects to alter the lifestyle of people and perk up the overall city infrastructure and functionalities. Smart wireless sensor networks and Internet of Things with associated technologies are the key solutions for smart city implementation.

10.6 Challenge and Solution of Big Data for Smart City

10.6.1 Challenge in Big Data for Smart City

The reason of discussing these challenges for big data is to give research directions to new researchers in this domain.

10.6.1.1 Data Integration

In smart cities, data can be collected from different organizations, varied environments, and a broad variety of sensor devices for the data integration. Data integration is still a challenge for the organization to collect the data from of open-standards across the IT and communications industry. However, the political and organizational for data integration is even harder ones to address. Therefore, there must be an effort to developed a proper focus and standards, to collect the data in an easy way with less effort and also helpful for the further processing of data integration.

10.6.1.2 Security and Privacy

Security and privacy are important parameters for the smart cities which are connected with variety of devices. Viruses can be easily transfers from one device to another device by weak pairing and discovery protocols of the devices which require insufficient authorization and weakly encrypted communication. This can expose sensitive data, and susceptibility in the devices/sensors that can allow an invader to access remotely. Therefore, for successful protection of the huge data, the following issues must be addressed.

1) Government/agencies should have a policy for ensuring the privacy of the data collected from the users, i.e., citizens.
2) The data centers must be simple, available, and lightweight.
3) A continuous risk evaluation must be prepared to scrutinize the present fear and recognize new upcoming attacks.

10.6.1.3 Data Analytics

Data analysis is an enormously vital functionality on which the performance of a smart city depends. New data-mining algorithms and visualization techniques are required for useful insights from the variety of voluminous data acquired by a smart city. For their better functioning, real-time analytics play a much greater role than the traditional store-and-process-later scenario. Thus, the challenges are brought forward not only by the size and heterogeneity of data, but also in terms of strict time-bound processing that can affect a smart-city performance. It should also be ensured that with an increase in data volume, the robustness, efficiency, and effectiveness of the existing data-mining algorithms are preserved. Other challenges are furnished below.

10.6.2 Solution of Challenge Smart City

10.6.2.1 Conquering Difficulties with Enactment

Lawmakers may face major difficulties by incorporating valuable approaches to releasing financial development, direct partners for the city's populace, and this problem may also continue at the time of development in the field of research-and-development scheme. Policymakers may use their own information and adjusting exchange offs to get members to their share for some tests.

When different IoT sensors and cameras on shrewd road lights are placed in roads and streets, then the person/public will feel that they are viewed by their regional office. This will create worries over the protection of their own information.

To process the gathered information by the task will increase cost and provide the income to the business activity.

Despite these protection challenges and after providing subsidy, it has been observed that some of the brilliant urban areas are facing problems to establish a good security system. Open private associations can play a vital role to reduce the monetary cost problem of the government and manage the issue in low cost.

Adjusting different city divisions and partners on shared view, and permitting interoperability and the sharing of information among them, helps in the assignment of the underlying monetary speculation on the grounds that before executing brilliant city activities, government offices and private accomplices have been working in their very own storehouses.

This storehouse outlook is one of the fundamental issues governments and framework integrators must survive. An adjustment in the board style, which presents open joint effort and information sharing among city bodies can help diminish the money-related bar, enabling keen urban communities to accomplish their objectives.

Officials in each district of the world know about the interoperability and subsidizing difficulties looked by savvy urban communities, so they are attempting to figure normal enthusiasm among task accomplices. Enactment can enable nearby governments to execute savvy city innovations and defeat the different difficulties they face.

10.6.2.2 Making People Smarter—Education for Everyone

Education is an additional path that smart cities can relieve anxiety among the populace. Regional authorities can plan innovative education programs and provide promptly accessible benefits to the public to make these activities effectively fruitful.

It will be a wise decision to not choose all cities as the smart cities strategic at the same degree of improvement because they have different administration and speculation models.

The concept of smart city idea is quite new, and due to this, it is facing a huge number of difficulties in different aspects, but smart cities such as Singapore, Dubai, London, and New York are using more grounded computerized systems and high-end digital security to improve the availability of information and data for better education. These cities used the bottom of approaches for their need.

These organizations have taken the view of developing cities expert and going with joint venture programs to create smart activities in their smart cities. In the future, we see faster development in different cities in our locality.

10.7 Conclusion

This work has presented a big-data oriented smart-city paradigm. We have provided a big-data taxonomy of smart cities based on computing infrastructure, storage infrastructure, data variety, data analytics, and data visualization for the understanding of the readers. Further, we provide the major big-data analytics platforms for the ease of researchers. Concerning the heterogeneous data types, often with conflicting processing requirements, we present a concise mapping between them and the most appropriate analytical techniques that can be used. Likewise, ten chose contextual analyses of smart cities over the world have been accounted for to uncover an expanding pattern of smart-city arrangements. At last, a few open research difficulties have been talked about, for example, security/protection, information reconciliation, and information examination, which request consideration from the exploration network and should prepare for future work.

References

1. Al Nuaimi, E., Al Neyadi, H., Mohamed, N., Al-Jaroodi, J., Applications of big data to smart cities. *J. Internet Serv. Appl.*, 6, 1, 1–15, 2015.
2. Hashem, I.A.T., Chang, V., Anuar, N.B., Adewole, K., Yaqoob, I., Gani, A., Chiroma, H., The role of big data in smart city. *Int. J. Inf. Manage.*, 36, 5, 748–758, 2016.
3. Pantelis, K. and Aija, L., Understanding the value of (big) data, in: *Big Data, 2013 IEEE International Conference on IEEE*, pp. 38–42, 2013.
4. Khan, Z., Anjum, A., Kiani, S.L., Cloud Based Big Data Analytics for Smart Future Cities, in: *Proceedings of the 2013 IEEE/ACM 6th International Conference on Utility and Cloud Computing*, IEEE Computer Society, pp. 381–386, 2013.
5. Sobolevsky, S., Bojic, I., Belyi, A., Sitko, I., Hawelka, B., Murillo Arias, J., Ratti, C., Scaling of city attractiveness for foreign visitors through big data of human economical and social media activity, in: *Big Data (BigData Congress), 2015 IEEE International Congress on*, IEEE, pp. 600–607, 2015.
6. Sun, Y., Song, H., Jara, A.J., Bie, R., Internet of things and big data analytics for smart and connected communities. *IEEE Access*, 4, 766–773, 2016.
7. Strohbach, M., Ziekow, H., Gazis, V., Akiva, N., Towards a big data analytics framework for IoT and smart city applications, in: *Modeling and processing for next-generation big-data technologies*, pp. 257–282, Springer, Cham, 2015.
8. Rathore, M.M., Ahmad, A., Paul, A., Rho, S., Urban planning and building smart cities based on the internet of things using big data analytics. *Comput. Networks*, 101, 63–80, 2016.

Index

Printed and bound by CPI Group (UK) Ltd, Croydon, CR0 4YY